*A Real-Life Christian
Spiritual Journey*

A Real-Life Christian Spiritual Journey

A Story of Real Life Spiritual Experiences
on the Way Back to God

Richard Ferguson

iUniverse, Inc.
Bloomington

A Real-Life Christian Spiritual Journey

iUniverse books may be ordered through booksellers or by contacting:

iUniverse
1663 Liberty Drive
Bloomington, IN 47403
www.iuniverse.com
1-800-Authors (1-800-288-4677)

ISBN: 978-1-4620-1672-3 (sc)
ISBN: 978-1-4620-1674-7 (dj)
ISBN: 978-1-4620-1673-0 (e)

Printed in the United States of America

iUniverse rev. date: 8/8/2011

To my beloved Marilyn,
who waits for me in heaven and
with whom I will spend eternity.

Contents

Introduction

As I WENT THROUGH THE graduate pastoral ministry program at Santa Clara University, I realized I was with a special group of people who were not afraid to open themselves up and share their deepest feelings and experiences with others. I had never experienced this before. In my life experience to that point, I had seen that the vast majority of people never share intimate details of their spiritual lives, even with trusted friends. Rather, they keep things to themselves, even their desire to know more about the Spirit. They prefer to "wonder in silence" because they do not know whom to ask or confide in, or because they fear sticking their necks out and revealing more of themselves than they are comfortable with. While this latter feeling is understandable—after all, none of us wants to expose much of ourselves for fear of embarrassment—the result of this fear is that we lose out on important spiritual growth possibilities.

If we'd start asking questions and reaching out to others, we might just be pleasantly surprised. For one, we might discover that others have problems that are similar to or even worse than ours, in which case, we might no longer feel we are suffering alone. And after that, we might learn to fix our problems by seeing how others have handled theirs; without such insight into others' experiences, we doom ourselves to repeating the same mistakes over and over, and wondering why.

Second, as we go through life, each of us travels through different stages of psychological and spiritual growth. Yet, by keeping our feelings to ourselves, we never become aware of those inner changes. It's almost as if we are going through life asleep.

When people share their stories with one another, they come closer together and unity is created. This lightens the load for each individual while increasing the loving bonds among the group. Theologically, this is exactly what God wants—a unity of mankind.

And that is why I am about to share my story with you. I hope by opening the door between us and revealing my own real-life experience with all of its psychological and spiritual implications that you will learn about your own life. God has guided me from hating—yes, openly hating—anything to do with religion, even up to the time I got my master's degree in theology and pastoral ministry and became a third-degree Reiki practitioner. (Reiki is an ancient Asian healing practice that involves the channeling of God's healing energy and universal life force through the practitioner into the patient.) In time, however, this foot-dragging, hostile, Christian little boy went from being emotionally guarded, looking at people as only threats, to being open and loving toward God's other children.

Along the way, I have learned a lot about life and God, and it is in my sharing those lessons with you that I pray your life will improve, your heart will see peace, and a glint will appear in your eye for the wonderful things God has in store for us who love Him.

My experiences include lessons about Christianity that the average parishioner may have never been exposed to—lessons that paint a picture of Christian doctrine that is more people-friendly and less legalistic (that is, based solely on adherence to doctrinal rules merely to appease God). We do indeed need to share the load with others—for, as it has been said many times, no man is an island.

In this book are dozens of true stories, each with a spiritual lesson, as well as a number of true mystical experiences, each of which point directly to the love of God and the reality of heaven. The stories I will tell you are real and actually happened as described. The person who lived these stories is me, your author. I will not exaggerate or change facts for dramatic effect. Some stories are tragic and painful; others are downright amusing. All of them point to real spiritual experiences that brought God's light into my life. All these stories have a spiritual dimension to them—as does everything in life. These experiences taught me something, and now they can illuminate you with the light of learning as well.

In addition, to make the lessons of my personal spiritual journey clearer, I will reference two giants in the fields of psychology and spirituality: Erik Erikson and James Fowler, both famous psychologists. The events I will present to you will use the framework developed over a lifetime of research by Erikson and Fowler. Erik Erikson is called the father of psychosocial development. His books *Childhood and Society* and *Identity: Youth and*

Crisis were milestone texts on child development. James Fowler is the recognized authority on spiritual growth and the stages of faith in God that humans go through. His book *Stages of Faith* is foundational for understanding how our faith in God changes as we grow from infancy through old age. Other theories of development exist besides those of Erikson and Fowler. I used theirs because I feel that, together, their theories offer a framework that is both complete and yet understandable in terms of the human experience.

Part one of this book chronicles the average human's journey through this life, including the various stages of spiritual and psychological growth from infancy to old age. I will use incidents from my own life to better illustrate these stages.

Part two asserts that there is an overriding unity to everything and everybody in the universe. It contends that people are people no matter where you encounter them, and that things are not as different across nations, religions, cultures, and, for that matter, the physical world as you have been led to believe.

Part three comes full circle, ending where we started with the stages of life. In this section, however, that life journey will be discussed in terms of both the physical and spiritual worlds. In this part, we look more closely at the end of life from the perspective of those who have lost loved ones. My own fascinating and true stories regarding the death of my beloved wife prove much about the reality of the spiritual world and heaven in this section, making it clear that death is not an end but rather a graduation to a higher, more loving, and more joyful existence. By the end of the book, I hope you will be able to see the bigger picture of how life unfolds for all of us—even when we are not paying much attention.

Lastly, I would like to give thanks to people like James Fowler, Erik Erikson, Thomas Merton, Carl Jung, H. Richard Niebuhr, John A. Sanford, Elaine Pagels, Dorothee Soelle, Eckhart Tolle, Huston Smith, and many others listed in the reference section. All these people have devoted their lives and academic pursuits to understanding, in great detail, the framework of spirituality and the open faith that I am presenting to you.

Reflection vs. Nostalgia

An important point about the reflection exercises: when you look back on your life, study it as objectively as you can and learn from it. If, instead, you wind up longing for the good old days, you will not make spiritual progress, because you will never stop mentally walking that journey in your memory.

Reflecting on life experiences is a spiritual practice. Reflection offers you the advantage of seeing how things turned out and sorting through the reasons they turned out that way, so that you can keep going forward. In short, you should use it to learn what you can from your past in order to live in the present and plan the future with more experienced eyes. As Robert Johnson says,

> The attempt to go back or romanticize the good ol' days is a common political theme in American culture. It usually marks the desire to avoid difficult times ahead, and of course it is always a lie. Nostalgia means business profit but psychological disaster. You must go forward from the Garden of Eden, through the painful time of transformation to the heavenly Jerusalem, which is a symbol for the wholeness of man restored.[1]

This is not to say, however, that reflection is not also an emotional experience. It is not easy at times. But it can be healing, too. Jim Burklo, in his book *Open Christianity*, says, "Spiritual practice can be difficult, because it requires conscious effort in the face of all the countless distractions of everyday existence. And there is risk: it can open one up to painful memories or repressed feelings. But in spiritual practice we rediscover that God is readily available, offering compassion."[2]

So look back, reflect, and learn, but don't ever wish that you were back where you were then.

---

[1] Robert A. Johnson, *Transformation* (San Francisco: Harper Collins, 1991), 62.

[2] Jim Burklo, *Open Christianity* (Rising Star Press, 2000), 143.

There are a number of reflection exercises in this book that will help you reach deeper understandings of the different topics presented. We will use a standard preparation for each of our reflections that has not only been successful in my life but has also been taught by many very talented spiritual directors.

Reflection Exercise Preparation
(Standard Method for All Reflections)

Go to a quiet place, turn the lights down or off completely, and sit in any comfortable position you like. To eliminate sound distractions, you might use earplugs—or gun muffs, as I do. I even play soft meditation music inside the muffs, which is very pleasant.

Light a candle, which is a nice symbol for the light of God.

Try to ensure that, in the time and place you pick, you will not be interrupted. Lock the door, if necessary. I even post a sign on the door saying, "Serious meditation in progress. Knock, and God may strike you with lightning at my request!"

Then close your eyes, take a deep breath, and clear your mind. Perhaps you may need to use a mantra. One of my favorites is, "Open unto thee, dear Lord, open unto thee." But use whatever you feel comfortable with. Using what is called an *om* chant (simply chanting "ommmmm" over and over again) often works well, too. Whatever you choose to do, wait until you feel your mind has completely cleared before proceeding with meditation. Make sure you do this when you have the time to do a good job, however, because you are worthy of a good job.

PART I

The Human Spiritual Journey

1

In the Beginning:
Our Prehuman Existence

SLOWLY, I BECAME CONSCIOUS OF my surroundings. I was being born into a place of magic, love, and complete harmony among all beings who were there with me. The most gorgeous golden light I would ever encounter in my existence came from what seemed every direction. Somehow this light nourished me at my very young age—that is, I would have been young, had time had meaning where I was, and had age been something real. Neither was space real, as I was formless; I had no body yet, no arms, no legs. I worried about none of this, though, for I intuitively knew it would all come later.

But now, as the beautiful light sustained me in complete security and happiness, wrapping me in its warm embrace, loving me with an indescribable intensity, I could see in all directions at once. I felt immense love within every particle of my being from God's golden light and from all my brothers and sisters. I was extremely happy, knowing nothing negative, for it did not exist here.

The other children felt the same. There were millions of us, but we were in unity such that we could know one another's feelings and thoughts. We all knew we were in an exalted place of wonderment, a sacred place of joy and endless bliss that went in all directions for as far as we could perceive. We moved around our world effortlessly, sometimes by ourselves and sometimes with friends.

We children all knew and deeply loved one another just as we loved ourselves and God the Father and God the Mother. Though much the same, each of us was different, too. Each of us was unique, as God had already bestowed the gifts of individuality and free will. Out of the love of our Father God and our Mother God, we became ourselves, each unique, yet each reflecting an image of Father and Mother.

To emphasize our individuality, God gave us each the gift of a holy name, which was to be ours for eternity. My name, Joseph, will be for all time. All other names like Richard that I may be given throughout the ages are temporary, for I am Joseph.

I was grateful and humbled He chose this name for me, since millions of years in the future, it would be the name of the father of Jesus Christ when He would go to earth. We all knew what was to come, and we all would participate in the wonderment of creation with our Father and Mother. We would become co-creators with God.

We knew, too, that infinite potential lay before us in other realms, but we did not want to venture that way, for fear of leaving the love and security of our sacred home. As time passed, however, we slowly began to see what we could become in those realms. It became clearer that if we wanted to fulfill God's original intent for each of our lives, we would have to journey outside our wonderful home to explore the other areas that God had created. We realized that our doing this for Father and Mother would bring them joy, as they watched us gain all different kinds of knowledge and experiences, and reach our full potentials.

Even then, we were still hesitant to leave, but as in all divine communication, God infused us with what we needed to know before we set out on our journeys. He promised to be with us each step of the way. We would never be away from Him, He said. He would be closer to us than we each were to our own breath.

He told us we would experience trouble and pain for the first time in our existence. And although He promised to help us when we were in trouble and to freely give us what we needed, He said he would not give us everything we wanted. If we succeeded in handling our troubles, all the while loving Him and loving our neighbors as ourselves, He said that not only would He be very proud of us, but also that we, upon our return to heaven, would grow to enjoy the higher realms even more than before.

He assured us that our free will would allow us to make the right choices, to avoid dangers in our path. Each journey we took gave us the opportunity to gain more knowledge about God's creation, the least part of which was not ourselves. It was then we began to understand that His creation was infinite and that in it our little place of love and security was but a very small part.

Before it was my time to leave, God told me that He created a special female person for only me. In this life her name is Marilyn. She and I would be married multiple times during our many journeys together in different places and various eras. And after our journeys were finished and we had achieved our full potential, we would spend eternity together, our souls intermingled in rapturous and unending love for each other. We would then be free to roam all of creation at our pleasure, enjoying and learning together.

When came the time to begin our journeys, millions of my brothers and sisters and I used our spiritual wings to fly to the Earth and other places within our Father's creation, keeping in mind that we must always remember the rules God had set forth, which were quite simple actually: focus on and love Him first, and then love others as ourselves. To follow these rules, we were to use our inborn talents and free will to always choose the right path. He would always be with us in the form of the Holy Spirit to help and guide us along our journey.

As so we came to Earth, born into different situations, cultures, and geographies, beginning our human lives and personal adventures complete with emotion, joy, struggle, pain, and pleasure.

Our Common Spiritual Journey

I INVITE YOU TO COME with me on a fantastic journey. It's a spiritual journey of real life that all of us are on right now whether we realize it or not. Although this book has many stories of my personal journey, much of these experiences are ones that you will be able to identify with from your personal journey. Our life experiences and stories are signposts along our collective spiritual journey ordained by God.

CHAPTER 2

The Journey of Faith, Spirit, and Self

MY SPIRITUAL JOURNEY BEGAN WITH a shock.

I was young, still feeling the afterglow of the sacred place I came from. We lived in a yellow brick apartment building on the corner of a busy street in Chicago. To get to our unit in the basement, we had to go down some steps, turn left, and go down another set of steps. There were also steps on the right, but they went up to somewhere I never went.

I was happy, crawling on the kitchen floor, playing with my favorite yellow plastic truck. Bare, silver-colored pipes crisscrossed the ceiling. They must have been pretty old, because they groaned and squeaked a lot. High on the wall above the sink, there were windows, small and right up by the ceiling. I could see the snow piled against them now, and because our apartment was in the basement, the floor was cold to the touch as I played. But I didn't care. I was fascinated watching the little wheels on my truck turn as I zoomed it across the floor, making motor sounds. I was in my own little world of make-believe where my toys were as real as everything else and where I felt all was well.

From time to time, I saw people's legs walk by our kitchen windows and heard our upstairs neighbors. The ceiling would creak and groan as they walked across the floor, and small snippets of conversation would occasionally float down through the vents: "Harold, did you pick up my dry cleaning?"

Mom was cooking as I played, and I could smell the gas burner and hear its hissing. The smell of food told me eating was not too far away. If I was lucky, Mom would give me a taste of what was on the stove before we ate.

Mom always wore a white apron when she cooked. If she spilled something, the apron protected her. And no matter what she spilled, her apron was always washed clean on laundry day. For me, in time, that white apron would come to represent the warmth and resilience of home.

Suddenly, my dad came home from work. There he was in the kitchen, and he immediately started to scream at Mom. His voice was so loud and frightening; I hid behind Mom's skirt and started to cry. My body quivered from fear as I held tight to her white apron.

I remember very clearly him yelling, "I told you he is not to play in here!" right before he kicked my toy truck across the room, smashing it to pieces. I began to sob. I cannot begin to describe the terror I felt in that instant as the broken parts of my truck scattered across the kitchen floor. My little world was shattered. To this day, I can still feel the soft cloth of my mom's skirt on my face and the terror I felt when I looked up and saw the rage in my dad's face. Pain was seared into my heart's memory, where that evening's thirty-second moment would last a lifetime.

A child's trust for the mother of the house is very important. It is where the child forms a basic trust of the world. My mom was always there for me. Whatever I needed, I could always count on her.

Likewise, the behavior of both parents toward the child affects the young one's rudimentary images of God. And so for me, because of what my father did that evening, this was the day I walked through a new spiritual portal. That portal was the threshold of a new stage of my spiritual life, the beginning of new understandings and experiences of which I had never before been capable. On the other side of that threshold, the little boy that had existed just a few minutes earlier was no more. My developing brain was now tainted and my nervous system bumped off-course down a new, damaged path. My innocence and perceptions of trust were forever changed.

I viewed the world differently after that, becoming much more aware. I began to grow up and recognize just the kind of reality I had been born into. It was a painful awakening, but an awakening no less. And it was an awakening not only to the dangers of what this life could hold for me but also to the potentials.

And so it was, that on that linoleum floor in a basement apartment on Mango Avenue in Chicago, my journey to God began.

Not until I was an adult, of course, did I know the changes that took place in those few minutes. I did not know that I had indeed started a new spiritual chapter. And this is the way it is for all of us. Not only are we changed by our experiences and perceptions throughout life, but each of us can also refer back to a starting point for that change—usually in our early childhood. For some children, that starting point may be a positive memory, full of love, warmth, and good feelings. However others, such as I, were not so lucky. Though I realize I am not special in this regard; millions were worse off than I in their early childhood experiences.

Decades later, when I confronted my father about what he did that evening, he acknowledged remembering it. I was actually surprised. He told me he'd known that all I'd wanted was a hug, but he never expressed any kind of regret. He didn't even try to give me a reason—even a poor excuse—for what he'd done to my mom and me.

It was not until my teenage years, after putting up with behavior like this for what seemed hundreds of times, that I finally concluded my father was just plain mean. He had a lot of rage stored within him, which he apparently felt he had the right to take out on others whenever he wanted, as, afterward, he always felt justified in doing so. This was, and still is, terribly sad to me.

The Beginning Stages of Faith

ACCORDING TO JAMES FOWLER'S BOOK *Stages of Faith,* basic feelings formed by children around the age of two or three will stay with them their whole lives.[3] It is at this age when children are just beginning to form ideas of trust in the world. Is the world a place that you can trust to meet your needs or not? Little vulnerable brains are answering this question based on their experiences, either for better or worse.

In fact, from infant age until about seven or eight, children develop all sorts of ideas about relationships and attitudes about the world around them. During these years, the brain is "wired" as to how it should relate to the world.

When the event with my father took place, I was around age two or three, and just beginning to form my ideas of trust in the world. So with this one crucial moment, I began to feel the world could not be trusted. Even though my mom took excellent care of me, the violence that occurred that day, not to mention on a multitude of days that followed, rewired my brain for good.

The fragility of a child's mental and emotional state is not a new idea. Even the Romans recognized that treating children well was vital to their development. As Juvenal, the Roman poet and satirist, put it, "Be gentle

---

[3]   James Fowler, *Stages of Faith* (San Francisco: Harper Collins, 1976).

with the young … Refrain from doing ill; for one all-powerful reason, lest our children should copy our misdeeds; we are all too prone to imitate whatever is base and depraved."

This moment in each of our lives, the moment when we set in motion a basic trust or mistrust of the world, marks the beginning of both our faith and what I call our "mode of existence." *Basically, it marks the beginning of our spiritual journey back to God and to discovering who we are as His children.*

You, too, had a beginning point in your personal journey back to God and the discovery of yourself, even if you are not yet aware of it. It is a journey we all travel, a journey of healing from past hurts, a road to discovering God and our true identities. But most of all, it is a fantastic journey toward the knowledge of just how wonderful and peaceful our relationship with God really is, no matter how dreary or filled with suffering this world can be.

Each of us is a unique creation of God, and as such, each of our journeys on this planet is different. We are each on our own path through life. But even as we are unique, we pass through identical stages of faith and psychological development as we walk our way back toward God.

In the remainder of the chapter, I will walk you through two different aspects of these various stages of development, which we all share: the spiritual aspect and the psychological one. After all, our spirits and our minds are interconnected, each affecting the other intimately. This is what makes us human.

Psychological Development

ERIK ERIKSON, KNOWN AS THE father of psychosocial development, says we pass through eight stages of mental development as we age from infancy to maturity. Psychosocial development refers to the ways in which our personal psychology affects our interactions with other people and God. Each stage has its own set of challenges to master and dangers to avoid. He also says we will never notice our passing from one stage to the next, and that *trying* to notice it would be like staring at a wall of wet paint, waiting for it to dry; the process is just too slow, not to mention the boundaries between each stage too blurred. There is no definite moment where a cosmic diploma descends from the sky announcing we have now graduated to the next phase of development. As Erikson put it, "Transitions represent an upheaval in one's life at any point and can be protracted in its process for five to seven years or longer."[4]

As mentioned, Erikson also thought that each phase of life had its own set of challenges and dangers, and that it was up to the individual to meet those challenges. More, he thought that if we did not overcome those hurdles, we could not progress to the next phase of our development, even as we aged. Intuitively, this is a truth we all know: we all change as we get older, and those who do not, we often call "immature." As Henry David Thoreau said very simply, "Things do not change; we change."

Take a look at the eight stages that Erikson categorized, along with their defining characteristics and challenges.

1. **Infancy.** This is the stage where we form our basic trust or mistrust of the world we've just been born into. Our level of trust depends on whether our infantile needs were met. The mother's role is vital in this stage. Healthy children are the result of a mother who is always there to provide for their needs, such as those for physical comfort (hugs, for example), cleanliness (bathing and grooming), and hunger (feeding). Otherwise, children end up mistrusting the world as they grow through succeeding stages.

2. **Early childhood.** Here, we form our self image. Depending on our experiences, that image can be one of self-worth or of shame. We pick up on what the adults around us think of us, and we believe that defines our value to the world.

3. **Childhood.** As we begin to work with others to achieve things during this phase, we notice we have certain individual talents. We then display these talents in our individual social groups— for example, showing our friends that we can throw a baseball the farthest.

4. **Late childhood.** We become more aware of our own competence, understanding that the skills and talents we recognized in the previous stage can be useful. We then feel we have something to offer, whether it be to our family, our friends, or the world in general.

5. **Adolescence.** We go through a kind of identity crisis, trying to figure out who we are. This is where the weird hairdos and

---

[4] Erik Erikson, *Childhood and Society* (W. W. Norton and Co, 1950).

goofy pants appear, and where the love our life changes each week as we search for our own unique identity.

6. **Young adulthood**. As we desire to share our newly found identity with others, we develop virtues of love and intimacy. (Of course, hormones play a big part here, too.) As a result of it all, we search for a mate.

7. **Adulthood.** At this point in life, the challenge is to move beyond a particular intimate relationship into a concern for wider society, becoming more open to the suffering of others. If you are paying attention, you will not be able to avoid noticing the beggar on the street corner and feeling sadness in your heart, hopefully to the point you do something about it.

8. **Old age.** Here, the challenge is to accept the life we've lived as something that "had to be." An inner acceptance of "what is" marks the virtue that, if attained, increases our awareness of oneness and wholeness with all of creation.

I saw an elderly woman on the nightly news that was interviewed right after a tornado totally destroyed her house and everything she worked for in her life. She told the reporter, "Well, life goes on and we will, too—just without a few things." Now that is a mature person who can say that and mean it.

Spiritual Development

THE SECOND ASPECT OF OUR growth is spiritual. James Fowler, in his book *Stages of Faith*, points out six different stages of faith development. As with our psychological development, each phase builds upon the previous ones as we progress toward what Fowler calls "Universalizing Faith"; however, we may not all progress through all the stages for one reason or another. Fowler described the following stages in our faith, or images of God, in our growth toward being a mature person.

When I say spiritual development, I mean our changing image of who God is, as well as our relationship to Him and to all of the other parts of His creation, including His people. Our perception of how we fit into that matrix of creation and our relationship with it evolves over our lifetime, affecting who we are.

1. **Infancy.** In this first stage, we have what is called undifferentiated faith: we cannot tell where we as an individual end and the world begins. This may seem odd, but in essence, it is the idea that infants have yet to acquire a sense of self; they are not aware that they are separate from other people. As such, as infants, we form our first "pre-images" of God based on a sense of mutuality with those around us. An infant does not form an image of God per se, but becomes aware of his surroundings and other people that he cannot differentiate from himself. This stage is fundamental to forming more advanced understandings of God.

2. **Childhood.** This stage of faith is where kids develop first self-awareness and then awareness of what they think are the conditions of existence (for example, they form ideas about authority and fairness and God). It is the age of asking "Why?" about two billion times a week and driving our parents crazy. It is first the age of pretending and playing make-believe in order to learn more about life; then, in the school years, it is the age where stories take on meaning. Kids at this age can tell stories, understand religious symbols in a very literal sense, and grasp a basic sense of fairness. This is where kids drive their parents nuts by saying things like, "Why can't I do that? Johnny's parents let him do it!"

3. **Adolescence.** Stage Three is where a person begins to put all the diverse pieces together—family, community, God, work, school, and faith—into a consistent picture that also includes a sense of individual identity and future. It's a time when people unconsciously conform to group beliefs and expectations without much reflection on their personal beliefs. For example, someone might say, "I believe that because Billy Graham said so." Unfortunately, many spend the rest of their lives at this level of faith. That's because transition to the next stage of faith is not necessarily age-dependant but, rather, is marked by serious questioning of religious authorities and principles.

4. **Young adulthood.** In many people, this stage does not occur until the mid-thirties to forties, if ever. As mentioned, it is marked by more serious reflection on one's own responsibilities, identity, and religious beliefs and attitudes. At this stage, it

becomes no longer acceptable to believe something just because someone in authority said to. A person becomes more self-reflective and identifies what they really believe in, particularly when there is a conflict between self as an individual versus self as a member of a group. Serious questions about the religion one grew up with frequently occur at this stage. For example, you might hear a young adult say something like, "Can you believe the stupid thing the pope said to Latin America the other day?" In essence, young adults are spreading their spiritually independent wings.

5. **Midlife and beyond.** Many never make it this far in their spiritual development. At this stage, the last vestiges of group thinking are challenged, and an expanded, though still somewhat ambiguous, religious ideology emerges. Along with this ideology comes the realization that all of humanity is united in some way that we cannot explain; it is best thought of as a blurring of self and the world. The once-clear boundary between "I am here" and "there is the world" becomes more porous and fuzzy, and things no longer seem so black and white.

   As a result of this blurring, things that once seemed very opposite appear less so; rather, they appear more porous and continuous, and the mind tries to unify them by gaining an expanded readiness to be close to that which is "other," even if it seems strange.

6. **Maturity.** The sixth and last stage of spiritual development is very rare. The vast majority of people do not come this far. Spiritual maturity is characterized by outgrowing the fuzziness of stage five's ideologies. It features a radical commitment to justice, love, and selflessness, as well as a passion to transform this world. Think of the following people and you will understand this stage: Gandhi, Martin Luther King Jr., Mother Teresa of Calcutta, and Dag Hammarskjold.

Change: The Universal Constant

Change is the one constant in the universe—now there's an oxymoron. But the amazing fact is that it is true. Did you know that the cells in your body change each day? And that every seven years, new ones have replaced all the old cells in your body? (Though my new cells seem to have more wrinkles than the previous ones!)

In the universe, that which is made of matter cannot remain the same. It must change due to a law of physics called "universal increasing entropy." The surface of the earth constantly changes, as does the sun. Everything in creation changes a bit each day.

And, every day, you change—your attitudes, your knowledge, your maturity, your perspective on life. It may certainly not seem so, but you do. Because these changes take place so gradually, however—just a little bit at a time—we hardly notice that we have become different over time.

Nothing stays the same. Or, as Heraclitus put it, "Nothing endures but change."[5] We all know it; we just tend to forget. Each of us is at a different point in our spiritual and psychological development. I am not necessarily where you are in your faith journey. But where we are is not important; God will meet each of us exactly where we stand. The important thing is that we are making progress.

And once you reach a certain point in your physical and psychological development, you can take charge of that progress. As Andy Warhol so aptly said, "They always say time changes things, but you actually have to change them yourself."[6]

Reflection Exercise: Your Life Development

I suggest taking some time by yourself to reflect on how you view God and the world and yourself differently today than you did at earlier points in your life. Use the reflection preparation steps described at the end of the Introduction. Make sure you do this when you have the time to do a good job, because you are worthy of a good job. When you are ready, take a look at the three sets of questions below to help guide your reflection.

If you are making progress in your psychological life, your views of yourself and of the world will be both different and more positive than they have ever been.

Whatever your answers, though, remember that you are a special creation of God, deserving of His love and of your own respect. And with that in mind, let's start a spiritual and psychological journey together by viewing in more detail the thoughts and feelings that accompany the various stages of human development.

---

[5] Heraclitus, from Diogenes Laertius, *Lives of Eminent Philosophers*.

[6] Andy Warhol, *The Philosophy of Andy Warhol* (Harvest Books, 1975).

Reflections on God

Remember to prepare for this exercise as described in the last part of the Introduction

Do you view God now the same as you did five years ago? Or as a child? Use the following questions to help you think about how you see God and religion:

- Is God judgmental? Does He send people to hell?
- Do you have to appease God and follow all church doctrines and rituals and rules?
- Where is God? Is He here with us on earth and throughout creation, or is He somewhere "out there"?
- Have you gone beyond what you were taught as a child? Do you disagree with any religious teachings you grew up with?

If your answers reflect ideas of God and religion that are the same as they've always been, you are not making progress in your spiritual life. I say this because a natural result of spiritual growth is that your vision of God gets bigger and more open, until we can no longer define Him by a set of doctrines because you see that He goes far beyond that.

Reflections of the world around you. Ask yourself these questions regarding how you view the world and others around you:

- Do you view humanity as a unit—all in the same boat? Or do you consider yourself, as well as every other person on the earth, an individual?
- Do you concentrate on differences between people or on similarities?
- Has your trust in others grown over the years or diminished?

Reflections of you. Now consider your view of yourself, by reflecting on these questions:

- Is your view of yourself different than it used to be at any point in time?
- Have you formed ideas that are different from those of your parents?

- I have a family member who used to say that the world has more horse's asses than horses. Have you departed from such "given" knowledge, or do you cling to it?
- Do you consider yourself a kinder, gentler person than you were years ago? Or has life taught you that in order to survive, you must get tough—that living in the world is all about survival of the fittest?

CHAPTER 3

Stage One: The Faith of Infants

AFTER READING THIS CHAPTER'S TITLE, you might be asking, "How can infants have faith?" Let's answer that question by looking at one of the definitions of faith: complete trust.

What does trust have to do with newborns? As mentioned in the previous chapter, it is at this very early stage in life when we form our basic sense of trust in the world and in others. It is this sense of trust that then becomes a fundamental building block of our faith. That is why Fowler calls the faith of an infant "undifferentiated faith"—faith in which seeds of trust, courage, hope, and love are just being planted.

Undifferentiated faith grows out of how reliable our external world is—that is, whether the world can be counted on to provide for our needs, and then, if so, how promptly and how well; for example, how soon we are fed, cleaned, and nurtured after we feel the need for such things.

Undifferentiated faith also is responsible for forming in each of us a "pre-image" of God. By pre-image, I mean a view of God that arises from emotional experiences rather than from rational thought. Because rational thought does not exist in the infant, emotional impressions are all we have at this early age. And those emotional impressions are made through our experiences. By leaving us lasting impressions of how trustworthy others are, as well as how worthy we are of being cared for by others, these experiences shape the way we relate to those others—including God. In this way, there is a direct connection between what we experience as small children and the basic "felt" image of God that we form for life.

These ideas of God and trust and others stick with us because of something called *emotional memory*. In their book *Ghosts from the Nursery*, Robin Karr-Morse and Meredith S. Wiley say, "Events early in life, particularly those experienced with strong emotion, can and do remain an influence throughout our lives. Memory, as it turns out, is not just a matter of rational or even verbal recall. We also have nonverbal, essentially emotional memory, particularly for experiences, events, and people that carry a strong emotional valence."[7]

Simply put, as infants and small toddlers, we soak up everything around us, and these experiences "in the cradle" affect us the rest of our lives because, though we have no conscious memory of them, we remember them emotionally. This emotional memory, according to Fowler, is what ultimately and fundamentally affects our faith in God. He says that the "trust, autonomy, hope, and courage, or their opposites, [which are] developed in this phase [of life] underlie ... all that comes later in faith."[8]

There is also a physical dimension to an infant's emotional development that is worth mentioning here. In *Ghosts from the Nursery*, Morse and Wiley say,

> When the brain is first forming, both the quantity and quality of tissue and chemistry can be changed by sensitization to trauma. Experiences can change the brain of an older child also. But in the beginning during infancy our brain is at its most malleable. It actually organizes itself around the conditions that it experiences. Hypersensitivity can become wired into basic brain chemistry and bodily functions. Attention span and other capacities in the brain originally available for learning and other skills may be deflected by negative experiences to help defend against future trauma.[9]

In other words, any experience that an infant or small child perceives as traumatic can permanently change his brain, which, in turn, will affect his abilities and emotions throughout his lifetime.

This is why one of the worst things a caregiver can do is to neglect or abuse a child. The effects of such abuse and neglect leave invisible

7   Robin Karr-Morse and Meredith S. Wiley, *Ghosts from the Nursery* (Atlantic Monthly Press, 1997), 39.

8   James Fowler, *Stages of Faith* (San Francisco: Harper Collins, 1976).

9   Robin Karr-Morse and Meredith S. Wiley, *Ghosts from the Nursery* (Atlantic Monthly Press, 1997), 158.

scars on a person's being, causing emotional suffering and a host of other problems—sometimes even suicide. (If you want to explore this topic in more detail, I highly recommend reading chapters 4 through 21 in Fowler's *Stages of Faith*.) Quite simply, because of what happens to us as infants, we become who we are—good or bad—without even realizing it. That means if our needs are not met in infancy, our spiritual and psychological growth will suffer; for example, we may become excessively selfish, have the desire to dominate others, or exhibit behaviors of isolation and failed relationships.

We Are Not Alone

BY NO MEANS AM I the only victim of childhood abuse. In fact, countless others have experienced much worse. In your early years, you, too, may have been subjected to incidents that altered your faith and development. Though the time and place and severity of traumatic events certainly vary from person to person to some extent, we have all had what we probably perceived at the time to be just such an incident. This is a common thread shared by all humanity.

Fortunately, there comes a point in all of our lives when we can question *why* we have become the people we are, and understand our childhoods and the effects they had on us. God has provided us with this ability to reflect on our lives as a way to help us heal from past hurtful events, grow closer to him, and become more of the person he had always intended.

In addition, God provides us with help along the way. We are never alone, even though we might feel that way from time to time. We are inseparable from God, and He is always far closer to us than we can imagine. Our spirit guide, angels, and a host of others are also always near to help guide us through our journey of healing and faith. I believe that God has already made each of us stronger than the pain we experience—but with His additional support, I have no doubt that we can truly work toward an understanding of why we are the way we are, and ultimately toward healing.

Come with me, then. Let's travel together toward God and healing by doing the following reflection exercise.

Reflection Exercise: Your First Memory

Pause for a moment and reflect on your first memory in this life. Use the reflection preparation described in the Introduction. Make sure you do this when you have the time to do a good job, however, because you are worthy of a good job.

Next, transport yourself back in time—as an adult, but in a child's body—and try to recall your earliest memory in this life. Remember where you were, what you were doing, what was said, and who was present. Recall the sights, sounds, and smells. Then remember how you felt. Was it a happy moment, in which you felt loved and secure? Was it a moment of discovery? Or was it more of a negative event that caused you fear? If you need to, get out an old family album or other object that brings you back as early as possible in your childhood. And don't forget to ask God for His guidance in remembering.

Once you have a grasp on your first memory, ask God to guide you to a deeper understanding of the incident and the effect it had on you. If the experience was negative, ask Him to help you begin the healing process. Do not assign blame to anyone; rather, treat behaviors as fact and move on to what you need to do to heal yourself and forgive others.

As you recall and feel, remember that you are a loved child of God and that nothing can separate you from Him—nothing. So be gentle with yourself. See yourself as a flower shining in the sunlight of God's love—its beauty emerging for you to behold.

Part of the reason we are on this planet is to discover who we really are, and this reflection exercise will help you do that. Even if you do not particularly like the memory you unveil, know that your discovery of it is something valuable, because it will help you change direction and move toward your full godly potential. Use the negative experience for the good by asking God to guide you toward fulfilling His intent for your life. After all, only in the prayerful understanding of past events can healing begin.

My First Memory

I FOUND THE ABOVE EXERCISE very painful, even forty years after my first experience on the kitchen floor in Chicago with my little yellow truck. But after reflecting upon it more, I learned a lot about how my thoughts and ideas had not only formed and but also affected my life for several decades. I learned that, due to the trauma I experienced in that moment, I grew up holding the subconscious belief that the world was a hostile place and that people could not be trusted. As a result, I developed this overriding feeling that I must be on guard at all times.

Of course, at the time, I was not conscious of my choice not to trust the world. At three years old, I was incapable of the self-awareness and rational thought required to make such a choice. But reflecting back on that time as an adult, I realized that I had begun to prefer playing in the corner or behind the couch, and that I had become more quiet and withdrawn in general. I see now that, without my knowing or understanding it, this was the point in my life when I began forming a protective crust around myself. One outward sign of this change inside me was that I stopped singing. I used to sing while I played but I just stopped that without thinking about it. One night while I was being put to bed my mom asked me why I stopped. I did not know.

In time, I also became hypersensitive; to this day, loud noises are still very distressing to me. I also now have a boatload of allergies and asthma. What does that have to do with childhood trauma? My doctor told me there are two causes of asthma: (1) a genetic predisposition, and (2) something—usually a traumatic event or series of events—to trigger the genetics to take hold.

Despite those difficulties, however, this Reflection Exercise ended up being my gateway to becoming a better person. Asking God for help in healing, in particular, has lessened the emotional impact of this memory on my soul, and has brought me to a greater understanding of who I am and why I sometimes act certain ways.

It has also given me a new perspective on parenting my own children. Essentially, I learned, as Phyllis Diller once aptly put it: "Always be nice to your children, because they are the ones who will choose your nursing home."

Different Starting Points, Same God

EACH OF US BEGINS OUR spiritual life under different circumstances, in different places and times, and in different cultures. But no matter where we start, we, as God's children, are all on the same path—the path toward God.

As mentioned, my Christian spiritual journey began decades ago with abuse, fear, trauma, and cigarette-filled rooms that caused me to develop asthma later in childhood. Your journey's starting point is different.

When I look back at the turning points in my life, I can see God's loving fingerprints all over them. At the time, I did not know He was there, working within the events and within me. Likewise, His fingerprints are on your journey, although you likely did not notice when His hands made them. It is only in the prayerful looking back that we can see God's work in our life and His gentle nudges on our soul toward the proper path. Soren Kierkegaard said it best: "Life can be understood backwards, but it must be lived forwards."

Just like gently flowing water smoothes out the hard, jagged rocks in a stream, so God gently removes our rough edges by flowing through and caressing our lives, day to day, as we live unaware of His work. Only when we look back at the long channel over which we've come can we see how we were often saved from destruction even while being allowed to experience the pain that led to our learning and growth. And only when we look back can we see how far we've come and be truly amazed at how far that is. Through such hindsight, we realize that, in the end, we are all loved children of God.

Reflection Exercise: Seeing God's Fingerprints

Use our reflection preparation steps, and then look back over your life for moments in which God might have been working in you or helping you.

Remember, most times, you will not have noticed His nudges when they happened, for they always come so naturally and silently. For example, you'd have never literally heard His voice speaking to you, as He neither has the need to speak out loud nor one particular language to speak in. Instead, God "speaks" through the events and people in your life, to get His message through to you.

His nudging could come in the form of something a friend said that resonated within your spirit. It could come as a feeling in a quiet moment as you look at your garden or watch children play in the park. It could even come in the form of a blank, peaceful state of mind in a moment without noise and distractions.

Focus on only one event or situation at a time. See where He nudged you to bring higher understanding, deeper questions about life, and certain feelings that would lead you to behave in ways that were loving and beneficial, not only for yourself but also for others.

CHAPTER 4

Stage One: The Faith of Young Children

CHILDREN BETWEEN THE AGES OF three and eight are at what Fowler calls Stage One of the spiritual journey: Intuitive Projective Faith. Forget the fancy label. Fowler explains it as "the fantasy-filled imitative phase, in which the child can be powerfully and permanently influenced by examples, moods, actions and stories of the visible faith of primally related adults."[10]

In other words, these children's perceptions of authority figures (including God) is permanently formed by witnessing and then imitating the behavior of their caregivers and teachers of religion. Fowler goes on to say that negative perspectives formed during this time can be corrected when the child becomes an adult and has the analytical tools and life experience to see the inherent flaws in those ideas.

Regarding the behavior of religious teachers, in particular, Fowler goes on to say this: "The dangers in Stage One arise from the possible 'possession' of the child's imagination by unrestrained images of terror and destructiveness or the exploitation of his or her imagination in the reinforcement of taboos and moral or doctrinal expectations."[11] In other words, religious teachers are in a position to scare the crap out of children by presenting images of hell and sending them there if they do not behave as perfect little students.

---

[10] *Stages of Faith*, James Fowler, Harper San Francisco, 1981 pg 133
[11] James Fowler, *Stages of Faith* (San Francisco: Harper Collins), 133–134.

If you tell a child that God will throw him into hell for being bad—for committing the mortal sin of missing Sunday Mass, for example—that terror-filled image will stick with him the rest of his life, unless he overcomes it. Or, if you were that child, you might now feel afraid, say, if you missed a single Sunday Mass, even because of illness. That's because the lesson you were taught became a subconscious feeling, such that it controls your behavior without you realizing it.

Cults are born out of adults stuck in this stage of faith. They have given themselves over to an authority figure who controls them through fear of terrible punishments unless they do exactly what they are told to do. They have failed to think for themselves. The cult of Jim Jones, a leader who incited nearly a thousand people to mass suicide, offers a prime example of the tragedy that can occur when this happens.

Catholic School: How Not To Treat Children

RAISED A ROMAN CATHOLIC, I went to Catholic school in the first through fourth grades. This is prime time in Fowler's Stage One. The thing I learned most there was to hate religion. For a very long time after I went to St. Tarcissus in Chicago, I did not like God much, let alone trust Him. Why? Because of the cruel way we kids were treated at school. My stories about Catholic school provide a good example of how school-age children tend to project the characteristics of their immediate authority figures onto the ultimate authority figure—God. In my case, I could not stand the nuns who taught our school because of the way they treated us, so I projected those feelings onto God.

I remember very clearly my first day in school. I had to wear a tie for the first time in my life. Dark pants, a white button-down collared shirt, and a blue tie was the official uniform of the prison … er, I mean, school. My first impression of the sister in charge of our class was one of fear. She was big and wore a black dress and a hood. Her mean-looking face had a thousand wrinkles. Later that day, I guess I'd figured that I had had enough of the place, because I simply got up and walked out. I walked out of the classroom, down the hall, and through the front door. And no one stopped me. Wouldn't you know it, as I was headed down the street toward home, I saw my mother walking toward me, a surprised look on her face. She was not mad about my stealthy escape, but, to my dismay, I did have to go back the next day. And this is how I began my foray into

Catholic school. Little did I know that years of negative experiences had yet to follow.

I am not going to hell for telling you the following stories. But first, let me just say, "Dear Pope, please forgive me for what I am about to say." On second thought, never mind.

For those of us who were raised in the fifties and sixties, doctrinal abuse was an all-too-common occurrence within the Catholic school system. In those days, I think we imported more nuns from Germany than we did Volkswagens or Heineken; they ran my entire school. And to say they were strict is an understatement.

Looking back, I now see St. Tarcissus as more of a detention center than a school. At even the slightest infraction, the sisters would react as if you'd just farted a big one in front of the pope at St. Peter's Basilica. If you stepped out of line even the tiniest bit, all hell would descend on you in the form of a large black-robed woman with a rosary dangling from her waistband. The floor would shake and the wall-hangings rattle as the sister rumbled your way, her thunder thighs slapping together under that big black tent, and her rosary beads clicking together as she went. Then, setting her sights on her newfound prey (you!), she would swoop swiftly down upon you with a speed that was remarkable considering the tonnage of her girth.

Then, zeroing in on you, she would scowl from inside her big black hood, her face so intensely red in anger that it almost made you pee your pants. Some kids did. One nun I remember even sported a blue vein in her forehead that would pop out whenever she got mad.

In class, if you committed something unacceptable, the standard procedure was to call the offender up to the front of the room and humiliate him in front of his fifty-nine classmates (yes, classes were typically this large) by shouting at him and then hitting him in a wide variety of ways— whacks on the back of the head, rulers across the back of your hands and ass.

One time I passed a note to a kid next to me that said something like, "This sucks," and next thing I knew, a black-robed bellowing beast shouted, "Rickard!" (The German nuns of the eat-a-lot-of-sausage order never knew how to say my name right.) I made my death march up to the front of the class, thinking, *Dead kid walking!*

All eyes were on me as I made my way up, pondering my bloody death. When I got to the front, I stood at attention next to the hooded one's desk. If possible, the room fell even more silent, as my classmates and I waited for the verdict. The old, wrinkled executioner proceeded to shout at me and told me to bend over. She then whacked the back of my head three times. Nuns seemed to do all beatings in threes, as if thinking holy thoughts of the Trinity while whacking away. I remember hearing their rosaries click as their hands hit the back of my head: *whack, click, whack, click, whack, click.*

One such classroom humiliation that sticks in my mind was the time a kid did something wrong and was standing at attention next to the black-robed probation officer's desk. He announced that he felt sick. Even though it was just after lunchtime, apparently the sister did not believe him, as she proceeded to instruct him to bend over. Bad move, sister! This kid's digestive system had other demonic ideas—Satan had taken over, prompting him to puke on both the sister's desk and the floor next to it. Sister Darth Vader had chunks of his lunch right smack dab on the top of her desk. The horror on her face was an expression I will remember for all time.

We students gasped. Although the kid was officially now our hero, we also knew he was as good as doomed. He had committed the king of mortal sins before our very eyes. I imagined what his confession would sound like that week: "Dear God, I am heartily sorry for puking on Sister's desk—not because I dread the loss of heaven, but because I stunk up the place." And, boy, did he. Even after the sister had herded the rest of us into the hall, we could smell it. The rancid odor seemed to permeate the classroom walls and down the hall. We guys, in the finest tradition of St. Tarcissus, held our official blue ties up to our noses, giggling.

Then a squadron of reinforcements—more black-robed centurions— arrived to control the mob of giggling third graders. With their black robes swishing and rosaries clicking, they all frantically called out for the janitor, though amazingly, they somehow still found time to berate the kids for giggling and being too loud. Threats of "shut up or you will stay after school" echoed down the halls. (Remember I am talking about eight-year-old kids versus German sumo women. It just was not fair.)

Life in Catholic school brought other minor challenges. On a normal day, we were marched, military style—single-file, no talking, etc.—into the church for Mass. Squirming in the pew was not allowed. Ever. Squirm in church, and the sisters had you believing that the guy on the cross would climb down, walk over, and swat you. Meanwhile, the guy in the fancy gown up there on the altar squirmed quite a bit. He would always mumble something and wave his arms around, and for reasons beyond me. I often thought he just had a drinking problem like my uncle, the way he always raised that goblet of wine in seeming praise.

Perhaps I was even altar-boy material. Then I could wear one of those goofy white thingies around my shoulders and press the button that rang the bells. My problem would be trying to act so solemn and holy while holding one of those twenty-foot-long candles during the procession. I'd probably start giggling, lose control of the damned thing, and set some little old lady's wig on fire. (They always seemed to sit near the altar, where I would have a good shot at them with the blowtorch of holiness.)

Confession, too, required no squirming, but this task was harder to achieve while standing in line, feeling anxious because you had to remember what to tell the guy behind the screen regarding how rotten a kid you had been.

Whenever someone was in the confessional, a little red light was on. When it turned off, it was the next person's turn. You would kneel, waiting, hearing the poor kid in the confessional next to you mumbling. Then you would hear the screen slide shut, silence, and you knew your time had come. The screen would slide open and you would see the outline of *him*—the priest—just waiting for you to say how truly bad you had been. When you got in, it was like facing torture in the dark.

For what seemed an eternity, I'd roll around in my brain just what I should say.

Bless me, Father, for I have sinned. Of course, I cannot remember any of my heinous sins, Father, but I saw a good episode of the Lone Ranger the other day ... want to discuss that?

No, I need to make something up, like I talked back to my mom ... yeah, that's a good one. I should get just a few Hail Marys out of that. Let's see, now I need something else to make it seem more real. I know: I punched a kid for stealing my sandwich. Wow! Another good one. I might get a few Our Fathers out of that one, since it involved physical violence.

And so it went on more than one occasion, after which I was told to recite the Act of Contrition. I did, of course, but in my mind, the recitation always sounded a little different. "Oh, my God, I am heartily sorry for having offended thee, and I detest all my sins ..." *No, I don't. Throwing rocks is fun, and I like the F-word, whatever it means.* "... because I dread the loss of heaven and the pains of hell ..." *Well, I guess so, if that's true.* "... but most of all because they offend thee, my God." *God who? That guy hanging on the plus sign in church? Who cares?*

My goal was just to get through it with a standard fare of five to ten Hail Marys and five Our Fathers, and then go to the railing in front of the altar where I could act holy and say my prayers and get my one "Get Out of Hell Free" card, good till I screwed up again … which in my case, might last until I got out the door of the church.

A Doctrine of Fear: Learning Lifelong Unconscious Guilt

THIS TELLS US THAT THEOLOGIES and teachings that appeal to any element of fear are not of Jesus Christ, despite what we were taught as children. In fact, such fear-based theologies constitute what I consider to be spiritual abuse. Strong words, perhaps, but I believe they fit. After all, folks, God is rarely found behind a loud, bellowing voice; more often than not, he is found in the soft sounds of a gentle breeze.

(As a side note, I will go into this idea of fear and religion more in a later chapter, as I observe Eastern religious traditions such as Hinduism or Buddhism. These traditions seem less susceptible to invoking spiritual abuse, since they are focused less on rules and more on the inner life of a person than are Western religions.)

The above stories speak of a human experience that is far broader than that of fifties-style Catholic schools. They speak of an all-too-common scenario, in which an organization uses fear as a tool to invoke obedience to and belief of its own dogma and doctrine. For that reason, I pray that this chapter brings light and peace to your soul, particularly if you, too, struggle with past religious teachings that still evoke fear inside you. If you often find yourself in such a struggle, I ask you to remember what Jesus himself said: "Fear not." It is just that simple. That this quote can be found in Matthew 10:31, Luke 12:7, Luke 12:32, and John 12:15 speaks volumes about its importance.

One of the biggest fear-invoking principles we were taught in Catholic school is that we could not talk to God directly, making God seem like this invisible, looming eye in the sky. The priest had to be our representative, talking to God on our behalf, forcing us to go to confession a lot—just so our sins could be forgiven. So what happens to us if he goes on vacation?

Another terror-filled idea we were fed: if we ever died in our sleep, we had better not have any "mortal sins on our soul," or we would go directly to hell. Now, those words make good ingredients for a sound night's sleep.

Looking back at all of it, I can see now that the establishment was instilling fear into us as a means of making us psychologically and emotionally dependent on the church. I tell you now: reject any doctrine that contains fear as an ingredient. I don't care who's teaching it; if the doctrine has an element of fear, reject it. It is really that simple.

Why? God loves you unconditionally. He is not waiting for you to screw up so that He can send you to hell. Unconditional divine love means just that—there are no requirements you must meet to have God love you. You can squirm at the confessional, giggle in class, even puke on a nun's desk for that matter, and not a lightening bolt will hit you. Heck, God might actually get a chuckle out of some of those things. I can just envision our loving God looking down on that boy in my class that day and saying, "Hey, little Johnnie just puked on Sister Sausage's stuff! Good shot, my little loved one, good shot!"

If you are still uneasy about rejecting establishments that try to bash your brain with their versions of religion, then let's take this issue from another angle.

Much of what we were taught at Catholic school was based on the fear of God rather than the unconditional love of God—the "you'd better obey, or God will smite you" kind of teachings. (Granted, I didn't know what *smite* meant back then, but I did know it didn't sound too good.) We learned there were a whole host of sins, not to mention designated punishments for each kind. In fact, I always imagined the nuns consulting their own table of sins and corresponding punishments whenever a student committed a grievance in class. "Let's see now," the sister would think, "Richard passed gas in class. That will be five Hail Marys." (If it smelled, it would go up to ten.) Of course, no one needed a table to tell them the punishment for missing Holy Mass. That was a mortal sin, which meant it demanded immediate confession or else risk a direct trip to hell.

Anne Katherine, in her book *Boundaries,* has this to say on the subject: "We have spiritual boundaries. You are the only one who knows the right spiritual path for yourself. If someone tries to tell you he knows the only way you can believe, he is out of line." [12]

The Bible also supports this idea of rejecting others' religious ideas if they do not fit your own spirituality. Check out Philippians 2:12 (New English Bible): "You must work out your own salvation with fear and trembling." So while it is okay to be assisted in our beliefs, it is not

---

[12]   Ibid.

acceptable to be forced. Our spiritual development can only come from our inner selves.

The Buddha mirrored the same idea when he said, "Do not go by what is handed down, nor on the authority of your traditions."[13] Instead, he advised making a prayerful individual effort at spirituality, which will help you grow closer to God.

If you still believe this bilge about God always wanting to send you to hell, then stop it right now! God loves you and hears every prayer you've ever said. It is impossible for Him *not* to hear your prayers, and you do *not* need a priest or any other kind of clergy to intercede for you. Remember that God knows even the number of hairs on your head (Matthew 10:30). So why would He not listen to you? He always and forever can and wants to hear your prayers. In fact, He wants to hear everything you have to say, no matter how boring you might think it to be. I am not saying that you should not go to confession or go to a priest for help. Heck, no. There can be great value in involving others on your spiritual journey. But you do not need an intercessory to talk to God.

So when I got older, I rejected everything I was taught. Why? Because I thought the theology was wrong? Heck, I didn't care about that. I just hated how I'd been treated in Catholic school, and consequently, I hated everything having to do with God. In fact, not until I got my master's degree in theology and pastoral ministry forty-five years later did my negative feelings have a firm place on solid theological ground.

Many people today who were exposed to the Catholic school's culture of fear still have lingering feelings of obligation to go to church, lest they go to hell. This is very sad. You should instead go to church because you love Jesus Christ, and you should celebrate the Eucharist out of love. God will not send you to hell if you miss Mass. If that is true, Mahatma Gandhi, the Buddha, Muhammad, and all the previous Dalai Lamas are all roasting in hell right now rubbing shoulders with Adolf Hitler. I don't think anyone believes that is where they are right now. Pray out of love, not out of obligation or fear. Repeat this last sentence until it soaks in. It is that important.

---

[13]   Huston Smith, *The World's Religions* (San Francisco: Harper, 1991).

After All That, My Kids Went to . . . What? Catholic School?

AS A MATTER OF FACT, all my children went to Catholic schools, all the way from elementary through college. Funnier yet, both my oldest and youngest daughters teach at Catholic elementary schools.

How in the heck did that happen? There are a number of reasons. First, in hindsight, I realized that the public schools I attended after leaving St. Tarcissus were even worse than the private ones had been. My deep-seated fear of nuns and God was replaced with the fear of bullies and violence.

In all of the public schools I attended—in Chicago, as well as in Oakland and San Lorenzo (both in California)—I was exposed to a lot of small-time punks who enjoyed pushing others around. These future felons would spit, throw things, and make obscene gestures—anything to pick a fight and get control over classmates. It seemed the playground was always one step away from a fight breaking out.

Further, I began participating in my share of these extracurricular activities. Once, I got pushed a step too far, and the other kid lived to regret it. It got to the point where the sight of blood did not bother me anymore.

At the time, however, I found public school better than the alternative. At least in public school, I could fight and win. In Catholic school, with a two-hundred-fifty-pound nun thundering toward you, winning was impossible. To boot, since I'd gotten the impression at Catholic school that God was like this huge cosmic nun just waiting to send me to hell, I figured, "If I am going there anyway, I may as well give up and fight these nasty little brats."

But then, over time, even though I did not realize it was happening, God was working within me, softening my attitude toward Catholic school. And I began to realize that through the years, Catholic schools had changed for the good in a very big way. These two things—a change in attitude and a change in the Catholic school system—lead me to sense that the "new and improved" system might just instill some good in my kids. In particular, I had a sense that my kids would learn how to feel love toward others and to understand the divine order of things and their places in creation.

So when my kids became school-age, Marilyn and I investigated the local parish schools, and we saw many good things. The class environment was light years away from what I had experienced as a child. It provided a positive atmosphere for kids. And there were no future prison inmates to fight either!

Thus, we decided to send them to Catholic School. To this day, I am glad I did.

Unfortunately, however, even though my attitude toward Catholic school had softened, my attitude toward God did not. Though my wife and I took our kids to church and did all the things we thought necessary to be good Catholic-school parents, I personally still had too many internal disagreements with what I thought it meant to be a real follower of Christ. Not until I took graduate classes in pastoral ministry did I find out that I had actually been standing on solid Catholic doctrine all along. I just hadn't known it.

A Doctrine of Conscience: Learning about Vatican-Blessed Freedom of Faith

IF YOU STILL FEEL UNEASY about going against church doctrine because of what you learned in childhood or in some class somewhere, forget it. If you have prayerfully—and I do mean with sincere prayer—considered a view not blessed by the church, consulted with other Christians about it, and still disagree with it, you must go with your conscience. Yes, even if that means going against a church teaching. How can I say this? Because I happen to know that, as a Catholic, you have a cosmic get-out-of-jail-free card issued by the pope himself. Actually it comes from God, not the pope.

Few people realize there is a Catholic Church doctrine that addresses just such an issue. According to the Freedom of Conscience Doctrine, it is not a sin to follow your prayerfully considered conscience, even if that means deciding upon an action or philosophy that goes against the Church's teaching.

Put another way, if you have a clear conscience while disagreeing with a Church teaching or doctrine, provided that you have spent time in prayer about it and that you accept responsibility for your actions, this doctrine says you are free to do so; you are not sinning. See? Even the Church recognizes that it may not forcefully impose its dogma upon a person who has formed a sincerely prayerful conscience.

Under the Freedom of Conscience Doctrine, I am free to criticize the nuns at St. Tarcissus and any other so-called Christian institution that operates in a culture of fear. And so are you.

In your life, reject fear-based doctrines and compulsions, and remember that *God loves you unconditionally.* What does that really mean? Let's reflect on that now.

Reflection Exercise: What Exactly Is Unconditional Love?

First using the meditation preparation steps, ponder the following thoughts and questions to help you reflect on the idea of unconditional love.

- God loves Adolf Hitler as much as He loves the pope.
- God loves you as much as Albert Einstein.
- God loves you as much as the beggar on the street.
- What does the word *unconditional* mean to you?
- How does the dictionary define the word? What does
- the Catholic Encyclopedia say about it?
- If you said "Fu*k you God" and meant it, would He still love you? Why or why not?
- If you were an atheist would God still love you? Why?
- Think of the person who has hurt you the most on purpose. Have you forgiven that person? Do you love that person? Does God?
- Do other people love you unconditionally? Why or why not?
- When in your life have you displayed unconditional love? When have you failed? (Think of *fail* as just another word for "opportunity for improvement.")

Meditating on the meaning of unconditional love in your life will help you become the best person that you can envision becoming. And, in the process, it will bring you closer to God.

In summary: whether or not we are aware of it, each of us looks at the world through our own experience-based lenses, and we do so mostly subconsciously. That means people who experienced Catholic school as I did, or any other fear-based religious organization when they were young, may well have one or both of the following: (1) subconscious negative attitudes toward God or (2) fear of departing from "official orthodox" doctrine, because they were taught God would punish them. This kind of subconscious thinking is so destructive to the inner beings of people who are indeed made in God's image.

So understand this now: God will *not* punish you if your image of Him is different than what you were taught it should be. Repeat that last sentence until it sinks in, my dear friend. God loves you unconditionally no matter what your sincere beliefs are. You may experience unpleasant consequences of your own making, but God will never stop loving you. Think about this. If God is everywhere, He can never turn His back on you. Why, if He is everywhere, in every direction, He has no back to turn. It's impossible for God to turn away from you—yes, impossible. In fact, this idea is so fundamental that I encourage you to stop and reflect on it.

I can only hope that Jesus asks the St. Tarcissus nuns after their deaths, "Why the hell did you do those horrible things to my children?"

Reflection Exercise: Departing from Childhood Teachings

Do you believe, to this day, all that you were taught as a child? As you ponder this question, certain teachings may come to your mind first. These teachings, for you, are the most important ones to focus on.

Now make a list of all the beliefs and doctrines you still believe in, as well as the ones you don't, and consider the following:

- Why do you still believe in the doctrines you do?
- Why do you not believe in the other doctrines you have listed?
- Do you believe God, with His unconditional love, will send us to hell if we believe something other than what we were taught?
- What is hell? Is it fire and brimstone, or is it separation from God at our own hands?
- Does God dole out punishments to us on this earth? Why or why not?
- Did God allow Moses to kill three thousand people upon his return from the mountain because they made a golden idol? Is Moses in heaven or hell now? Meditate on the implications of both scenarios.
- Do you believe the stories of the Old Testament really happened as described, or are they metaphorical tales meant to drive home a point to the ancient Hebrews?
- Establish in your own mind your image of what God is like and not like.

The above questions, in addition to any others you may come up with, should help you establish the answer to this singular question: What do I believe today?

A Prayer for Divine Guidance and Healing

I MET A MAN QUITE a few years ago who mentioned that he, too, had gone to Catholic school and then proceeded to tell me, in very animated, forceful tones, that he considered the pope a fascist. Wow! I was shocked to hear someone express such strong negative feelings about the pope so openly. I could only wonder what pain he must have endured as a child to feel so intensely even as an adult.

This experience proved to me that many people not only still deal with the spiritual damage inflicted on them as children by all flavors of religious zealots, but also carry varying degrees of it. In other words, while the man in front of me seemed to have extreme bitterness against the Church, religion, for me, amounted to just a pain in the ass. Fortunately for all of us, regardless of our degree of pain, God has plans for each of us.

In my experience, He loved me despite how I felt about Him, and His power was far greater than any of the nuns or my abusive father could ever wield. God used that power in ways that I never suspected at the time, but looking back, I now see how certain incidents led me to where I am today: in a deep and loving relationship with God. In spite of all the suffering I had to endure growing up and all the healing I had to do as an adult to overcome its negative effects, He guided me here. And I really mean *guided*. He did not force in any way. He opened doors of understanding, and it was up to me to go through them. (Remember, God never forces Himself upon anyone; that would violate His gift of free will to us.)

I promise you that God will do this for you, too, if you ask Him to come into your life. You do not need any fancy prayers. You do not need a priest or anyone in the clergy. All you need is an open and sincere heart. And if you are a victim of religious abuse, I pray that you will understand what happened and work to overcome your feelings toward God and Christianity (or any other religious institution that may have used fear tactics on you).

The following prayer is a good start:

My Dear Father and Mother in heaven,
I hurt now. I am aware of hurtful emotions within me.
I feel defective inside, but I hide it from others,
for if they knew my thoughts, it would bring me even more pain.
Dear God, I open my heart to You.
Please guide me to heal from my past.
Please give me what I need to heal.
You know what that is, even though I do not.
I want to return to the road that leads to the real, loving me.
I want to shed this false outer me and heal inside.
Then I can be who You intended me to be;
then I can shine my unique light of You into the world.

Amen.

Review

FROM THE AGES OF TWO to about six, everything we experience is new and not understood. This is the age of wonderment and excitement, the age when kids drive their parents nuts with questions of "why."

Although I was only in the first grade, I began to be fearful of God because of what the nuns taught. I started to equate God to a bunch of rules that, if broken, you got punished for. It's sad that the nuns used prayers like the Our Father and Hail Mary as punishments for us. This is a great way to drive kids away from prayer, as they did with me.

The age range of three to six is when self-awareness begins. It's during this time that "Mine!" is heard frequently. The first real awareness of death occurs at this age also. About this developmental stage, Fowler wrote, "In league with forms of knowing dominated by perception, imagination in this stage is extremely productive of long lasting images and feelings, that later more stable and self-reflective valuing and thinking will have to order and sort out."[14] Or, in simpler words, long-lasting images and feelings, both positive and negative, are formed during this stage.

---

[14]   James Fowler, *Stages of Faith* (San Francisco: Harper Collins, 1981), 134.

Contrary to what Fowler says, however, I feel many people do not go back and reprocess those childhood lessons, and the results are spiritual stagnation and, in many cases, a continuing fear or dislike of God and religion in general. When a child does begin to question those lessons and try to clarify just what is real and what is not, the transition to Stage Two starts.

CHAPTER 5

Stage Two: The Faith of Older Children/Preadolescents

THE TRANSITION TO STAGE TWO happens to most children at age eight or nine, although there is no definite point when it occurs. The end of stage one is not like the end of trading in the stock market, when a bell is rung. It's more of a transition period where certain attributes drop off and others begin to make their presence known.

Ideas about Self, Relationships, and Authority

PRE-ADOLESCENCE IS THE PSYCHOLOGICAL AGE bracket in which kids must feel they are important and loved by others. Close relationships with peers as well as with parents and other authority figures engenders the older child with self worth. In addition, older kids who feel loved and valued can become productive, creative, and successful with the responsibilities given to them.

Conversely, negative relationships with parents and peers at this stage can lead to deep feelings of inferiority and inhibition. The virtuous feeling of being competent in life is lost, which can lead to frustration and rage against others. Yet another example of the point that I cannot stress enough in this book about the power parents have on their kids' lives.

As Anne Katherine in her book, *Boundaries,* says, "A parent has the power to validate or invalidate the worth of his or her child. The potential for harm is overwhelming … Many children are like miniature radar receivers. They pick up on everything. They are highly observant and aware of nuance, implications at a glance. Their interpretations and conclusions stem from five delicate senses. These interpretations can have the force of a bullet."[15]

In my case, my father doled out spankings and slaps across the face for my doing whatever little boys do. He also yelled, threatened, and belittled me to gain my compliance to whatever he demanded, often while stating his philosophy that "kids should be seen and not heard." It's no wonder I felt so greatly inferior.

Of course, this phenomenon about a parent's influence on a child also applies to other close authority figures—teachers, grandparents, day care providers, or, in my case again, the nuns at St. Tarcissus. Worse yet, it applies to all religious authorities, who are in a position to do great damage to children's self-images as well as to their images of God.

New Life, Same Fights

AFTER I COMPLETED THE FOURTH grade at St. Tarcissus, I went to the local public school, Farnsworth Elementary. I loved getting out of the Catholic prison, and life in public school was good. I did well and even participated in the fifth grade talent show with a magic act. Now that the school pressure was off, I "just" had to deal with the rage of my father.

My father's second-hand cigarette smoke and ever-present threats of punishment had an unhealthy effect on me. I was so sick at times my mother worried that I had leukemia. It was only after a series of serious sicknesses that one doctor discovered I had severe chronic allergies and asthma. After several doctors' visits, my parents were told that the best thing for me was to move either to California or Florida.

I was eleven years old when we moved to California. My parents chose California because my father had seen San Francisco on the way back from Guam after WWII and liked it. I was excited to move. In fact, I still view the move to California as one of the two good things my father did in my life. (The second was not to stand in the way of my college education. I would be the first Ferguson ever to go to college, and he liked that. Also, I would be remiss not to say that it seems to take ten good things to cancel out one rotten one, so I'm not convinced my dad made up for his shortcomings.)

---

[15]   Anne Katherine, *Boundaries* (New York: MJF Books, 1991), 89.

Going to school in Oakland was a new experience for me in several ways. For one, it was the first time in my life I had gone to a racially mixed school, and this opened my eyes to racism like I had never seen it before.

I also saw abuse and violence anew, in two different respects. First, I discovered that many of my classmates lived in homes far more abusive than mine. Second, because I happened to move to this school at an age when anger begins being acted out on the playground, I witnessed more violence among my peers. And not only at school, but around the neighborhood, too, which was … well, let's say it was not the cream of the crop. There was a hard edge to the people there and many of the kids had abusive personalities.

So for me, home was a source of fear, school was a source of fear, and the streets were a source of fear. All of that fear piled together made me feel generally distrustful and defective. Often, I wanted just to be invisible, because I thought I would stay safe that way.

The result of all this for me was a deep-seated fear of authority figures, which persisted until I got the psychotherapy I needed to realize the error in my thinking and the true source of these negative feelings and actions. Even in my college years, I did not ask questions in class many times, for fear the professors would think I sounded stupid. Every time I even considered raising my hand, an invisible war would take place in my head, unnoticed by everyone. It was: raise your hand, risk embarrassment; keep it down and risk a lower score on the test. Back and forth I went. I developed other attitudinal problems, as well; to name a few, I became angry at small things and was overly critical of myself when I made a mistake.

Experiences are constantly forming the ultimate mental conditions under which a child will understand human existence and create a personal image of God, both of which will last a lifetime.

Ideas about Fairness and Justice

ANOTHER ASPECT OF SPIRITUAL AND psychological growth among preadolescents is a growing sense of fairness and justice. For example, kids this age will often complain, "It's not fair!"

As part of this new awareness, kids will have made the connection between wrongdoing and punishment. That means, in most cases, if an older child knowingly does something wrong, he or she will accept the punishment.

Likewise, however, if a parent punishes a child unfairly, the child also knows that acutely. Abused children actually have a strong sense that they are being abused, even if they cannot articulate it; they simply feel violated, treated unfairly, and build up rage as a result. Then they either turn their rage outward, directing it toward others, or inward (as I did), following a course to adult depression.

The following story is a good example of how that was a process for me. It was a hot summer afternoon in Chicago. I was on my roller skates, going up and down the cement sidewalk in front of our apartment building. I had the kind of skates that you needed to tighten onto your shoes with a key. The sun was shining, and I was having fun listening to the skates growl over the pavement, as they were metal and made lots of noise across the cracks.

After a while, I got thirsty, so I went through the back door into the kitchen to get a drink. Dad's rule was: no skates in the house. But the kitchen sink was only about eight feet from the door, and I was so thirsty. I did not want to have to take my skates off just to walk a few feet, get a drink, and walk back, only to put them back on. So I skated to the sink to get my drink of water.

Then my dad walked in from the other room and saw me with my skates on. I was not aware of the trouble I was in, though. I was still just looking forward to going back out for more skating.

"Here comes the Cheerio Kid," I said to him, mimicking a popular TV commercial at the time. With that, Dad grabbed me by the arm and started yelling about how he would not tolerate skates in the house. He then led me to my bedroom and told me to take down my pants and bend over the edge of the bed. When I did, he proceeded to whip me with his belt. I still can remember the sound his belt made as he took it off; sounds like that stay with you for the rest of your life. Not until I was crying uncontrollably did he stop hitting me and say something to the effect of, "Let that be a lesson to you."

I don't remember if I ever got my drink of water. I definitely did not skate anymore that day. I did not do anything else, for that matter. I just stayed in my room, feeling crushed, embarrassed, and humiliated.

That night at dinner, my dad told me that he'd had a hard time not laughing at my "Cheerio Kid" joke while he was beating me with his belt. Somehow, it seemed, he thought the whole thing was funny! Other times in the summer I would be thirsty and ask for a Coke. He would respond by asking me in a very stern voice, "What's wrong with water?" When

I got older and had developed my "marketing mouth" more acutely, I would answer by saying, "You know it must taste a lot better don't you?" As an adult I spoke before large crowds of customers as the corporate representative, hence I needed my "marketing mouth." My response usually would start an argument. I usually lost.

According to Fowler, in the same way that kids this age begin to see similarities between parents and authority figures and their developing image of God, they also project human characteristics relating to judgment, anger, forgiveness, and mercy on God. They assume that the emotions and actions of humans in this area are also the emotions and actions held by God.

As such, my image of God was not good. He was just another potential source of getting into big trouble. And so in the same way I tried to stay out of my father's way to avoid undue punishment, I gave no thought to God. I wanted nothing to do with Him and what I had always heard called "the wrath of God." As a side note on this topic, however, my mother in all of this was the compassionate one, who never failed to support me and provide me what I needed. She took very good care of me. In fact, I credit her with preventing me from going over the edge.

Reflection Exercise: Childhood Injustice and Pain

Using our standard reflection preparation steps, pause for a moment and reflect on events in your life that, either good or bad, had a strong effect on your ideas of what it means to be treated fairly. Here are some thoughts and questions to get you started:

- How did your teachers treat you?
- Does any one teacher stick out in your mind as being very good or very bad? What is your attitude and memory toward this teacher today?
- As a child, did you feel that you could be yourself at home? If not, why not?
- If you messed up as a child how did your parents handle it? In your mind at the time did you consider that fair? Today, what is your opinion of their treatment of your violation? Is it the same or has it changed over the years?
- Did your parents outwardly show love and affection toward you? Did you feel loved?
- What person gave you the roughest time growing up? Does that still hurt?

I have already said this in many of the other reflection exercises, but it bears repeating: do this exercise while remembering that you are a loved child of God and that nothing can separate you from Him—nothing. Ask God for His guidance in remembering what you can and His help in healing from whatever hurt. Ask Him, too, to guide you to a deeper understanding of each event you ponder, as well as the effects it had on you. Be gentle with yourself as you remember these events of so long ago.

Vocal Expression

ONE DAY, I WAS PLAYING ball with a boy across the street from me, named Gary. Looking back, I can see he took out all of his aggression on me. Sometimes I would go home hoarse from all the yelling I did at him. On this particular day, his usual harassment commenced because he was losing the game and did not like it one bit. He would try to cheat and then argue about how many outs there were, and so on. He blatantly broke my sense of fair play.

In response, after using my big mouth as always, I did something new—I got physical. I shoved him to the ground and he fell right on his butt. His face blossomed with surprise and flushed red. I then threatened to beat him up so bad and pound him so low that the ants would pee on him. And that's when Gary said, "F— you!" Well. This was new.

I'd never heard that word before. What could it mean? I didn't know, but from the way he'd used it, it did sound like a word that would come in handy some day. After all, Gary was a whole two years older than I was, so I figured he'd probably learned it somewhere really good.

That said, I yelled back. "F— you and your mother too!"

With that, he shoved me back, and the game was over. Whatever I had just said, it apparently had worked.

Later that afternoon, I went home and asked my mom, "What does f— mean?"

There was a dead silence, a long silence. The earth stood still, birds stopped singing, airplanes halted in midair. I immediately knew I had hit upon something. Finally, she turned to me. With the look on her face, you'd think I'd just dropped the communion wafer in church.

"Where did you hear that?" she asked.

Then I really knew something was up. I told her that Gary had said it to me.

"You should never ever use that word again," she said. "It's a very bad word. If I hear you use that word again, you will get soap in your mouth."

That was the day I expanded my vocabulary by one fun word and gained a new tool to express my rejection and anger—well, as long as some adult didn't hear me say it. Isn't it funny how banning something increases its popularity?

Soon there were lots of kids around the block using this great word. We found many creative uses for it too. But the point is it was so expressive, so it felt good to yell it at someone. That's because as kids this age begin to develop a sense of reciprocal fairness and divine lawfulness, anger begins to build in response to what they perceive as the many injustices in the world. They need a way to express that anger. And vocabulary is just such a way.

Fowler says the following about this idea: "The limitations of literalness and an excessive reliance upon reciprocity as a principle for constructing an ultimate environment can result in ... an abasing sense of badness embraced because of mistreatment, neglect or the apparent disfavor of significant others."[16] In other words, the world already seems unfair, so if you add abuse or neglect to that experience, a child forms a very negative view of him- or herself and, as a result, takes the pain out on others. It's no coincidence, then, that this is the same age range in which behavior problems begin.

I remember all the ways my father mistreated me as a child, and at the time, deep down, I knew his behavior was not right. In addition, because I naturally projected the human qualities displayed by my dad onto God, God, to me, was like an old man watching everything I did. He was very much like Santa Claus, who could always see who was naughty and nice. The result: I felt indeed that I was a bad boy. I felt I was defective. But I could not articulate all the anger and pain I had. I never questioned why I felt so angry with everyone, but felt helpless to do anything about it.

Now, I can see that my use of the F-word was an attempt to let off the steam that had built up inside of me as a result of my inability to express my anger toward my dad. In turn, using foul language enabled me to be in touch with my inner being. By using these new choice words, I began to realize that there was anger inside of me, although I could not yet express those feelings directly (for example, by realizing and saying, simply, "I am angry"). Besides, from a faith perspective, using this word will not send you to hell. If that were true, there would be no teamsters in heaven—and that cannot be true. God has heard it all, and more, anyway.

Here's how Fowler described this idea of vocalization in Stage Two: "The great gift to consciousness that emerges in this stage is the ability to narratize one's experience."[17]

You've probably heard this story about two brothers, but it perfectly exemplifies this concept of verbalization, particularly in dealing with words that are typically considered forbidden. The story goes that a nine-year-old and a seven-year-old are alone in their bedroom.

"You know what?" the nine-year-old asks his smaller brother. "I think it's about time we started cussing."

The seven-year-old nods in approval.

The nine-year-old continues. "When we go downstairs for breakfast, I'm gonna say something with *hell* and you say something with *ass*."

The seven-year-old agrees with enthusiasm.

---

[16]   James Fowler, *Stages of Faith* (San Francisco: Harper Collins, 1981), 150.

[17]   Ibid., 136.

Later, when the mother walks into the kitchen and asks the nine-year-old what he wants for breakfast, he replies, "Aw, hell, Mom, I guess I'll have some Cheerios."

Whack! He flies out of his chair and tumbles across the kitchen floor. When he gets up, he runs upstairs crying his eyes out. His mother is in hot pursuit, slapping his rear with every step. Then his mom locks him in his room and shouts, "You can stay there until I let you out!"

She then comes back downstairs, looks at the seven-year-old and asks with a stern voice, "And what do *you* want for breakfast, young man?"

"I don't know," he blubbers, "but you can bet your ass it won't be Cheerios!"

Though this little anecdote is meant as a joke, it is interesting when you apply it to the principle of increased vocalization in Stage Two. While our little heroic seven-year-old is getting verbal, his self-expression doesn't include questioning his mother's punishment of his brother. In other words, the younger brother is indirectly expressing his anger toward his mother, without knowing it. Fowler would say that it's because our seven-year-old has an "understanding of reciprocal justice as an immanent structure in our lives."[18]

Looking back, I marvel at how God rescued me from all of my pain and helped me to be where I am today. No one can ever convince me there are not miracles.

Aggression

WHEN I WAS ABOUT EIGHT, I used to play with two brothers about my age named John and Russell. One day, they came over to play marbles, and I saw that both of them had broken their left arms. Yes, *both* of them, each in the same spot and on the same arm. Both had casts from their wrists to their elbows, both held in place by white slings. Now being only eight, I never saw past the obvious. Frankly, I had thought it was neat. *Gee, look at all the attention and sympathy they got*, I thought. *I like that.*

After a time, the slings and casts came off, and life returned to normal. But about eighteen months later—guess what? Again both of them broke their arms—same arms, same spot, and on the same day. They told me it had happened while playing. *Well how about that!* I thought, *What are the chances of two brothers breaking the same arm on the same day accidentally ... twice?* Later, I realized that chances are better finding Elvis alive and living

---

[18] Ibid., 143.

in a Florida retirement home playing Mozart. Apparently, I wasn't the only kid in the neighborhood who was abused. But at the time, all that mattered is that we could still play marbles together, so not much was said about it after that.

In *Ghosts from the Nursery*, Morse and Wiley write the following:

> In an abusive environment … internalizing children may develop generalized anxiety and later depression or panic disorders. These are often the children who seem the easiest to socialize because they comply to avoid negative consequences.… But like little pressure cookers, they also may repress negative feelings and then explode in aggressive behavior. In an overly punitive or critical environment, the price to children who internalize is self-directed emotional violence resulting, at a minimum, in the erosion of confidence and competence and, in the worst cases, suicide.[19]

I really see myself in those words. They explain why I have post-traumatic stress disorder, which requires drugs to this day: kids' nervous systems get damaged permanently due to abuse, and that damage stays for a lifetime.

However, these words also explain how violence gets transmitted from one generation to the next. These damaged kids, once adults, express their pain through further aggression. In the same way that using foul language becomes a way to unconsciously express the pain and anger resulting from mistreatment, aggression becomes a means to convey negative feelings as a result of abuse. In the book *Ghosts from the Nursery*, the authors say, "Physically abusing a child is another way to handle anger or frustration or feelings of being trapped and overwhelmed. The parent beats the child to relieve his or her own emotional needs."

The foundation for physical aggression is laid long before a child becomes an adult, however. In fact, Fowler says the basis for aggression is built as early as age four or five (see more on this topic in the next chapter).

When I got angry, for example, it came out on the streets. (Of course, the neighborhood I grew up in was not exactly where Ozzie and Harriet or Beaver Cleaver lived.) Even though I was pale white, skinny, and frail, I got into multiple fistfights and rock fights. The standard procedure in rock fights was to stand about fifty feet apart, yell a lot, and heave as many

---

[19]   Robin Karr-Morse and Meredith S. Wiley, *Ghosts from the Nursery* (Atlantic Monthly Press, 1997), 140.

rocks at the other kid as you could—and, yes, with the intent to do real harm. I got good at throwing accurately and dodging incoming rocks while yelling, "You missed me, you big %*&^@#!"

One rock fight in particular stands out in my mind as the epitome of this idea that physical aggression is the result of pent-up anger. It was with a kid from my fifth grade class, and we were throwing rocks at each other over traffic on a busy street. Hell, we never hit anybody's car, so we thought we were okay. At one point, I heaved a pretty large rock over. I watched it arch over the tops of the cars, and, a few seconds later, saw the kid fall to the ground. I'd made a direct hit on his head while he'd been bending down to get another rock. *Great shot!* I thought. And that was it. I had won. So I turned around and walked home, feeling very satisfied with myself.

The next day at school, I learned that the kid had needed five or six stitches in his head. I still didn't feel bad about it. I was spilling over with so much anger from school and home and the streets that I did not care how much the other boy was hurting or about what my teachers thought. My hands were too full with surviving my environment. And as far as what God thought … God who? The guy in the sky could wait as far as I was concerned. I just hoped that my parents would never find out. (Mom, if you are reading this, sorry! You had to be tough in that neighborhood!)

I did not realize at the time how damaged I was on the inside. I was not aware of the serious emotional distress, depression, and anger I felt. I was not aware of feeling worthless and suspicious of everyone around me, both of which controlled my aggression.

Another fight that sticks out in my mind happened when we first moved to Oakland. Being the new kid on the block, I had yet to build a community of friends, so I hung out with one guy for a while who liked to antagonize others and push people into doing things he knew they did not want to. One day, he was playing at my house, and for some unknown reason, he wanted to throw a toy of mine over the edge of the balcony. I tried to stop him, telling him he'd better not, and so, of course, he did. He threw my toy off the balcony and broke it. I got so mad, I punched him as hard as I could, smack dab in the face. He wound up on his back in the bushes. You should have seen the look on his bloodied face. He was shocked that someone had not only stood up to him, but had hauled off and plastered him right in his bugger locker.

"You hit me!" he said, with a look of shock and pain.

I started yelling at him and said, "Do that again, and all of you will hurt next time! If I ever see you again, I will kill you."

He ran home holding his nose, and that was the last I played with him. This boy had just gotten a taste of the crud that had been cooking for years in my personal pressure cooker; unfortunately for him, it tasted like my fist.

Later in life, when I looked back on these events, I could see how I had begun turning into my father. This occurred in my forties, during therapy, when it was discovered that I was very abused as a child, and I was diagnosed with Post-Traumatic Stress Disorder.

The Spiritual Ripple Effect: How Attitudes Are Transmitted through Generations

It's often clear that the things we say and do have immediate effects on those involved. What we may not realize is that our words and actions also impact people from whom we are far removed, both in space and time. This idea is something I call the spiritual ripple effect.

To understand what I mean, imagine throwing a stone into a still lake. Immediately, you can see the water ripple outward from the place where the stone went in—those ripples, which are sudden and conspicuous, are like the immediate effects of our words and deeds on others. But what you often do not see in the water are the dozens, even hundreds, of additional ripples that result from just these first few. These other ripples usually go unnoticed because they are more distant and subtle, and can happen quite a bit after the original impact of the rock—much like the effects of our behaviors go unnoticed in future generations and distant places.

Let me give you an example. My father's father was a self-centered, dishonest man. There was an absence of love in his house, not only in the way he raised my dad, but also in the way he treated the dogs on their farm. As such, my grandfather painted for my father a picture of what normative behavior should look like and immediately affected my father's inner being. This was the first ripple in the water. The effects on my dad then rippled through time, as my father treated me likewise, resulting in incidents like the time I got a beating and my father pushed my face into the urine on my bed after I wet it, saying, "this is what we do to dogs on the farm."

Unfortunately, when my father became an adult, he didn't stop the destructive ripples from moving through time and to me. My father accepted hitting, yelling, and issuing punishments and threats for every little misstep as a valid way to parent.

It seems hard to believe that the cruel parenting and dog-training methods in a Virginia farm during the 1930s, combined with my father's acceptance of those methods as legitimate, would result in me spending time in psychotherapy and dealing with emotional depression the rest of my life. That's not to say my father's problems were the only cause of my own issues—it takes more than one brick of abuse to build a house of depression—but they did play a very large part.

I chose to stop the destructive ripples. I would not pass it on. Without my awareness, this decision began to take form in my mind when I was just ten or eleven years old. I started to really see the destructiveness in my father's actions, not only toward me but toward others as well. I began, on some level, to become aware of the fact that I was showing aggression toward others with little concern over whether I hurt them. It was not long after that realization that I began to think about how I never wanted to become like him.

I started *mentally* rejecting his behavior, though I still acted out physically. Fully rejecting my father's behavior was a gradual process. It took years for the idea to crystallize in my mind, and not until I was fifteen or sixteen did I realize that I had choices in my life, thanks to God and my mother. Finally, though, I stopped behaving like him altogether. God had other plans for me. And for that, I am eternally thankful.

The idea of abusive behavior rippling across generations is not new. Thoughtful people back in Roman times were even aware that it happened. As Roman poet and satirist Juvenal (55 AD–127 AD) recommended, "Refrain from doing ill, for one all-powerful reason, lest our children should copy our misdeeds; we are all too prone to imitate whatever is base and depraved."[20]

The spiritual ripple effect also applies to positive energy. Positive words and actions work their way down the line, as well. I would be remiss not to mention that the definitive example of the spiritual ripple effect is Jesus's crucifixion and resurrection. This event has rippled across the entire world and over two thousand years in time. And those ripples continue to this day, thankfully for us.

Remember this spiritual principle, and it will help you better understand the world you live in as well as your own behavior. And then beware of

---

[20]   http://www.quotationspage.com

what you say and do; you create spiritual ripples in this world and to the next generation.

Fiction as Fact

Most kids in Stage Two love fictional stories. The story becomes a powerful way for kids to relate to existence. It provides them with a model of how to relate to their surroundings, and as such, it also creates or recreates their images of authority figures and God. Fowler wrote, "Stories of lives and of great adventures, true or realistically fictional, appeal because of their inherent interest, but they also appeal because they become media for the extension of the child's experience and understanding of life."[21]

Books and TV are powerful mediums for delivering stories to children. I loved reading Jules Verne's *Twenty Thousand Leagues Under the Sea,* and TV was a big influence in my increasing understanding of life and the rules of existence in my pre-adolescence.

My favorite back then was the Western, which was actually more of a morality play, with good guys fighting bad guys. The good guys always wore white hats and the bad guys wore black. Shows like *Davy Crockett, King of the Wild Frontier* by Walt Disney showed a man of high principles, who lived an ethical life and was an excellent role model for kids my age. Thank you, Walt Disney.

I also liked series that depicted kids and families in real-life situations. In that vein, thanks to Disney again for *Spin and Marty,* a daily show about two kids at summer camp who were treated with love and kindness by the adults around them. Also among these series were the *Ozzie and Harriet Show,* which depicted a family with a loving father and mother who responded to the trouble their kids got into with kind but firm guidance. *Leave It to Beaver,* another show depicting loving parents and the travails of growing up, was a series I really identified with—or, maybe better said, wanted to identify with. *Father Knows Best* and *The Donna Reed Show* featured the same basic theme: kids my age who had a father who gently responded to their mischief and treated his kids with kindness even when he was angry.

I did not know it at the time, but these shows gave me the priceless knowledge that not all fathers treated their kids the way my father treated me. They gave me a context, a background against which I could see the blatant contrast between others' dads and mine. Against that backdrop, my

---

[21]   *Stages of Faith,* James Fowler, Harper San Francisco, 1981 pg136

dad's anger stuck out like black dot on a white wall. I began to understand that his treatment of me was not normal, and to see him for what he really was. I began to know that things did not have to be this way and that there were better ways for fathers to treat their children. Unlike the TV show, I began to know that Father—at least my father—did *not* know best.

On the other hand, it was also in this context that I saw that my mother acted very much like the idealized moms on TV. My mother was the Donna Reed or the Harriet Nelson in our house.

Now, I certainly did not have any of these thoughts consciously, and so I did not react to them at the time. But a context of conduct was forming in my mind that made my mother begin to appear as a saint and my father as the cruel person he really was. This context was important later on, when I began looking back on my life. It brought light and understanding to my life, leading me to a deeper understanding of myself, which was the beginning to understanding God.

God and the Lone Ranger in the 1950s

You know how certain things just stick with us even though they seem relatively unimportant? The reason is that, at the time, the event carried a meaningful spiritual message which we happened to be open to, so it resonated within us as something that just "rang true." In other words, a godly truth was being revealed to us. Well, one thing that has stuck with me all these years is a particular *Lone Ranger* episode.

Back when I was about ten or eleven, one of my favorite Western series was the *Lone Ranger*. If you are older than dirt like I am, you probably remember the popular phrase from this show: "Who was that masked man? Look, he gave me a silver bullet!" which was always followed by the Lone Ranger and Tonto riding off into the sunset, after doing great good by defeating the bad guys in black hats.

Well in this one particular episode I remember, an old Indian chief and a minister, who'd been passing by on a wagon train, were talking about God—or what the chief called "the big spirit in the sky." The chief was interested in what the "pale face" worshiped as God. The minister told him about the Christian God, but the Indian chief did not seem all that impressed. So the minister showed the chief the Bible, and again, the chief had very little reaction. So finally the chief asked the minister a series of questions, the first of which was, "Do you believe in the Great Spirit beyond the mountains and sky?"

The minister said yes.

"Do you believe in the Great Spirit that makes the rivers run, the buffalo herds for our meat, and the papoose inside our squaws?"

The minister said yes to that also.

"Do you believe that the Great Spirit makes the rain and sun for our crops, and calls to us when we die?"

The minister could only agree with that, too.

So then the moment came that I will remember always. The old Indian chief concluded, "Hmmmm. You got same God as us."

I will pound the drum again and say that looking back will show us spiritual truths that we learned as kids but did not know it at the time. In this case, the truth I learned was that this Indian chief, someone whom the white man considered a savage, was actually so spiritually evolved that he could see that the same God was in all things—including what the minister was preaching as Christianity, which the chief had never heard of before. The chief's faith was an example to me of healthy, open spirituality, and I wondered how much better a place our world would be if more people were as wise as he. (As a side note, after studying theology and pastoral ministry, I came to believe that all the world's religions, no matter how different they may seem on the surface, are actually worshiping the same loving God that we Christians do. In fact, I have devoted a whole chapter to this subject on the world's religions that I think you will find eye-opening.)

Isn't it interesting that a theological truth can be found almost anywhere, if only you are paying attention? If you look under the surface of things and think about it, you will begin to see enormous spiritual forces at work in everyday life—even in our childhood viewing of the *Lone Ranger!* That may sound a bit weird, but remember that God did not shut up two thousand years ago, so follow me on this one. God is continually revealing Himself to us through events, people, and even our own feelings; this idea is actually an orthodox Catholic doctrine too.

People who disagree that God's revelations continue to this day just are not paying attention. Their minds are too occupied with the material things in life to see the spiritual things. But, if you have spiritual eyes and ears, you can see the existence of God all around you and the presence of God throughout your past. So on that note, here are some additional spiritual lessons I learned from the Lone Ranger during my second stage of faith. Now let's take a quick look at the Lone Ranger's creed. These are the values and beliefs that he lived his fictional life by:

I believe that to have a friend,
a man must be one.
That all men are created equal
and that everyone has within himself
the power to make this a better world.
That God put the firewood there
but that every man
must gather and light it himself.
In being prepared
physically, mentally, and morally
to fight when necessary
for that which is right,
a man should make the most
of what equipment he has.
That "This government,
of the people, by the people
and for the people"
shall live always.
That men should live by
the rule of what is best
for the greatest number.
That sooner or later—
somewhere, somehow—
we must settle with the world
and make payment for what we have taken.
That all things change but truth,
and that truth alone lives on forever
in my Creator, my country, my fellow man.[22]

This creed is actually quite biblical. Check out what the Bible says in the following areas:

- **Regarding friends.** Jesus said in John 15:13, "Greater love has no man than this, that a man lay down his life for his friends."

---

[22] http://www.endeavorcomics.com/largent/ranger/creed.html

- **Regarding equality.** Jesus ate with sinners and outcasts of the Hebrew society. This action is a powerful statement of the equality that Jesus regarded these people with.
- **Regarding God providing for us.** St. Paul said in 2 Corinthians 9:8, "And God is able to provide you with every blessing in abundance, so that you may always have enough of everything and may provide in abundance for every good work."
- **Regarding fighting for what is right.** 2 Timothy 4:7 says, "I have fought the good fight, I have finished the race, I have kept the faith." (But remember that Jesus said to forgive your enemies, too.)
- **Regarding doing good for the most people.** Speaking of the second most important commandment, Jesus said in Matthew 22:39, "you shall love your neighbor as yourself." Also, St. Paul wrote in 1 Corinthians 10:24, "Let no one seek his own good, but the good of his neighbor."
- **Regarding settling with the world.** In one of the synoptic gospels, Matthew 13:49 says, "So it will be at the close of the age. The angels will come out and separate the evil from the righteous."
- **Regarding that all things change.** Ecclesiastes 3:1–8: "For everything there is a season, and a time for every matter under heaven; a time to be born, and a time to die; a time to plant, and a time to pluck up what is planted; a time to kill, and a time to heal; a time to break down, and a time to build up; a time to weep, and a time to laugh; a time to mourn, and a time to dance; a time to cast away stones, and a time to gather stones together; a time to embrace, and a time to refrain from embracing; a time to seek, and a time to lose; a time to keep, and a time to cast away; a time to rend, and a time to sew; a time to keep silence, and a time to speak; a time to love, and a time to hate; a time for war, and a time for peace."

The Lone Ranger creed, then, is actually biblical material in a different form. Interesting, isn't it? The writer of the Lone Ranger Creed had to get the idea to write what he did from somewhere. I believe that "somewhere" could have been God.

Bottom line: God lives, and you will find His continuing self-revelation in many things around you, if only you pay attention and look into your past. Look for God and I guarantee that you will indeed find Him.

You may remember that Tonto always called the Lone Ranger "Kemosabe." Tonto was a very loyal friend to the Lone Ranger. One day after the Lone Ranger and Tonto had retired on their ranch, they were walking through the cattle area, reminiscing about all their adventures. Suddenly, Tonto grabbed the Lone Ranger by the arm, pointed to the ground in front of them, and said, "Lone Ranger, watch out! Don't step in the kemosabe!" (And you thought a theology book couldn't be funny.) So, for all those years, it seemed Tonto had been calling the Lone Ranger ... well, you get the gist! As it turns out, however, this was only a joke, as the word "kemosabe" actually means "faithful friend" or "trusty scout." But in knowing so, we see that in the preceding jest, there is a spiritual value. Did you catch it? Tonto was showing love for the Lone Ranger in the "afterlife" as he always had on the trail. Pay attention, and you will find God.

Preadolescent Faith: A Summary

PREADOLESCENTS START TO UNDERSTAND GOD as a kind of cosmic human; that is, a being who has human characteristics and emotions, such as anger, forgiveness, and other qualities that they see in their parents. Kids also begin to see a similarity between the role of their parents and other authority figures, and the role of God in their lives.

As their sense of fairness and reciprocity develops, they see a connection between wrongdoing and its subsequent punishment. They begin to decipher "big wrongs" versus small ones, and to understand how the punishment should fit the violation; consequently, any mismatch feeds their view that the world is unfair.

This developing sense of justice carries over into their view of God, and there is an emerging concept of divinely instituted lawfulness.

From a psychological perspective, adolescents become able to verbalize their life experiences, telling and listening to stories, and thus learning from the common experience. As such, the story becomes a powerful way to understand life.

Finally, kids at this age need the love and support of significant others in their lives, especially of parents and other close caregivers.

CHAPTER 6

Stage Three: The Faith of Teenagers

Interpersonal betrayals can give rise to ... nihilistic despair ...
—James Fowler, regarding the dangers of Stage Three faith

IN THE TEENAGE YEARS, IMAGE is all-important. This is the age in which kids begin forming their own unique identities in terms of how they fit into the larger human race. It is the age in which girls primp endlessly in front of the mirror and guys learn the phrase "I have to freshen up" from the girls.

It is an age of great and rapid change, physically and emotionally. Puberty hits and hormones start to rage. Body parts grow and hair appears where it never was before. To boys, girls start appearing as more than longhaired aliens with various-sized bumps on their chests. High school boys compare notes on dates, and baseball metaphors abound. For the first time in their lives, the brains of these newly minted teenagers allow them to see themselves from the outside, reflecting on their own thinking. As a result, new feelings, anxieties, and attitudes spring forth, often creating internal turmoil.

To get their bearings during this time of chaotic change, teenagers become involved in social cliques and seek social acceptance. Being an accepted member of a like-minded and like-talented group is vitally important to legitimize the adolescent's newly forming personhood. As James Fowler says, the social group gives a teenager the "eyes and ears of a few trusted others in which to see the image of personality emerging and to get a hearing for the new feelings, insights, anxieties, and commitments that are forming and seeking expression."[23] Erik Erikson confirms this idea when he says adolescents "are now primarily concerned with what they appear to be in the eyes of others as compared with what they feel they are."[24]

You've seen these small groups of like-minded kids walking down the mall together: the "in" crowd, the dweebs, the geeks, the jocks, the socialites, the smart ones, the freaks. These are just a few of the social groups named by teenagers based on emerging personalities and talents.

Social acceptance is important for more than a teenager's self-image and sense of belonging, however; it is also vital to a healthy image of God. After all, we need a healthy image of self if we are to have a healthy image of God. That's why adolescence is also a time for curiosity about just who God is and how He fits into the overall scheme of existence. On the flip side, kids are trying to figure out where they are in the universe too, and how God relates to them.

In the end of life, this link between image of self and image of God are inextricably linked. The need for social acceptance drives adolescent behavior so strongly that, if not fulfilled, independent judgment and action can be inhibited through adulthood. Rejected as teenagers, some continue to seek acceptance by others to the point that it becomes the driving force for their entire lives. Traumatic experiences such as abuse—especially sexual abuse—can also bring out extremely strong emotions that drive behavior for a lifetime, with the person not even understanding what is happening within themselves.

This drive for social acceptance in adult life thwarts the emergence of the individual and inhibits his or her getting to know God in a more intimate manner.

As the opening quote to this chapter says, betrayals from friends or loved ones can bring about lifelong nihilistic attitudes as well; these are attitudes in which there is total rejection of established laws and institutions of society, and destructiveness toward the world, including oneself. This last one is a powder keg. This is where many criminals are born through abusive treatment from parents and other authority figures.

---

[23] *Stages of Faith*, James Fowler, Harper San Francisco, 1981 pg151
[24] Erik Erikson, *Childhood and Society* (W. W. Norton and Co, 1950), 261.

Aggression Times Two

AFTER FINISHING SIXTH GRADE AT Farnsworth, at about twelve years old, I went on to McChesney Junior High in California. This is the age in which kids, now teenagers, begin forming their unique identities. And not coincidentally, it is also the age in which the more aggressive personalities—which started emerging in kids as young as four or five— become more cemented, visible, and threatening. In other words, teenagers bring the full force of whatever aggression they've learned at home out into the world. Erik Erikson describes this process of ever-developing aggression as such:

> The child of four or five is faced with the next step (in development) and with the next crisis (challenge). Being firmly convinced that he is a person, the child must now find out what kind of person he is going to be. And here he hitches his wagon to nothing less than a star: he wants to be like his parents, who to him appear very powerful and very beautiful, although quite unreasonably dangerous. He identifies with them.[25]

Aggression, then, becomes part of a person during the years that identity is first forming, which happens at around age five. Later, as the adolescent further cements his or her identity as being separate from others and part of the larger human race, which also happens during this stage, the child might express social anxiety in this way: "How can I be gentle when all I have learned is to be tough and when I must be tough to feel safe?"[26]

Applying that idea to my experiences, I see now that the school bullies were simply learning how to feel safe; they felt they needed to act tough and dominate other kids in order to keep from getting hurt themselves. This meant being outwardly aggressive and picking fights with anyone they could—like me. I think bullies often saw me as the perfect victim, because I tended to stay under cover to avoid fights. (Though it usually didn't take them long to find out I could stand my ground if I got angry enough. And many a time, I did.)

---

[25]   Erik Erikson, *Identity and the Life Cycle* (W. W. Norton and Co., 1980), 78.

[26]   Ibid., 28.

Unfortunately, at this age, violence often goes beyond schoolyard bullying. The anxiety and pain picked up from home has now built up to an inner rage against everyone. In *Ghosts from the Nursery*, the authors state that if a child is abused early in life, they become "like little pressure cookers" who "repress negative feelings and then explode in aggressive behaviors ... who act out their anger in aggressive ways against other people and things."[27]

A Shot in the Dark

ONE EVENING AFTER DARK, I was riding my bike home after my paper route for the *Oakland Tribune*. Pedaling down my street toward home, I noticed two kids walking in the opposite direction. With a closer look, I recognized they were a couple of notorious bullies from McChesney, whom I had so far made it a point to stay away from. One of them was carrying a rifle of some sort. Finally, I passed them. I looked at them and they looked at me. No words were spoken, no gestures or looks were exchanged, no nothing.

Several seconds later, when I reached my house, something told me to keep on going, to ride past the house without stopping. It was a strong feeling that seemed to come from deep inside and to say (not in word, but in feeling), "Don't stop pedaling. Keep on going."

I should have listened—I know now that the feeling was my spirit guide warning me—but I did not. I stopped, got off my bike, and opened the garage door.

Just then another feeling hit me. It said, "Whatever you do, do not look in the direction of those kids. Look away as if you do not know they are there." With that, I felt a tingling sensation in the back of my neck, and then I heard a gunshot followed by a cracking sound against the garage door. Immediately, I felt a painful stinging in my right calf.

I'd been shot at! And for no reason at all except that I just happened to be there right then—a convenient target and nothing more. Lucky for me, it was only a pellet and left nothing but a welt on my calf under my thick blue jeans; the garage door had absorbed most of the blow. The psychological damage I received was more severe. The event was shocking, traumatic, and shattering, and it would be one of my first paranormal experiences, even though I didn't know what that word meant back then.

---

27   Robin Karr-Morse and Meredith S. Wiley, *Ghosts from the Nursery* (Atlantic Monthly Press, 1997), 140.

Many years later, what I did know was that I'd just been the victim of the spiritual ripple effect. I knew that the parents of those bullies had transmitted negative energy to their kids through words and deeds, and that, in turn, those kids expressed that negative energy by shooting at me. The parents of those kids had never seen me, but I was a victim of their violence.

Sylvia Brown, the famous psychic, says that a full 30 percent of people on the earth today are dark spirits. She defines dark spirits as people who have rejected the loving ways of God, and have put their own interests above all else to the point that they will destroy whatever gets in their way. These people are full of negative energy, which comes out in their words and deeds. You will never see their souls in heaven, for they have made an eternal choice. That is not to say God will condemn them, as He loves all His children unconditionally—even the ones who shot at me that dark night. Instead, after death, these dark souls will be shuttled back to Earth to try to get it right the next time.

(By the way, Sylvia is the real thing. She is not a hoax like many so-called psychics or mediums. I have spent a full day with her and read many of her books, and after discussing it with my Christian spiritual advisor, we agree that Sylvia has spiritual gifts that the rest of us do not. I recommend her books to anyone who wants to better understand God's creation beyond the context of religion.)[28]

The All-Important Self-Image

I DID NOT HAVE THE social acceptance that both Erikson and Fowler have said is necessary for a healthy self-image. In a space of eighteen months, my family moved from Chicago, to a motel in Oakland, to a rented house in Oakland, and then to San Lorenzo, California. As a result, I had no circle of friends to accept me and to pal around with for some time. Even though I had some "friends" in Oakland, I did not belong to a peer group that validated me as a person worthy of respect. On top of that, I was an only child, so I had no siblings to relate to. I felt completely isolated.

It didn't help that our move to San Lorenzo from Oakland happened mid-school year, after curriculums had started and social groups had formed. As you can imagine, the school punks felt the need to demonstrate their control to the new kid; surprising, however, was that they did this right in class. When the teacher turned his back to write on the board, one

---

[28] Sylvia Browne Corporation, Campbell, California.

of them would lean over and spit on me. In just my first day, this happened quite a few times.

The next day, I put on a tough act. With an evil glare, I warned those kids to stop it and did not back down. Then I told a few other kids that back in Chicago, I had gotten into serious trouble with authorities and had never lost a fistfight. Well, the second part was true anyway. As I'd hoped, the word spread and the little future criminals stopped harassing me. No one spit on me again. It's still hard for me to believe that a pale, skinny kid could pull off such a bluff.

With the bullies out of the way, I could now focus on more interesting things—like girls. In fact, one girl in particular. In one of my seventh grade classes, a wonderful-looking blonde sat across the room from me. Her name was Vikky. She was the most beautiful girl I'd ever seen. We got to know each other that year and then became an item. This girl was the first person, outside of my mother, who showed interest in me just as I was. I had never experienced that before from a peer. She was something called a Lutheran, whatever that was, and we talked about God sometimes. For the first time in my life, I felt a close, intimate love, and believe it or not, we stayed together for several years. We were voted cutest couple at our Junior High graduation, and continued going together until I was a sophomore at Santa Clara University.

Meanwhile in San Lorenzo, I made a lot of friends, and for the first time in my life, felt accepted and part of a community. I took to sports. First, I played baseball, but I was a mediocre pitcher and knew I would not make varsity. But I wanted ever so desperately to get a varsity sweater for Vikky to wear around school. So over my freshman summer, I practiced tennis every day. (It turned out hitting something was good for me, considering my background.) I had such great success that I got the number two spot on the team the following year, along with my varsity letter in tennis. I enjoyed letting Vikky wear it on Fridays, as this was the school custom. And possibly because of my newfound athleticism, I had begun to get healthier because my asthma and allergies were weakening.

Finally, things were looking up.

Stopping the Spiritual Ripple Effect

AT SEVENTEEN, I BECAME A sergeant in the Air Force Civil Air Patrol. The Civil Air Patrol was an official auxiliary of the US Air Force for high school students. The group was based at Oakland Airport, where we met every other week, but we also got to spend time on the Air Force base, training and taking flights. As head of the color guard unit, my special duty was to greet incoming dignitaries that landed at Oakland Airport.

One particular Saturday morning, the color guard was called in to greet Jacqueline Cochran. Cochran was famous for being a record-setting pilot and a good friend of Amelia Earhart. She had made national news for doing an around-the-world demonstration flight. One Saturday, she was to land her four-engine JetStar in Oakland as part of the tour. My color guard was to greet her at the end of the steps coming off the plane.

When she landed, there were news cameras all over the place. The four of us in the color guard were ready, and I have to say we looked good. We all wore our chrome helmets, white gloves, and Air Force uniforms. I carried the United States flag. The second cadet held the California flag. And the last two carried show rifles with white straps. When the stairs came down, I stood at attention, and upon Cochran's exit, I saluted her with the stars and stripes. Apparently, she liked that, because she came over to speak to me. She graciously thanked me for all the work we'd put into arranging her welcome, and I said it was a pleasure. All the while, lots of news cameras were pointing at her and me. She shook my white-gloved hand and proceeded with her business. As it turned out, because of that one handshake, I had made it on the six o'clock news that night! And, boy, did I want to see me on TV.

When I got home that afternoon, I told my mom about the incident and called my friends and my girlfriend to tell them to watch. (Back then you could not tape TV shows. If you missed the show, it was gone.) Everyone was excited for me. Well, almost everyone. When my father got home from work, my mother and I told him the news. His reaction was immediate: he said I needed a haircut and was immediately to go get one. And, he added, he would hear no backtalk.

I felt a rage build up inside me, and my stomach muscles tightened, ready for a fight. How unreasonable could one human get? I was not due for a haircut for at least another week or two. That is, until he found out about me being on TV. Then suddenly, my hair became the most important thing on earth to him.

I argued profusely. I said I could get a haircut the next day. I said my hair was already too short per his orders regarding my hair length.

"You had better get your ass out the door now to get that haircut!" he said in an increasingly angry voice.

Then I knew that it had to be today, or, as usual, he would find out what social events were most important to me and then ground me from going to them. The worst part was he knew exactly what he was doing: purposely destroying my chance to see myself with a famous aviatrix on the major local news. Purposely robbing me of my chance to feel noticed. So there I was, sitting in the barber's chair, while my fifteen minutes of fame was dribbling away into oblivion.

That night when I got home, my mom told me she'd seen me and that I'd looked great. The next day in school, a bunch of friends also told me they'd seen me. It seemed the only one who did not see me was me.

The incident left me tremendously hurt and angry. I hated my father for what he'd done. Many years later, my psychologist said that my father had been jealous of me and that this was his way to hurt me. I truly believe she was right. Let me tell you, if you want to damage a teenager's self-image and create rage that could potentially be acted out on others, this is a good way to do it.

I remember the precise point in my life when I decided to stop the spiritual ripple effect that my father's father had started. It actually happened long before the haircut incident, but because the above incident seems to drive home the importance of this decision, it seems appropriate to bring it up now.

It happened when I was about fifteen, right after an argument I'd had with my dad about something I do not remember. What I do remember vividly, however, were the exact words I said to myself in that moment: *I will never treat my kids the way he treats me.* I remember the thought as clearly as if I'd had it yesterday.

Little did I know at the time that with that one thought, I was declaring my freedom from my dad and from the seeds of destruction he had planted—and continued to plant—in my mind. After all, as Ramakrishna said, By the mind one is bound, by the mind one is freed ... He who asserts with strong conviction, 'I am not bound, I am free,' becomes free.

That's not to say, however, that stopping the spiritual ripple effect altogether is quick and easy. In fact, at that point, with that one thought, I had only just planted the seeds of freedom. My independence would not really start to flower until much later. But flower it did, and I thank both God and my mother for that.

On that note, there is another lesson here, and it is probably the most important of all. That lesson is this: God is stronger than any other person in your life. Let me write that again. God is stronger than any other person in your life. That means if someone hurts you badly, asking God for guidance and then following your heart and conscience will get you back on track. It may take a lot of time, crying, and effort, but don't give up, because you are worth it. There is no situation on earth that God cannot lead you out of, and the above story is proof. If God could lead me out of my emotional pit and out of the tangled mess of self-identity I was in, He can do it for you, too.

Reflection Exercise: Talking with God

This reflection exercise is a bit different from the others, as it doesn't require a lot of time and is best done every day. But use the standard reflection preparation.

Once a day, take just a few minutes to talk to God as if you were talking to your best friend. Use plain English and just speak from your heart. No fancy prayers necessary. If you are struggling to overcome a situation of some kind, as the one described above or anything else, you can also ask God for His guidance.

If you begin the habit of talking to God every day, things will ultimately get better for you. After all, it is impossible for God to fail you.

You could start out this way:

Father and Mother in heaven, hallowed be thy name. My dear Father, today something has been bothering me. It is about ... [now you fill in the blank, saying whatever is on your mind. It could be a problem, or it could be your thanks, adoration, or love for God or any other kind of prayer].

Then end with something like this:

I pray for Your guidance, and will do my best to be open to You and the ways You might use to answer my prayer. Dear Father and Mother in heaven, I remain open unto You. Amen.

God Remains "Dog" Spelled Backward

AS THE SCOPE OF TEENAGERS' brains expand to people outside the family (e.g., to peer groups and to the larger human race), they become more aware of the world in general. This increased awareness changes their perceptions of how all the elements of existence fit together, including those relating to God. Thus, teens essentially begin to ask the question, "Where do I fit in?"

That's not to say God tops the list of typical teenage thoughts and concerns. I know I sure didn't hear any of the guys standing around campus, saying, "Hey, did you hear the sermon at church on Sunday?" More likely, the discussion was about the girls and included nicknames for them, such as Swivel Hips and Pizza Face. (Well, we were guys, what do you expect?) But faith during these years does go through significant changes, of which adolescents are often unaware.

On a deeper, subconscious level, adolescents begin to realize that God is mysteriously present and that He loves them. Their image of Him becomes more open and goes beyond that of the human-like old man with a white beard to that of someone who is able to know them to depths they could never understand. In fact, Erik Erikson goes so far as to say that teenagers hunger for God to know, accept, and confirm them, no matter their social standing.

At the same time, because teenagers still view authority as external to themselves, God continues to fall into a hierarchical framework as well. However, images of God may take on more compassionate, fatherly overtones than before, assuming qualities such as companionship, guidance, love, wisdom, and support.

Interestingly, research by Fowler suggests that many never get past this level of faith.[29] For one reason or another, they never overcome the psychological and spiritual hurdles of this mode of spirituality that would enable them to move on to Stage Four. (Just a reminder: this is not a spiritual failure; rather, Stage Three simply defines their permanent understanding of existence. God still loves them as much as He does the pope or Mother Teresa or any other person.)

For me, because of my inability to form a healthy self-image at the time, I rendered God essentially nonexistent. In the rare moments I did think of Him, He still came off as some cosmic authority figure who could

---

[29] James Fowler, *Stages of Faith* (San Francisco: Harper Collins, 1981), 322.

send me to hell—where, incidentally, I would probably see a lot of my friends. And because I also still equated religion with behemoth German nuns whacking me in the back of the head, not to mention humiliating me in front of my peers, I was more than happy to leave religion behind in Chicago.

My mother must have been concerned about my spirituality, though, because after living in San Lorenzo for some time, she forced—and I mean forced—me to get confirmed in the Catholic Church. It did little good. All that oil-on-your-forehead stuff was nonsense to me, and the words I had to recite were a joke.

What I was going through reverts, once again, to Fowler's statement "interpersonal betrayals can give rise ... to nihilistic despair ..."[30] Such betrayal happens not only in peer relationships, but also in parental ones. If a parent betrays the personhood of a teenager by abusing, disrespecting, or demeaning him or her, the teenager begins to cement those deep feelings, which began in childhood, that said, "I am worthless" and "everything I do is futile." Those feelings then easily descend into hostile attitudes toward God and the world in general.

Moving to Sunnyvale

If you have children in this stage in life, please do not move around a lot. The price to children in self-identity, as well as in psychological and spiritual development, is too high. Providing a stable home and giving them a chance to find themselves through their network of friends will provide them with a solid foundation for knowing themselves and then ultimately knowing God. As my children were growing up, I turned down two corporate marketing-manager jobs so that we could continue to live in Santa Clara. I am very glad I did; my children have friends from elementary school even to this day. Unless you are starving, the money is not worth it.

Unfortunately, about halfway through my senior year, my family moved yet again. This time it was to Sunnyvale, which was about thirty miles from San Lorenzo. I was completely shattered to have to leave behind my whole network of friends, especially my sweet Vikky. And worse, still,

---

[30] James Fowler, *Stages of Faith* (San Francisco: Harper Collins, 1981), 179.

was my father's draconian limitation on how often I could drive back to see her. He said he did not want me "wearing out his car" to see my girlfriend, when there were other girls in town—as if girls were replaceable car parts or something.

What a TURD (Theologically Underdeveloped Rotten Doof)! I thought. And then, because I lost what little respect I'd had left for him, I didn't mind lying to get around his rules. In order to see Vikky, all I'd have to do is dress up in my Air Force uniform and pretend I had a Civil Air Patrol meeting back in Oakland. My father would have to let me have the car, since he couldn't prevent me from officially attending squadron meetings. I just had to make sure there was no blonde hair on my uniform when I got home.

At Fremont Union High in Sunnyvale, I was again the new kid on the block. This time, however, I immediately got on the varsity tennis team as the number one man and captain. Fortunately, it seemed my varsity letter jacket was enough to insulate me from the local members of the Future Criminals Society.

But I was lonelier than you can imagine. I deeply missed Vikky and my friends at Arroyo High. Looking back, I now see that this was when I developed the depression that would—as depression typically does—haunt me for decades, even until now.

In my loneliness, I took refuge in books and academics, especially science and chemistry. My grades then became good enough to get me into the California Scholarship Federation, which gave me the privilege of access to the loft in the school library. I would sit at a desk up there and look down on the kids on the main floor, thinking that I was finally separated from the riff-raff and where I belonged: above them. Arrogant, yes, but it made me feel good about myself, even if superficially. It was the first time in my life that I had received positive feedback from authorities (teachers)—and not just from Vikky and the guys on the tennis team.

That's not to say I had become truly happy, however. The seeds of depression, loneliness, and my dislike for God persisted. Even through my final teenage years when Mom still dragged me to Mass every week, God remained completely off of my radar screen. Religion had not changed for me since St. Tarcissus. Mass still consisted of this guy up on the altar, waving his arms, looking all holy as he drank wine in front of us. There was a lot of pomp and circumstance, as if the ritual meant something. To me, it was all a complete waste of time.

Forming Self-Image in the Larger Family Context

TOWARD THE LATER TEENAGE YEARS, the adolescent has formed his or her own code of morals and ethics, which serve criteria for liking (or disliking) other people. It was in this context that I began to form my own opinions about my extended family. My mother's side, I liked very much, and enjoyed being with them. Her family was not perfect, but they showed togetherness and spoke lovingly and respectfully toward one another. I found myself really wanting to be like them, although by then, I had already picked up at least some of the less-desirable attitudes from my dad's side, whom, I came to the conclusion, I did not like very much.

What was the difference between the two families? In a word: love. My father's family was boorish, ill mannered, and easily angered, treating one another with rudeness. When I was just five and visiting them back in Virginia, I had gotten five helium-filled balloons. It was great. However, my uncle, (my father's brother) delighted in popping my helium balloons, all the while laughing—even though I was, all the while, crying. This is an occasion that proved actor George Burns exactly correct when he said, "Happiness is having a large, loving, caring, close-knit family, but in another city." Looking back, I can now see that my dislike for most of the Ferguson family had extended itself to my dislike of all authority figures, which inevitably also carried over to my view of God.

Grandpa Ferguson Comes to Town

HERE'S ANOTHER STORY THAT EPITOMIZES that quote from George Burns. One time when I was in high school, my grandfather from my dad's side and his new wife came to visit us. For reasons unknown to me, the two had also moved out to California, after which they had paid us sporadic visits. Once a Baptist preacher and farmer in Virginia, Grandpa had become a traveling salesman in the business of patio awnings. (How anyone got from preaching to patio awnings was beyond me.)

So on this particular visit, Grandpa pressured my parents to buy an awning from him. They did. But it cost them $500, which back in 1963 was a tidy sum for my family, so they had to take out a loan on the house to pay for it. I still remember the discussion at the dinner table while Grandpa smoked his ever-present cigars.

About a week later, my parents procured the loan and paid my grandfather. Grandpa told them the awning would be delivered in a few weeks.

Then guess what happened next. Are you ready for this? That was the last time any of us saw Grandpa again, ever. He skipped town with my parents' money and we never heard from him again. He had told so many lies in his life that he had apparently desensitized himself from cheating his own son's family out of $500.

Years later, I learned that God has a great sense of humor. Some people call it karma; others call it ironic justice. The bottom line is that the things you say and do come back to you. What happened exactly? We heard from family in Virginia that Grandpa had developed cancer of the tongue. Can you imagine that? Due to those cigars he always had hanging out of his mouth, he got cancer in his lying tongue, and would have to have most of it surgically removed.

Honestly, my first reaction to the news was not very Christian-like, so I will not repeat it here. Suffice it to say, I thought, *So there is a God, after all!* It was the first time in my life when I saw, firsthand, that bad guys get what they deserve. I was learning that life does give you back what you give.

Though to us, it sometimes seems to take too long for the boomerang of holy smite to come back and hit someone, this spiritual truth is part of God's creation that operates as automatically as gravity. The Hindus call it Karma. New Agers say that what you give to the universe, it will return to you. Christians quote Matthew 7:12: "As you give, so shall you receive." It is a truth that speaks to all of us in this life on Earth. It is God's way of teaching us what we need to learn, if we are paying attention to our actions and their consequences.

I took no pleasure in my grandfather's fate. He ultimately died from the cancer, making an extremely sad ending to an already sad life. To this day, I pray for him, that somehow, somewhere, my grandfather has learned what he needs to know so that he, too, can journey closer to God. At the time it all happened, however, you still couldn't get me near a church; the world began to seem different to me. I began to speculate that there really must be some kind of invisible force that operated around us. I was on my way to God but did not know it.

The College Years

AFTER HIGH SCHOOL, I ATTENDED Santa Clara University as a chemistry student. No longer in the public school system with all its future felons, I was now in the company of students who were there to learn. All these kids had GPAs as good as or better than mine, so I had to kick it into academic high gear just to keep up. I worked part-time at IBM for tuition money and studied the rest of the time, leaving little room for a social life. Not that I knew many people anyway, since, once again, I was in a new school. By this time, Vikky and I had also broken up, leaving me lonelier than ever. So in any spare time I could find, I took flying lessons. It was something I'd always wanted to do, and some days, I felt being able to fly was the only thing that kept me sane.

Meanwhile, I found religion staring me in the face again. On the application for college entrance, I had checked the box that specified I was Catholic. Bad move. That doomed me to take five theology courses, which was a requirement for Catholics only. How I wished I'd said I was a Methodist. I should have known better, since the Jesuits run Santa Clara.

As luck would have it, my first theology class was on the gospels, and the oldest priest known to man, Fr. Androdie, taught it. Androdie was directly from the good-ole-time-religion factory; I think he knew Moses personally. His class was at the bottom of my list, right below English Literature 101 and cafeteria food.

Every time I went, it was like I was back at St. Tarcissus, except instead of nuns, I had an old priest whose face looked like ten miles of bad road. One day, particularly tired from studying late the night before, I momentarily stopped taking notes. Old, craggy Eagle Eye spotted my lack of action, walked over to my desk, and said in a very loud voice, "Don't be lazy!" *So nothing had changed in Catholicism since I was a kid*, I thought. They were all still TURDs.

For our final exam, we had to memorize the names and dates of all of the ecumenical councils since Jesus Christ. *Holy cow!* I thought, no pun intended. How useless and time-consuming. So yours truly, being the genius I thought I was, decided to write the answers in my bluebook before test day. I got an A. Obviously, not only was God not on my radar screen, but there was also something really telling about the fact that the only class I ever cheated in was theology.

Well, they say that when the student is ready, the teacher will appear. So when I was nineteen, I managed to get my pilot's license, which was a wonderful experience that led me to a very important person in my life: Br. Tom Bracco. After getting my flight-instructor rating, Tom, a Jesuit brother, became my student and a lifelong friend. We flew hundreds of hours together in small aircraft, and we always had a ball. We would throw rolls of toilet paper out the airplane's window, watch it unroll in the air in a vertical stream, and then circle around it before cutting it with the wings.

We would also have long talks on our flights together, as well as in between classes. In those talks, Tom told me things about God that felt good and right for the first time in my life. And he taught me many life lessons. As such, he was able to repair some of the damage my father had done. Spiritually, I was spreading my wings and cementing my own ideology, which put the behavior of my father and the Ferguson clan into a dimmer light.

I truly believe that God sent him into my life when I needed it the most. All throughout college and graduate school, Tom was my life mentor, and I give him credit for helping me become the God-loving person I am today. He was my friend before I met my beloved Marilyn and he continues to be my friend after her passing away. Tom has indeed been a Godsend, as well as the perfect example of how God will give you what you need if you open your heart to Him and pray for His guidance. God is active in all of our lives, even on this very day, and He loves all of us even if we do not pray, as it was in my case.

Looking back, I see now how difficult college was for me, but it also did me a lot of good. Education is one of the most powerful forces on earth. It changed me deeply and transformed my outlook on life. I was able to put more distance between my own views and the ones held by my father and the other Fergusons. And in the middle of it all, I had a God-given mentor to help me through. I can see now that God was preparing me for my entrance into Stage Four.

Express Yourself

As we each travel through our life's journey, it is important, if we want to be spiritually healthy, that we express the unique self we are. There is no real mystery in it; it simply means doing something we love, whether that be pursuing the arts or sciences, contributing time to a cause we find important, or doing any other activity that makes us feel good inside—just as long as it expresses the inner being that God created in us.

Our heart always talks to us in feelings, yearnings, and desires, and if we listen to it, it will guide us toward things that can put a smile on our face. Many times, however, we do not realize that desire, or the depth of it, until there is a trigger—an event that sets us off in a particular direction. When this one event happens, we get feelings that say things like, "This is me" or "I am happy when I do this." That is your heart talking to you and guiding you toward your true self. We must pay attention.

In my case, ever since I can remember, I had a love affair with flight and the freedom it brings. When we were visiting family back in Chicago, my cousin took me up for a ride in a small plane. Well, that was it. From that moment, I knew I had to get my pilot's license. Without understanding how or why, I was paying attention to the stirrings of my heart. I got my pilot's license one year later.

CHAPTER 7

Stage Four: The Faith of Young Adults

THE TUMULTUOUS TRANSITION FROM STUDENT to responsible adult, from Stage Three to Stage Four, can last for several years according to James Fowler. For many, this stage can happen through a person's thirties and forties. (Although, if you're like me, I considered myself an *old* adult when I was forty; however, now that I am far older ... well, forty looks young!)

For others, the transition to Stage Four never happens at all. Again, this is not a failure. It just means that a person has reached his or her full spiritual potential in this life during Stage Three. And again, God does not love this person any less. God meets each of us right where we are in our spiritual journeys, no matter where that may be. God loves the simplest, poorest, most uneducated person as much as He does the pope, Mother Teresa, Gandhi, or any other being on the earth.

If it does happen, however, Stage Four generally begins when the teenager or young adult starts charting his or her own course through life. They bring with them their individual personalities, values, life lessons, attitudes and behaviors, education, and desires for the future, but they now accept responsibility for their actions, beliefs, attitudes, and lifestyles. By this time, all or most of the wild oats have been sown, and a way has been made for bringing stability into life. Of course, some people have more wild oats to sow than others, and, in a few cases, never finish sowing. Generally, however, this is the stage in which careers and marriages and families start, and life as an adult begins.

Stage Four faith often occurs at a time in life when our relationships with others and the world are changing in profound ways. As such, many young adults expand their field of interest to include larger societal issues such as politics, economics, and community. I read the book *Conscience of a Conservative,* by Barry Goldwater, an Arizona senator who ran for president in 1964. I also enjoyed a book about Albert Einstein's theory of relativity. With this expanding awareness of existence and the rules of the universe, the young adult begins to question the values, assumptions, and views of life that he or she grew up with.

Though such second-guessing is very healthy, it also can make this stage difficult and scary, as it can lead to changes that are fundamental to a person's very existence and call into question issues of spirituality. Remember, spirituality is our manner of being, our way of existence, and the character of our relationships with other people, the world, and God; it goes far beyond one's belief in religious doctrines. So it is in this stage when we start to look past the surface meaning of religious symbols and ask what they really mean.

In short, one's values are modified to suit more closely the life experiences and perceived relationship that person has with the universe. As a result, his or her spirituality can become more open and expansive in character—but only if the person is paying attention and receiving the lessons God is offering.

God uses the events in your life and the people around you as a mirror, in which you can see yourself. So if you want to make spiritual progress, make sure your antennae are working, decide whether you are willing to make whatever changes are necessary, and then be open to feedback. Someone once said that God uses a feather to guide those who listen, but a brick for those whose ears are closed. So if you insist on not listening, you may end up with a lot of bumps on your head!

Reflection Exercise: Listening for God's Guidance

Prepare for this reflection in the standard way. The purpose of this reflection is to meditate on the guidance God gives you from all sources in your life. Here are some questions to get you started regarding feedback from other people during the normal course of your life, which many times is actually God giving you guidance.

- Do other people like you? If not, why not? If so, why?
- If someone dislikes you, why? Remember, it's not only that person, it's you too.
- Try to remember some of the things that have been said to you by people you respect. When they told you something, did they show respect toward you?
- Did you feel love from them?
- Consider whether anything you have done recently improved the well being of another.
- Do you love other people—I mean *really* love them?
- Does your love translate into action for the benefit of other people?
- Does something besides love motivate your relationships?
- How do you feel others treat you? Search for reasons why.
- What you say or do originates within your soul. When you receive feedback on your actions or words, are you really listening and willing to take action after thinking about what is said?
- Are you really seeing the consequences of what you have done?
- Will your ego allow you to admit you need to change in some areas? If so, which ones?

Asking yourself these kinds of questions will help you to use real life as a mirror to discover what others see in you, including what is good and what needs improvement. At the end of this reflection, thank God for His divine guidance in your life.

When children come along, as a parent you will know what you really believe in; you will naturally teach it to your children. Religious tradition's doctrine, rules, and your manner of being with your true values and what you really think works in the real world is what you will teach your children. Your true spirituality, your true values, and attitudes will become engendered in your kids in a thousand different ways. Don't bother to tell a kid that smoking is bad for you when you have a cigarette hanging from your mouth; all they will think is that you are a hypocrite. There is no hiding from kids who you really are.

Independence, Fear, and Loneliness

While sorting through the issues of early adulthood, people are largely on their own. Schoolmates move on, leading their own separate lives, and the young adult is faced with making new friends and redefining him- or herself within new groups of people. In addition, external authority figures, such as parents and professors, leave the picture.

Many questions come front-and-center to be faced head on. Will I have what it takes to succeed? Which direction should I take? Where will I find a job? Who will love me? Will I get married or be lonely for the rest of my life? Where will I live? How will I pay the bills? Do I really want to be like my parents? Does my ideology really work in this world or am I way off base?

With their social support structures all but gone, young adults must now depend more on themselves to answer these questions. In some sense, they become their own boss or authority figure. As such, the consequences of their actions and decisions—either joy or pain—become apparent and real and memorable for the first time, as do the lessons learned from these experiences. This is a frightening stage, for sure, but necessary, as it enables each individual to grow in a way that is best for him or her.

Reflection Exercise: On My Own ... Now What?

This is a good time to pause and reflect. First, remember what was going on in your life once you were out of school and trying to make it on your own. Then remember what you were feeling; in particular, remember what you were afraid of. Finally, reflect on how things worked out for you, and why they happened the way they did. Was God there in the background, guiding the circumstances? (Hint: He was, but how?)

Here are some questions to start with, but be sure to add others that pertain to actual events you experienced after you completed your education and were out on your own.

- How did I feel back then? Did I look to the future with positive anticipation or did I fear it? Why?
- What worried me the most? Why?
- Did I miss college or my friends or my old way of life when I got out on my own? If so, what did I do about it? Did it work?
- Did my friends drift away over time or not? Was I able to make new meaningful relationships?
- Do I yearn for those times again? Why or why not?
- In what ways am I better off now versus then? In what ways am I worse?
- How did everything turn out for me? Can I see where the fingerprints of God were guiding my life without my knowledge?
- Did God use a feather to guide me or did I need a brick in the head?
- Did some unexplainable coincidences occur that led to very positive things entering my life? Could be God; do I think so?

As you reflect, you will probably remember some moments fondly, while others will be painful. Both are a part of real life, so meditate on each and see what you can learn. Remember, it is easier to see the tracks of God from the perspective of knowing how things turned out.

A Fish Out of Water

DURING MY LAST YEAR IN college, I could see what was coming, and I did not like it. I was worried. Soon, I would be out of school, my academic security blanket pulled out from underneath me, and working God knows where. The only real chemistry jobs available at the time were in Houston at Shell Oil, but I did not in any way want to move out of Santa Clara Valley and stink like an oil spill.

I did want badly to move out of my parents' house. I had wanted to do so for a long time, but I was a day student at nearby Santa Clara and could not afford to live in the dorms. Besides, even though my father was still being a TURD, I was not home much now, except to sleep, so the frequency of our heated debates was a lot less. At the same time, his anger toward me did not diminish. In fact, by that time, probably because he realized that I had decided to never be like him, he seemed to resent me even more, if that was possible.

I was old enough now that I had learned to dismiss his tirades and just relegate him to "irritant" status (read: a pathetic pain in the ass). As a kind-of side note, I would learn later that this brush-off was only a temporary surface fix. The emotional scars that his rage had formed in me throughout my childhood were still buried deep. As with all who have been abused by a parent, I would not uncover and realize the extent of the psychological and spiritual damage that was done to me, let alone deal with it, for decades to come.

Another crisis that hit me in my last year of college: I realized I no longer wanted to be a chemist. Well, great. After four long years of academic blood, sweat, and tears, I was just now realizing that. Crap! Now what? Let's just say that I had a whopping case of existential angst after I figured that one out. With graduation looming, I had to make a decision. And since I knew I liked business, I enrolled in the Master's of Business Administration program, to start the following fall.

Graduation was depressing. My whole identity as a chemistry student evaporated in what seemed a single day. Suddenly, I was a fish out of water. It didn't help that there was a recession going on, and the job situation looked bleak as well. The real world was waiting for me and I was scared stiff. Despite my big mouth, I was still very introverted, wary of authority figures, and unconfident in my abilities.

As it turned out, however, I got a job at the NASA Ames Research Center as a technician. I analyzed upper atmospheric particles to discern how much of it was extraterrestrial in nature. This job turned out to be a great blessing for me. I had my own lab and had to shut the door while doing analysis; this allowed me to do my homework for graduate school.

I was busy but lonely. During the workday, I was mostly by myself in my lab, with little social interaction. Outside of work, it seemed everyone I knew either went to the Vietnam War or moved away to graduate school. On top of that, one of my closer friends got a scholarship to MIT graduate pharmacology school and was killed in a car crash a few months after starting classes. Any way I thought about it, life seemed uncertain and out of control. It was as if everyone had scattered to the four winds, and I'd been left standing there, a dumb look on my face, wondering what had happened. Fowler would say of my experience that I was starting to "be apart from my conventional moorings."[31] Though it's true such separation is crucial for Stage Four development, that benign quote sure understated the pain I felt. If only someone would love me. I wondered if anyone would.

False Confidence: The Enemy of Spiritual Development

As with the other stages of faith, this fourth one has both its opportunities and its dangers. One of the dangers: becoming over-reliant on your intellect. Development of critical thought processes and the ability to quantize reality according to your own personal formulas at this stage can lead you to thinking you "have it all figured out" by means of analysis and conscious thought. Reality does not work that way, but many smart people think it does.

When this happens, a feeling of superiority arises in the individual. Fowler calls it a "second narcissism in which the now clearly bounded reflective self over assimilates 'reality' and the perspectives of others into its own world view."[32] In other words, these people think they know better than everyone else. You have seen them. They're the ones who have an answer for everything but are experts in nothing, or know nothing but have an opinion on everything.

Unfortunately, such narcissism ends a person's spiritual development without his or her even knowing it. Why? It is because no one will never know God with a conscious intellectual mind. So for many, sadly, this is where the spiritual-growth party ends. Combating such narcissism means questioning your own beliefs, which can either bring change that will

---

[31]   James Fowler, *Stages of Faith* (San Francisco: Harper Collins, 1981).
[32]   Ibid., 182.

draw you closer to God or reaffirm your existing belief; either way you have grown spiritually.

In this case, a person may feel, after living within the descriptive bounds of Stage Four for some time, that something is missing. Familiar motivations, values, expressions of spirituality—even those used by a person for many years—may start to seem flat, making one wonder if that's all there is. (Interestingly, in the early sixties, Peggy Lee had a song on the charts with that exact title: "Is that all there is?".)

In short, the religious tradition that has served one's life so well may start to feel inadequate. It may seem to reach a limit, as the richness and depth that it brought before suddenly ceases, at which point, restlessness arises and seems not to go away. These symptoms may signal an incipient transition to Stage Five. So again, life refuses to remain comfortable, familiar, or static. The only thing that remains the same is change.

Love Lost and Found

YOUNG ADULTHOOD OFTEN REPRESENTS A real crisis point in life. It is when most look around and think, *Gad, I have a lifetime staring me in the face. Now what?* Consequently, a lot of young adults turn to forming more serious relationships. Fowler says that in this stage, "a person is forming a new identity, which he or she expresses and actualizes by the choice of personal and group affiliations and the shaping of a lifestyle."[33] Erik Erikson expresses this same idea about social affiliations in the young adult: "He is ready for intimacy, that is, the capacity to commit himself to concrete affiliations and partnerships and to develop the ethical strength to abide by such commitments, even though they may call for significant sacrifices and compromises."[34] In other words, people are ready to commit to others. They yearn for lasting, loving relationships and, as a result, often get married. I think this happens to almost all of us in our early twenties as it did for me.

Another response to the "Now what?" question is the realization that we could use some divine intervention—or at least divine guidance. I suspect that all of us have godly spiritual experiences but most do not recognize them as such. Many times, an experience is brushed aside

---

[33] Ibid., 179.
[34] Erik Erikson, *Childhood and Society* (W. W. Norton and Co., 1950), 163.

as being "weird" or "just one of those things," and then is quickly forgotten.

Since the need for close relationships and the need for God's help coincide in this phase of life, it's no coincidence that my first very memorable spiritual experience coincided with a failed romance. (Remember, to recognize experiences like this one for what they are, you have to connect the dots in prayerful hindsight.)

In my first year of graduate school, I met a girl from Hawaii. Aside from my dear mom, she was the first person to say, "I love you." She became everything to me, and it seemed everything was finally right with the world. I thought all my painful life experiences had been worth it, just because they led me to her.

I started to envision spending my life with this woman. She was finishing up her major in sociology, and we talked about getting married someday. I even got her a diamond engagement ring. Some of her family had issues about us. It seems that it was planned that she would take care of her mother, whose husband was a spy in Vietnam and gone for long periods of time, but other than that, things seemed great. That was, until she graduated. Then suddenly, she left town and broke off our engagement. I was devastated from top to bottom. I almost quit graduate school out of grief. My whole world went dark.

A few months later, it was already dark as I left my evening class to go home. I was feeling particularly heartbroken. I was so heartbroken, in fact, that I walked directly to the Mission Church on campus just to talk to God. This was a first for me. I still hated church, and though I had never flat-out rejected God, I had never really kept Him on my spiritual radar. That is until now.

There I was, sitting in the back of the mission, crying and asking God what to do. Then after what seemed a long time, something happened that, to this day, I couldn't accurately describe. A feeling came over me. It was something that came from outside me, and it was as if I was being told something without hearing any words. I had never experienced anything like this before, and I did not understand what was happening.

After my initial shock, however, I found myself focusing on the message being given to me. It was saying, in some fashion, that everything would be all right, and it came to me with a feeling of complete peace. Somehow, I knew instinctively that it was God talking to me.

This "communication" did not last long; it was over in less than a minute. But its effects were profound. For the first time since the breakup, I felt some measure of relief. I left the mission a little while later, still miserable, but with a new feeling that there was light at the end of my painful tunnel. Looking back, I can now understand the mystical nature of that event in the Mission Church. God's fingerprints were all over it.

Two days later, as it turns out, was my birthday. I went to work and then to class that evening, just as I always did. I was depressed. It was as if the world could not care less that it was my birthday. I felt invisible to everyone and everything. After class, I walked to the student center to get a soda before going home. On my way there, I ran into a girl I'd just met earlier in class. She was walking in the opposite direction. My first impression of her was that she was a little weird, since she asked me if I was half Asian. I was this white Croatian guy; how could she think that? She was very attractive though.

As she approached, she gave me a big smile, and when she did, it was as if darkness turned into day. We stopped and talked. I asked her how accounting class was going, to which she replied she was having trouble. I offered to help her, as I was good with numbers. I then told her it was my birthday and I was tired from a full day of work and class that evening. I summoned the courage to ask her if she would like to go have a cup of coffee with me off-campus, so we could talk about class and I could find out more about her. She said yes.

We went to a local restaurant and had a great conversation. I found out she was from the Philippines and also a member of the International Club, which I was too. I also found out that she was dating a guy named Wally.

Fortunately for me, a few weeks later, she found out that the cad had been married for two years. Needless to say, that was the end of that. I was convinced then that God had engineered two breakups, so that she and I could get together. And we did, indeed, get together. You see, that classmate I had coffee with that evening was my dear Marilyn, who later became my wife. We were married for thirty-eight years before she passed away from cancer in 2009.

Looking back at the way we met, I ponder what happened in the Mission Church that night, just one evening before I "accidentally" met Marilyn on the steps of the student center. When I connect the dots, I see the plan God had for me and how He worked in both of our lives to bring us together.

In that situation, God was trying to tell me He was in control, and that I should be looking forward, rather than grieving the past. He was letting me in on His plan for my life by giving me a sense of peace in my heart. Even as I was sitting in the mission, completely unaware of what was to come, He was blessing the relationship I was to have with Marilyn.

Chances are, a similar scenario has occurred to you. To recall such a situation, reflect on circumstances in your life that seemed like coincidences at the time. Look for God beneath the surface of those events by looking back with the wisdom of knowing what happened, and listen for His gentle whisperings. Don't just pass it off as "one of those things"; doing so will guarantee your spiritual stagnation.

Reflection Exercise: God's Silent Work

Prepare for this reflection exercise in the standard way. Do the following:

- Recall an event in your life that seemed totally out of your control. This situation seemed to offer no way out; every direction you looked, you saw only pain.
- Now, from the vantage point of knowing what happened, sit back and watch the story unfold.
- Get to the heart of the matter by examining the motivations, characters, and personalities of the people involved. Why did they do what they did? Was God an influence in their actions?
- Was God an influence in your actions?
- Think about the pivotal points—those moments in which things could have gone either way.
- Finally, reflect on the actual results. Through the lens of hindsight, determine how this event led you to an opportunity to become more of the person God created you to be. This does not mean you fell into a bed of roses, but that things got back on track, so you could do what you needed to, to gain an increasing sense of well being. Both positive and negative results can be learning experiences.
- Did things go the way of producing goodness and love? If so, be grateful to God for that, but then ask why. Be sure your mind is clear and listen for any stirrings in your mind, heart or feelings.
- If things did not work out well, ask why as well. Again, listen for the whispers of God.
- If you hear not a darned thing, that is okay, too. Even experienced meditators such as myself sometimes draw a blank on things. When this happens, wait a day or so and do this again. Ultimately, you will get the information you need.
- I hope this Reflection Exercise is filled with eye-opening spiritual lessons for you, as it was for me.

The Phone's for You; It's God Calling

THE DAY AFTER MY FIRST daughter was born, I was standing in front of the glass window at the hospital's nursery, when reality struck in a big way.

Oh, my God, I thought. *I am a father! Now what?* Then through my insecurity, fear, and self-doubt, I told my sleeping one-day-old, simply, "I will do the best I can for you, dear daughter. I will do the best I can." Then I made the very conscious decision to pursue a career that would provide financial security for the family, at the expense of working at something I enjoyed more. This life-changing incident was a fork in the road for me. From that moment, I knew things would be difficult, but, somehow, that was okay with me. Love does that, you know.

Many years later, in my late forties, my life was successful in worldly terms. My family had prospered and was secure, which was the most important thing to me. I had a good career in computer marketing and was invested in real estate. My children were graduating from college, and retirement was within sight. I loved my family dearly and still felt extremely lucky to be married to Marilyn. I was a pilot and played golf in my spare time. It was quite a nice life.

Underneath the surface, however, things were not so tranquil. I was good at computer marketing, but the intensity and stress of that business proved to be a formula for burnout, and I did not like it for a minute. I had long since lost count of the number of different managers I'd had and the reorganizations I'd participated in.

In addition, although I had willingly paid a heavy price for my career decision, added to the normal stress of that life, I also unwillingly—and unknowingly—dragged around emotional baggage from years of child abuse. Things began happening inside me that I did not understand. I felt, increasingly, that something important was missing. To fill the gap, I wanted to add depth and new meaning to my life, but I did not know how; I wasn't yet empowered with the awareness that much of the pain I felt traced back to my childhood. And because I felt hollow but powerless to do anything about it, I was often given to anger.

I did not know where these feelings were coming from. I did not know at the time that God was stirring my spiritual pot. Searching for answers, I considered taking philosophy classes at Santa Clara University. I talked to Marilyn about it and saw a friend of ours who worked in the admissions office. He said not to waste my time; I already had an undergraduate minor in philosophy, and, besides, he thought I'd be better off in pastoral ministry. I had never heard of such a program, let alone knew that Santa Clara offered it.

At first, it was way out of my comfort zone. Pastoral ministry was just not me. Or so I thought. But after a while, something drove me to look into it. Marilyn was very supportive of the idea and suggested I take one class to see if I liked it. So I signed up for a summer session called Spiritual Direction, whatever that was.

Looking back on that class, I now understand the Chinese saying about a long journey beginning with one step. Spiritual Direction was my first step to a very long journey indeed. In fact, I first attended with the thought that if I made it to the end of the class, I'd probably just chalk it up to experience and be done with the whole thing. If ever there was a fish out of water, it was me in this class, and I was nowhere near my pond.

But by the end of class, my eyes had been opened in a profound way, and more so from the impressions left on me by my classmates and professor than from what I learned in the class itself. These people were so loving and caring and accepting of each other. It was as if I had entered another world whenever I walked into class; I could not be on Earth, with the way these people were—so open and supporting of one another's viewpoints about their lives and images of God. The professor was so kind and gentle; I did not know how to react.

Interesting, isn't it, that the professor of that class would wind up being my spiritual advisor for all the years since? And more interesting still how all the parts and pieces would come together after that class to lead me to graduate with a master's in pastoral ministry, become a Reiki practitioner, and write this book about real-life spirituality. I can now see that God was using that experience to bring out the true me after all those years in computer marketing. I had to go through that experience before I could be prepared to switch gears, not only putting God back on my radar, but also finally making Him the centerpiece of my life.

Summary

THIS STAGE OF FAITH OCCURS during a very turbulent time of life. It's a tough life transition to leave the security of the academic life and get a job. All your friends seem to scatter to the four winds, so it's a time when existing relationships fade away, and it's up to you to foster new relationships. On top of this, there is an increasing need to form permanent relationships, get married, and start a household. Throughout all this, it seems we are floating on a stormy sea, ready to sink at any time. Yet somehow things seem to work out, and our lives start in a new direction. It is during this time of life that God is working behind the scenes, where you will never detect His presence. It is only in the looking back that you will see the action and fingerprints of God during this volatile time of life.

CHAPTER 8

Stage Five: The Faith of Midlife and Beyond

"Teacher, which is the great commandment in the law?" And [Jesus] said to him, "You shall love the Lord your God with all your heart, and with all your soul, and with all your mind. This is the great and first commandment. And a second is like it; you shall love your neighbor as yourself. On these two commandments depend all the law and the prophets."
                                                                —Matthew 22:36–40

AT THIS STAGE OF OUR lives, we have been adults for quite a while, having endured many painful experiences and challenges that have taxed our abilities to the limit. We have dealt with problems in parenting and family, employment and finances, and probably health and disease. We may have also watched and helped our friends deal with these same issues. By now some people we know personally may have also passed away, leaving us to attend their funerals.

With each passing year, there is a greater tendency to feel that life is a bitch and then you die. And who can blame us for feeling this way? Life is indeed very hard, many times bordering on the edge of what we can tolerate. During times of difficulty, we tend to lose our balance and stop doing the things we love; we stop being involved in those activities that express who we really are. Life becomes dark, dreadful, and foreboding with no joy or peace of mind in sight. It just plain hurts to get up in the morning. I know this from personal experience.

Right after I retired from computer marketing, my beloved Marilyn—the most wonderful wife anyone can imagine—and I were making plans for a joyful retirement where we could travel and live the good life we felt we deserved after all the years of sacrifice and raising three great children. However, life and circumstances had other plans for us. Only a little over one year after my retirement, Marilyn was diagnosed with metatastic colon cancer. After that devastating news, we lived through many years of daily struggle, four major surgeries, three minor surgeries and countless other medical procedures and chemotherapy sessions with all the awful side effects that they bring. I remember waking up numerous times in the morning only to think, *Oh, f—, I'm still in this mess!* just before a wave of intense dread and depression swept over me. It would leave an actual sour taste in my mouth, a kind of nausea in the pit of my stomach that prevented me from eating breakfast, and anxiety that only strong sedatives could alleviate. Many times, it was all I could do just to get out of bed, feed myself, and take care of my dear wife and her cancer. And, in my case, that was on top of coping with post-traumatic stress disorder, anxiety, and a fear of authority figures resulting from my abusive childhood. My asthma and serious allergies did not help the situation, either. Due to the stress, they got worse.

When rotten things like this happen in life, we tend to focus on the negativity that surrounds us and forget the larger picture of our existence. We forget that no matter what happens on this planet, our heavenly home is waiting for our return; at least, for those of us who do the best we can with the best of intentions. Remembering your role in eternity does not come to mind, for example, when your cancer-patient wife is throwing up, or when you are cleaning up diarrhea off the floor right after you get up in the morning. In these horrible moments, heaven and God seem millions of miles away, if they seem to exist at all. The eternal moment of now seems filled with endless anguish, as you act positive for your loved one, smiling when happiness is the last emotion you feel. Yet all of this is part of a bigger picture, even if you lose sight of that picture as you tend to what is at hand.

Already, we are participating in the eternal reality that transcends life on earth. This is not a new idea, but an age-old biblical truth. In a subsequent book, I will show how people who lived 200,000 years ago already believed in this truth. I know it's hard when life seems to be flying apart—we all get lost in the life situations that confront us—but do try to take time away from whatever the rotten situation is, collect your thoughts, and remember this spiritual truth, because our existence as spiritual beings is not dependent on what happens to us on earth. It's what we say and do that counts.

Reflection Exercise: Participating in Eternal Reality

Prepare for this reflection in our standard way. Then address this truth. Here are some questions to get you started thinking about the truth of eternal reality more:

- The Bible says we are co-creators with God. Do you believe this? In what ways do we co-create with God on this planet?
- What does this idea about our being co-creators say about our participation in eternity? Does this somehow hint at the existence of other realms that are now hidden from us?
- In about five billion years, scientists predict that our sun will turn into a red giant and destroy Earth. In fact, they predict that it will also fry Mercury, Venus, and Mars before blowing up itself. Where will you be when that happens? This is not a flippant question. It is very serious, for you will exist then, but where and in what condition?
- What is the role of the spiritual ripple effect in your participation in eternity?
- Do you really believe that what you say and do here on Earth will help determine where you end up in eternity? I mean *really* believe and live your life accordingly?
- God loves Hitler as much as you because of His unconditional love. Does this mean that you will be rubbing shoulders with Hitler in heaven? Hint: no! But where will he be and where will you be? What will Hitler's condition be in light of God's unconditional love?

These questions are aimed at helping you think about the divine status of human beings. Do we have a future with God in ways we cannot imagine? Or, like the popular song from the group Kansas says, are we but "dust in the wind"?

Remembering Eternity

In Luke 12:32, Jesus said, "Fear not, little flock, for it is your Father's good pleasure to give you the kingdom."

Fear not? This may be easy to hear, but hard to do. That's where Jesus's words from Matthew 10:7 come in: "And preach as you go, saying, the kingdom of heaven is at hand." What does that mean? Well, to me it means that we have already been given the kingdom, as spoken about in Luke 12:32; therefore, we have no need to fear. It means that the kingdom of God is at our fingertips; it is just that close. Heaven is not in another galaxy or universe. It is right at the end of your hands. It is near you even now, as you read these words.

If the kingdom of God is so near, then why can't we see it, especially in times of trouble? Let me begin to answer that question with another question. Ever wonder where you were a year before you were born? You were with God. I started this book discussing that. But because of His infinite wisdom, you purposely have forgotten that temporarily, so that you could come here to learn and grow closer to God through the human experience. (Note: If you are interested in learning more about where you were before you were born, the closeness of the kingdom of God, and why you are here, I suggest you read some of the books written by Sylvia Browne.)

Because we are here on this earth to grow spiritually, our perception of reality must exclude our perception of heaven. If it did not, we would never take anything on Earth seriously, and thus not learn anything. It's just that simple. We are here to learn, grow, experience, and do the best we can, while we suffer the illusion that heaven is mysteriously absent from us.

Put another way, if we could see heaven, learning to grow spiritually would be like learning to ride a bike by reading a book about it. We would know in our minds what life's problems were, but we could not learn how to overcome them and become stronger unless we experienced them. To learn to ride a bike, you've got to go out there and do it and fall a number of times.

So, take heart. Regardless of what happens, know that suffering is temporary. Death, the almost universal fear of humanity, is actually a return to our existing heavenly home for those who love God first and then love others as themselves. This includes people who have never heard of Jesus. God is bigger than any one religious tradition or, for that matter, all of them put together. So do not despair. Dark, evil spirits would never read these words. Since you are reading them, then, I think you will return to heaven with all of the other good people in this world. Besides, would you really want to stay here for eternity? I wouldn't.

Now, I don't want to sound like all problems on Earth should be ignored and everything viewed as all roses and light. We need to acknowledge that there is real suffering and pain and disappointment and loss here on this planet. We must simply remember that these earthly experiences are not the last word regarding our true existence. Our true nature and existence is with God in His kingdom.

The Midlife Experience: Gaining Weight, Arthritis, and a Sense of Interconnectedness

RECENT DEVELOPMENTS IN COSMOLOGY (the branch of astronomy that deals with the general structure and evolution of the universe) say that 96 percent of our universe is "missing." Yes, you read that correctly. What's missing is matter that scientists know exists but that remains unobservable by our scientific instruments. It just goes to show that the universe is interrelated in ways that we are far from understanding.

Those who reach Stage Five in the faith process gain this realization without scientific study. They get the sense that the universe is interrelated in invisible ways; it's a growing awareness that creation goes far beyond what we humans can perceive with our five senses. That just as we cannot see radio waves, sound waves, or even most of the spectrum of light, we cannot see love or other spiritual forces. (Although, if we are paying attention, we can often see the effects of their work.)

As a result of this growing awareness of unity, the boundaries of the self (you) and the "other" (other people and elements of creation) become blurred, porous, and less sharp and definable. In other terms, the point where I begin and you end becomes less clear. The black-and-white distinctions of Stage Four give way to a deeper openness and acceptance of the fact that there is a commonality among all peoples of the earth that transcends surface differences such as race, creed, tribe, nation, religion, or any other group definition. In addition, all these group categorizations become understood as nothing but artificial creations of the human mind that separate us from one another and breed conflict and suffering. In short, the beauty and unity of creation begins to settle into the consciousness of the mind.

Jesus' words in Matthew 22:36–40 epitomize this idea of beauty and unity in all creation. When one of His disciples asked Him what the most important commandment was, Jesus answered, "You shall love the Lord your God with all your heart, and with all your soul, and with all your mind. This is the great and first commandment. And a second is like it; you shall love your neighbor as yourself. On these two commandments depend all the law and the prophets."

I cannot understate the profound importance of these two thoughts within creation. In them, Jesus summarized the entire Bible and names the characteristics we need to search for in our spiritual lives.

I believe Jesus said this because He realized the deep interconnection among people, from which would follow that loving your neighbor is like loving yourself. And if, indeed, we are all sparks of the one divine being, then loving our neighbor is also like loving God.

The Spiritual Ripple Effect: A Model of Interconnectedness

IF YOU THINK ABOUT IT, the spiritual ripple effect is made possible by our interrelatedness to others. After all, our interconnectedness in the universe means we are united even with people we have never met.

As such, our awareness of the interconnectedness of all creation should not end there; it should carry implications for our growth through changed behavior. Remember, God gives us water, but we must make the effort to go get it. We will not make spiritual progress by lying in lounge chairs, tilting our ears upward, and telling God to pour spiritual knowledge in our heads.

In other words, remember this truth when you feel like lashing out or doing something negative toward another: if you do, you will send out negative spiritual energy that will ripple across time and space. So my advice is simple: don't! And, meanwhile, ask God for help. If you make the effort, God will reward you. As it says in Matthew 7:7, "Ask, and it will be given you; seek, and you will find; knock, and it will be opened to you."

From my experience, nothing has changed since this was written in about 80 BC. Kent Nurburn said it this way: "Spiritual growth is honed and perfected only through practice. Like an instrument, it must be played."[35]

---

[35] Kent Nerburn, *Simple Truths* (New World Library, 1996), 93.

Reflection Exercise: The Unity of Mankind and the Universe

Prepare for this meditation as in all previous reflection exercises. The goal here is to become aware of the many invisible connections among people, among people and the elements of the universe, and then among the various parts of the universe. In becoming aware of such connections, you will likely begin to understand the unity among all things.

Here are some questions to get you thinking:

- Have you had any mystical experiences, in which something happened that couldn't be explained by normal physical means? (For example, I am blessed with the presence of my dear, departed wife Marilyn, and even speak to her frequently. No, I am not crazy! Many others do the same thing, but often do not share the experience openly as I am here.)
- Pretend you reside on a satellite orbiting Earth from about 20,000 miles. Envision your view of Earth. What thoughts come to mind regarding human unity, war and famine, and sharing resources? Now envision your view of everything else around you. For example, you watch the moon and stars unimpeded, and see the universe as no one else on Earth. What thoughts might come to your mind?
- Do you feel "one" with the universe?
- Consider this scientific phenomenon: a particle pair is so united that if each one is sent in opposite directions until they become very far away from each other, changing a property of one particle will immediately change the other in the opposite direction. Information flowed from one particle to the other. The second particle knew instantly what happened to the first and changed to keep things in balance and preserve the unity of the two particles. It is estimated that this information between these two particles transfers at a rate that is about 10,000 times faster than the speed of light. How did the other particle know something changed to its pair partner? How did it react so fast? There is a unity between these particles. What does that say to you regarding the nature of creation and God?
- These questions about existence offer you the chance to expand your mind outside of the box it is in, so focus on them one at a time, and do each one slowly.

Richard Ferguson

Many Religions, One God

ONCE A PERSON REALLY INTERNALIZES the truth that there is unity in creation, a natural openness within the heart occurs, which breeds in him or her the ability to see many sides of the same issue simultaneously. Defining such openness as being *liberal,* I continue to like the following quotes after many years:

> A liberal is a man too broadminded to take his own side in a quarrel.
> —Robert Frost

> Liberals are very broadminded: they are always willing to give careful consideration to both sides of the same side.
> —Anonymous

As a result of such openness, "other" people and religious traditions tend to lose their strangeness in the eyes of the Stage Five adult, and are no longer feared as something to be avoided or even condemned.

This ability to see multiple sides of an issue at once comes from questioning existing rules and traditions, and prayerfully reasoning for yourself. This is why I have continually said throughout this book that you need to think for yourself. God gave you a brain for a reason: He knew that, one day, humanity would arrive at our current place in history and that we would need brains and hearts able to question the way things are and to investigate new ideas in order to grow closer to Him.

So why is it that many people shut off their brains the minute they enter the church? Why do they just accept religious doctrine that reason and logic say can't be true? Well, just don't sit there; think! Use your intellectual powers to discern truth no matter where you are, including church. And if your thinking leads you to disagree with what the priest is saying, that's fine. Being a committed follower who loves Jesus Christ does not require you to stuff your brain in your pocket when you go to Mass and blindly accept whatever the priest says during the homily. In fact, it's quite the contrary. Being open to all spiritual angles is healthy and dignified, because it recognizes that no one knows everything. On the other hand, putting your feet into spiritual concrete will freeze you where you are on your spiritual journey.

In fact, being spiritually open means going so far as to see that other religious traditions can be just as valid as your own. Yes, you read that right. If God is infinite, ineffable, and mysterious, then who's to say that any one religious tradition is the way. If you get hung up on what Jesus says in John 14:6 ("I am the way, the truth, and the life; no one comes to the Father, but by me"), just remember that Jesus was not a Christian; He was a Hebrew! Besides, what did Jesus really mean by the phrase "by me"? Did He mean that if you do not believe in Him, you will go to hell? Or did He mean that you must follow His teachings and in order to see the Father? What was Jesus really saying? Think about it, using reason and logic.

Here are two practices that you can consciously follow to help you arrive at a place of spiritual openness:

1. **See something as truth before you put it into one of your predefined mental buckets.** We all do this automatically. When we meet someone, for example, we tend to ask questions such as "What do you do for a living?" or "Are you married?" What is really happening here is that we're putting the person in a personally predefined mental bucket. In doing so, we are attaching all of the other features in that particular bucket to the person we've just met, without even knowing whether they hold true.

   Say you meet someone who introduces himself as an employee of the IRS. Likely, your first instinct will be to put him into a bucket that contains a particular set of characteristics (e.g., the "Mean IRS Agent" bucket). As a result, you have attached all of the other characteristics in that bucket to this person, long before you even get to know him.

   To prejudge people in this way is to deny them the truth of who they are in the eyes of God, and therefore, will keep us from spiritually advancing.

2. **Do not swallow religious doctrine without ensuring it passes tests of reason, logic, and the teachings of Jesus Christ.** God's universe is logical and so, too, should all religious doctrine be. If something appears unreasonable, it is either wrong or happening in a way that we do not understand yet. The bottom line, though, is that you must free your mind from the shackles of religious authorities that would tyrannize your thinking into muteness if you are to achieve the freedom

of Stage Five. So do not ignore the internal stirrings of discontent. They may well be a sign that God is telling you something. Pay attention to them and always pray to God for guidance; you will get it if you ask.

Reflection Exercise: Experiencing Creation

Do these reflections outdoors:

1. Stroll around in a backyard garden or a place nearby that can offer you beautiful scenery and solitude. Admire the beauty before you, while relaxing your mind. If you are in your garden, this means not thinking about your fertilizer or the irrigation schedule.

Transition yourself by using a mantra you feel comfortable with, such as "Love to all."

Now, don't think. Just perceive what is before you, using all of your senses: see the colors, hear the birds sing, smell the flowers or the earth. If a thought comes, gently usher it to the side.

Finally, zero in on something. For example, look at the next flower you see. Stare at it for a few minutes, just taking in its beauty and its expression of itself in the sunlight.

Don't categorize it as a rose or a petunia or any other type of flower. Categorizing something puts the mind in control. Instead, look, see, feel, appreciate, experience, and absorb the flower's essence without thought. Absorb what it is saying to you; the flower is sharing with you its truth. After time, you will discover it has a personality all its own. Appreciate it for what it is, where it is in the universe, and the effect it has on you right now.

If you have trouble keeping your thoughts out, then practice doing this over and over on several different occasions. You will be glad you did. Your perception of creation will change for the better as you exercise one of the characteristics of Stage Five spirituality.

2. I get up very early in the morning during the winter, and, weather allowing, hop into my plane and take off before sunrise. At about 10,000 feet, when the sun starts to rise above the Sierra Nevada Mountains, I set the autopilot to fly directly into the sunrise. There comes a time when sunlight is hitting the wings and the rest of the plane and the ground below me is still very dark, as the sunlight has not yet reached it yet. Taking it all in is a powerfully positive spiritual experience. It gives me a sense of oneness with the universe.

Alternatively, go just before sunrise to the nearest mountain or hill that provides an unhindered view of the horizon. Then just relax and watch. The first few seconds after the sun rises are said to be healing in their power. Sunsets have the same opportunity for meditative reflection.

Peace on Earth, Goodwill to Men

ACCEPTING THE IDEA THAT OTHER religious traditions are valid pathways toward God ultimately leads to the Stage Five adult's commitment to peace and justice for all, regardless of race, creed, color, or any other human-made label. The idea of "the human community" creeps into their thoughts, which is healthy and helps them sort out eternal values versus temporary ones.

Thus, people in Stage Five deeply feel for anyone on the earth who is suffering—not just for the people they know personally. Something as simple as watching the nightly news, with all of its stories of suffering—tornados, droughts, war, poverty, crime, famine, and disease—can be a painful experience. If you love someone and they hurt, so do you. But then when you suffer out of empathy for someone else, God suffers with you.

In that sense, remember that when you see another person on this earth suffering with you, you are seeing a reflection of God hurting with you.

Loving other people and hurting with them is characteristic of adult spirituality, but for a few special people on this planet, it is the doorway to an even higher plane of spirituality: Stage Six. This is what we will explore next.

CHAPTER 9

Stage Six: Universal Faith (The Faith of Few)

IN A PREVIOUS REFLECTION EXERCISE, I had you imagine that you were orbiting the earth on a satellite and to imagine what you might observe and feel. The reason I did this is because some astronauts have described their experience of looking at the earth from this perspective as one in which everything seemed to have a kind of unity. Here are just a couple of those descriptions:

> As you pass from sunlight into darkness and back again every hour and a half, you become startlingly aware how artificial are thousands of boundaries we've created to separate and define. And for the first time in your life you feel in your gut the precious unity of the earth and all the living things it supports.
> —Astronaut Russell Schweickart, upon his return in Apollo 9

> My view of our planet (from the moon) was a glimpse of divinity.
> —Astronaut Edgar Mitchell

One astronaut called the experience an epiphany, in which he felt "oneness with everything created and a deep sense of ecstasy." Another, after walking on the moon, said that our petty squabbles on Earth were dangerous to our well-being. And yet another said that although he went to the moon, in a profound way, he discovered Earth for the first time.

This profound feeling of community, connectedness, and unity with all creation is available to you, too, and you don't have to go into space to get it. As mentioned in the previous chapter, places of natural beauty can impart such an experience. Be aware of those things that make you feel closer to God. Seek them out and enjoy them, as they enrich your spirit in ways that are not totally understandable by any of us.

For me, my airplane is the place I get away from all the negative energy on Earth. Being a pilot has been one of the great blessings in my life. One solo flight I remember in particular was back to San Jose from southern California. It was winter, and a strong storm had just moved through the day before, cleaning the air to perfection. You could see for hundreds of miles in any direction. At about three miles' altitude, I activated the autopilot and just sat, my hands folded in my lap. I was too high to see the details on the ground (cars for example). Evidence of human existence and civilization were lost within the big picture of creation for a time. The only evidence of others was the white contrails of the jets a few miles above me in the perfect blue sky. Other than the muffled, steady drone of the engine through my headset, there was complete peace. Off of the right wingtip, I could see the Sierra Nevada Mountains peaked with snow. To the left, the rich blue colors of the Pacific Ocean. And straight ahead, the San Francisco Bay about 150 miles in the distance.

I had a sense of oneness, as if everything fit together. I knew that there was indeed a master plan and that I was an inexorable part of it; that I was where I was supposed to be at that very moment. How did I know? God was in the cockpit with me, whispering His truth into my mind and spirit. It was the memory of a lifetime.

Be sure to realize that it does not matter what level of spiritual growth a person is at as I did. That is always available to everyone. Anyone who might have been with me that time would probably have experienced the joy that I did.

There are not many on our planet who make it this far, as the sixth stage of faith requires a radical commitment to peace and justice at the expense of personal safety and comfort.

Think Gandhi, Martin Luther King Jr., and Mother Teresa of Calcutta. These three exemplify the Stage Six characteristics. All three had a clear vision of an all-inclusive state-of-being for humans, regardless of their artificial labels. They saw the universe as a unified human community in which each person was part of the others and in which all were one before God. And they recognized the divinity in every living soul, regardless of a person's worldly circumstances.

As a result of their views of humankind, people in Stage Six feel strongly that anything short of full human dignity and respect is to be pointed out and fixed, regardless of why, when, where, or how the injustice occurs, or who is involved. Absolute love, peace, and justice for all is an ideal that burns in their hearts. Further, it seems in their very natures to do anything possible to overcome those injustices. Their love for humanity as a whole as well as for individuals is so strong that they will put the best interests of others ahead of theirs, even if it means risking their own personal safety and survival. Two of the three people mentioned above were assassinated, and the third, Mother Teresa, suffered immensely, almost dying a number of times.

Unfortunately, the Stage Six person is also more susceptible to such suffering because his or her radical commitment to justice and love almost always flies in the face of the institutions of the times. These people seem to irritate the established powers, particularly political and religious institutions, because they're viewed as threats to the status quo. The result is conflict, as many times the martyr is dealt with harshly. Yet, the person in Stage Six will not back off from his or her commitment to universal love.

Many times, conflict also arises because people in lower stages of faith think those with visions of universal justice are disconnected from reality. But Fowler makes a clear distinction between people who simply have a utopian imagination and those in Stage Six who address real problems and injustices that exist in the political and economic environment. "These are not abstract visions, generated like utopias out of some capacity for transcendent imagination," Fowler wrote. "Rather they are visions born out of radical acts of identification with persons and circumstances where the futurity of being is being crushed, blocked or exploited."[36] By "futurity of being," Fowler means the spiritual, economic, and social progress that we are divinely entitled to, by right of being the children of God.

Coming Full Circle (Sort of)

I FIND IT AMAZING THAT there seems to be a circular aspect of going from Stage One to Stage Six. As infants, we cannot tell the difference between

---

[36]   James Fowler, *Stages of Faith* (San Francisco: Harper Collins, 1981), 203.

ourselves and the rest of the world; we cannot understand where we leave off and other people begin, because our perception of self has not formed within us yet. This is a kind of oneness or unity of being, is it not? If we then reach Stage Six, we seem to return to this feeling of unity, this blurring of self and others.

This, of course, does not mean that we return to where we started as infants. No, we have grown spiritually and have come to know ourselves as unique beings. We have learned how we fit into the grand scheme of things and have better understood the character of God.

Perhaps it is better to think of our progress, then, as the seasons of the year. We begin our human spiritual journey in the spring of our lives, growing and experiencing what we need to as we pass through summer and autumn. By winter, we have gained knowledge, wisdom, and the profound feeling that all was worthwhile, so that later, when we pass into another spring of our eternal existence, we are different, closer to God, and more fully who God intended us to be from the beginning. From oneness we came, and back unto oneness we return, but forever changed.

As far as we know in our collective consciousness of human history, Stage Six is the pinnacle of human spiritual development. But I do not believe that faith ends here. I do not believe that is all there is. I suspect there are many more stages that are not visible to us on this earth. It stands to reason, after all, since God is infinite, ineffable, and mysterious, transcending all that we can perceive.

PART II

Learning in This Life

Chapter 10

A Liberal View of Faith

What most people think of when the word *faith* comes up is a particular understanding of or belief in God, often based on a specific religious tradition. In the following chapter, however, *faith* will have a more expanded meaning.

Faith, as used here, does not refer to belief in a particular religious doctrine or God; it goes way beyond being Catholic, Hindu, Islam, or any other religion. Rather, the word will mean the unique way in which each of us relates to our world, to others, and to God. In other words, faith is the sum total of all your beliefs—the moral values that guide you and your manner of being (or behavior) throughout life, and everything that makes you tick the way you do and motivates you to do things in the world.

Here are just a few of the things that make up a person's belief system, or faith:

- How and what you've learned at different ages in your life.
- How you believe life works, including what you think about what makes people tick, how the physical universe is arranged, and what needs to be done to survive in it.
- What meanings you bring to life, including your definitions of joy and suffering, which are based on your unique experiences here on Earth.
- What you believe your identity is—your role in the cosmic scheme of things.

- How you react within your understanding of life.

None of these things are static, however, and so neither is faith. As we grow older, our ever-accumulating experiences serve to continually change our views of life (even if we are not conscious of those changes).

To remind you of this very inclusive meaning throughout this chapter, I will often substitute the word *faith* with other terms and phrases, such as *spirituality, guiding principles, view of existence, existential relationship with the "other," inner values, relationship with God, and beliefs.*

Reflection Exercise: What Does Faith Mean to You?

My definition of faith is very open and expansive, as described above; yours may be much different. And yet your definition of the word is just as legitimate as mine. That's because faith is a personal definition based on where each of us is on our faith journey.

Wherever you are on that journey right now, rest assured that God would meet you there. Do not despair if you have "faith" in some theological topics but not in others. Not accepting all of the Church's teachings is normal and healthy, in my opinion.

That said, what is faith to you? Here are some questions to get you thinking:

- What do you think are the underlying components of faith?
- Do you have faith in the people around you? Why or why not?
- Do others have to perform for you or meet a certain standard before you can have faith in them? Why or why not?
- Do you have faith in Jesus Christ? Really? How can you tell?
- Do you have faith in your husband or wife? Why or why not?
- What is your faith in others based on?
- What is your faith in God based on?

Liberal and Fundamentalist Theology: A Comparison

BEFORE LAUNCHING A DISCUSSION ABOUT a liberal view of faith versus a conservative or fundamentalist one, it will be important to define what I mean by the terms *liberal* and *conservative* in relation to theology. (Please note that these terms, as used in this book, have no relationship to liberal and conservative political views.) I have compiled below a list of the few main thoughts encompassed by each theological viewpoint. This list is not inclusive.

Conservative Theology

Among other things, a fundamentalist or conservative Christian generally believes in the following:

- The virgin birth of Jesus Christ
- The doctrine of the Holy Trinity: Father, Son, and Holy Spirit
- Substitutionary atonement, in which Jesus died to redeem us from our original sin
- The literal, physical resurrection of Jesus after his crucifixion
- The literal, physical return of Jesus to Earth at some time in the future
- The existence of both heaven and hell, and the condemnation of sinners to hell for eternity
- The infallibility and literal interpretation of the Bible, which contains no contradictions
- The idea that Jesus Christ is the only means of receiving God's forgiveness of sin
- The concept that everything we need to know is in the Bible
- The idea that we are all tainted with original sin and therefore have a sin debt to God

In short, the rules that govern a conservative fundamentalist are fairly black and white, stemming from the belief that the Bible is the inspired word of God, and that is that. Some conservatives believe the Holy Spirit Himself dictated the sacred scriptures to the writers of the Bible.

The conservative view of God is, in my opinion, a more closed view. I call it the "God in a box" syndrome, in which conservative beliefs define the dimensions of the box, and then anything that falls outside the box is considered false or heretical.

Liberal Theology

The beliefs of the liberal Christian, on the other hand, are not so set in stone. Rather, liberal theology encompasses a more fluid system of beliefs that combines different ways of thinking about God. Liberals try to reconcile biblical thought with the reality they experience all around them.

That is not to say that a liberal's views are necessarily different from a conservative's. In fact, a liberal Christian will usually hold at least some beliefs that are the same. The difference is in how the liberal Christian arrives at those beliefs. In the open, liberal view, there is no "God in the box" syndrome, where the edges of the box are defined by doctrine or dogma. Instead, God is viewed as an infinite mystery that can never be contained by a human-defined doctrinal or dogmatic container of any kind, no matter how big.

Liberal theology understands that we do not know all there is to know, or even that we know all that we do not know. (Think about that last sentence for a while.) That said, however, there are certain characteristics of liberal theology that should be noted. These do not so much denote a fixed, doctrinal system of beliefs; instead, they speak to a manner of thinking about and approaching theology and scripture. A person with a liberal theological perspective usually displays the following characteristics:

• Uses an individualistic method of understanding God
• Applies the same methods for studying the Bible as for studying other ancient and sacred scriptures
• Does not hold a belief structure molded by orthodox church doctrine
• Shows a willingness to interpret scripture without notions that it is inerrant or infallible
• Believes that the Bible was written by people we do not know and modified along the way by others equally unknown to us
• Sees value in reading the gospels that did not make it into the Bible like the Gospel of Thomas, The Gospel of Peter or the Gospel of Mary
• Is suspicious of literal interpretations of scripture, holding the belief that the Bible is littered with contradictions because it is the inspired word of God given through imperfect men

• Displays an openness to other religious traditions, and pursues whatever traditions necessary in order to grow closer to God.
• Sees some commonality between Christianity and other religious traditions
• Uses all the modern biblical hermeneutics, such as the historical critical method of biblical exegesis, but looks beyond the words for deeper meaning
• Believes in the ongoing self-revelation of God; in other words, that God still speaks to us today
• Thinks the Church is a fallible human institution

A lot of people think liberal theology is a kind of New Age thing—you know, a belief that might accompany tree-hugging. But it is not. In fact, liberal theology is not a new concept at all. In my estimation, it seems to have been around at least since Michelangelo. In this famous painter's work at the Sistine Chapel, in a depiction of the last judgment, there is a circle of people surrounding Jesus Christ: presumably those who are close to Jesus and will go to heaven. As you might expect, Mother Mary is at His side, in addition to many of the saints. But there are a host of other unexpected and unknown faces as well. A couple of notable images, if you look in the upper right corner of the circle, are unmistakably those of two Jewish men. Through this depiction, Michelangelo seems to be proclaiming that heaven is open to everyone, a viewpoint that, at the time of this painting, would have been considered scandalous by the Church (to say nothing about Michelangelo's original portrayals of nudity). This leads me to believe that liberal interpretations of Christianity have been around for quite some time.

The Pursuit of Theological Truth

LET'S FACE IT. I AM very much the liberal when it comes to theology. To me, this perspective is far more open to reality, nurturing healthy spirituality that recognizes the vast diversity of God's creation and His love for all of it. I arrived at this viewpoint, however, only after much academic study, prayer, meditation, life experience, and just plain paying attention.

The journey toward my current liberal spiritual viewpoint did not begin until I was in my late forties. As you read about in the previous section, it was at this age when I began to feel a tug toward God, which prompted me to wonder about Him more seriously. It seemed that something inside me was changing, but I was not in charge of what was happening. It was seemingly proceeding on its own, as I remained a spectator, merely viewing and feeling the changes take place. God was still not front-and-center on my radar, but something related to Him was undoubtedly growing within me.

As time progressed, I found my personal views of spirituality diverging from what I was taught as a child—in a big way. I grew serious doubts about where I was headed spiritually. Was I becoming a sinful heretic? Would my emerging beliefs lead me to hell? Was I becoming a fallen Christian? And because, in theology, doubt is the father of education, I wanted to learn more about the roots of Christian theology. I also, for the first time, realized that I did not dislike God. I was able to discern the difference between the humans in the church versus God. The result: as mentioned, at fifty-two, I enrolled in the pastoral ministry graduate program at Santa Clara University.

After planting the desire within me to know more, however, God, it felt, had left me hanging. He handed over no divine information, gave no signs in the sky or memos in the clouds that said, "Okay, Rich, this is what you do now." Woody Allen of Hollywood fame expressed my frustration best when he said, "If only God would give me some clear sign! Like making a large deposit in my name in a Swiss bank." I agree that would remove all doubt! In seriousness though, the situation was frustrating to me at the time. But, again, we must work out our own salvation using our own efforts. Remember? God provides the water, but we must make the effort to go get it.

So as any thirsty child of God, I became very serious in my academic pursuit of theology in order to satisfy my doubts and questions. During my studies I developed a more open idea regarding the definition of the word *theology*. I learned that whatever your image of God, it's always too small.

A New and Improved Definition of Theology

One dictionary defines theology as, "the study of religious faith, practice, and experience; especially the study of God and of God's relation to the world."[37] I feel this definition is too restricted, implying that God is "there," we are "here," and theology is the study of God's long-distance relationship to us; it's as if we are separate from God. My problem with this definition comes because I believe we are inexorably tied to God.

---

[37]   http://www.merriam-webster.com/dictionary/theology

Although it often appears that we are separate from God, that separation is just an illusion to help us learn. In some way, even Albert Einstein could be said to agree with this proposition. He said, "Reality is merely an illusion, albeit a very persistent one."[38] My spiritual advisor has always told me that God is closer to us than our own breath. Matthew 10:29–31 says, "Are not two sparrows sold for a penny? And not one of them will fall to the ground without your Father's will. But even the hairs of your head are all numbered. Fear not, therefore; you are of more value than many sparrows." God wouldn't be able to know us in such detail if he were "there" and we "here."

All this in mind, I propose to define theology as "The study of all existence, including the study of the relationships of all things physical; the human psyche; religion; the relationship between God and man; the spiritual; man's place within all creation; and so on." This expanded definition of theology includes the notion of existence itself. It removes the implied separation of God by recognizing that He not only is within creation but also transcends it. Creation does not limit God; He is within every particle and atom. Thus, He knows us more than we know ourselves.

I know that this notion is controversial. But I am in good company as I quote Einstein again: "Science without religion is lame. Religion without science is blind."[39] That is, if science is the study of pottery, then studying science will give us insight about the potter. Understanding the cosmos will shed light on God Himself. For example, for my bachelor's degree in chemistry, I studied quantum physics. Since then, I always wondered where the physical laws came from. What caused, or who created, the four basic forces in the universe: electromagnetism, the strong nuclear force, the weak nuclear force, and gravity?

After all my hours of studying, reading, praying, and meditating, I concluded that if there are six billion people on the planet, there are six billion different ways to God. Each of these ways may be narrow and we may have difficulty passing through them, like a camel passing through the eye of a needle—but then, I also believe there are six billion different needles. Each of us is a unique creation of God, which means that one size of theology does not fit all, as a more conservative or fundamentalist theology would have us believe.

I like what Daniel J. Boorstin, US historian, once said: "The greatest obstacle to discovery is not ignorance—it is the illusion of knowledge."

[38]   http://rescomp.stanford.edu/~cheshire/EinsteinQuotes.html
[39]   Ibid.

That's the trap many people fall into, and it blocks them from discovering new perspectives about God and His creation.

Your Personal Path to God

MOST PEOPLE'S BELIEFS FALL SOMEWHERE between the strict conservative and very liberal view of things. Mine do too, for that matter, though I lean much more toward the liberal interpretation.

The problem, however, is that most people are so busy with their day-to-day lives that they have little time or energy left to sit and ponder theological issues, such as where they stand on the spirituality spectrum.

Now, there's nothing wrong with that, since, as mentioned many times, God meets each of us exactly where we are on our spiritual journey. But if you are reading this book because you yearn to grow closer to God, then remember that one way to do that is to assess where you are, where you feel God's guidance is leading you, and what personal path that God seems to have set for you to follow to your intended destination.

Reflection Exercise: Where Am I on My Path?

In my experience, there are a few questions you can answer to help you measure where you are on your individual path. Take your time on this. Even do it over a period of time and not just one meditation session.

- How are you improving yourself by focusing first on God with all your heart, your mind and your soul?
- How are you helping other people by loving them as yourself?
- How many books have you read to expand your mind in spiritual matters?

Then bring to your mind your life's path and count the ways you are improving and helping others. If you find something lacking, this is good, as it offers you room to grow. Just be gentle with yourself and resolve to make the appropriate changes, as you continue to seek God's guidance. You will eventually get to where you want to be.

The most important thing is just to attempt to answer these questions to the best of your ability, since they get to the bottom of how you are handling the two most important commandments according to Jesus Christ. In simpler terms, as long as you are doing your best to achieve these two goals, heaven is your next stop—and don't let anyone tell you any different. If you never remember anything else I say in this book, remember this, and you will be okay.

My Personal Pathway to Liberal Theology

THOUGH IT WAS SOMEWHAT FRUSTRATING at the time, I now feel very blessed that I had the opportunity to study pastoral ministry at Santa Clara. Even from a purely human level—that is, barring anything academic—it was an eye-opening experience that led me not only back to God but also to a more liberal viewpoint of theology. My classmates and I all led disparate lives and held very different points of view regarding God and how to be closer to Him. This opened my eyes in two ways.

First, because we were all different varieties of Christian, the perceptions and opinions we brought to the table had a rich diversity that added much flavor and texture to our class discussions. It was wonderful. Second, it was amazing to me, that despite all of our varied opinions on theology, we held among us a strong bond of love. It was as if we could say without hesitation to one another, "You are different from me, I am different from you, and we hold different perceptions of God. But we are one in the eyes of God, so, through Him, you are my sibling." Beautiful, isn't it? Too bad the rest of the world cannot be that way. But unfortunately, I think Georg Christoph Lichtenberg had it right when he said, "With most men, unbelief in one thing springs from blind belief in another." People get too closed-minded about what they believe while rejecting others' beliefs.

Another thing that happened—in fact, probably what marked the beginning of my journey toward a liberal view—was that I began to study world leaders who, in my estimation, lived in Stage Six spirituality. I admired Mahatma Gandhi, for example, and read a lot of what Siddhartha Gautama, the Buddha, had to say, and liked it very much. Neither of them were Christian, however—at least in the more traditional sense of the word. They were not baptized. They did not accept Jesus Christ as their personal lord and savior. So, if the conservative Christians were right, I reasoned, they must be in hell right now, alongside Adolf Hitler and others of his kind.

I had to disagree. I believed that God's loving light shined through these two and that the world became a better place because of them. On that same token, I also greatly admired Reverend Billy Graham. What a wonderful man of God he was. I attended many of his revivals and felt the presence of God in all of them. He was a conservative Christian, but that was okay with this liberal; God's love shined through him very brightly.

A Liberal's View of Basic Christian Doctrine

WITH ALL THAT IN MIND, where do I stand on the most pivotal doctrinal issues? Not that my views are any more important than any other Christian's, but since I do have a big mouth and have thought about this a lot, I will offer up my ideas for your consideration. Then, as Sylvia Browne often says, "Take what you want and leave the rest." Don't accept my viewpoints just because you read them in this book. Instead, research the different aspects, ask God for guidance, and meditate on each one until you feel comfortable in your heart that it is right for you.

Also keep in mind as you read that thought above, I might be accused of heresy for expressing the following viewpoints; that is okay with me. Jesus Christ himself was accused of blasphemy. Mind you, I am not comparing myself in any way to our Lord. What I am saying is that all religious progress is necessarily born out of what may be viewed at the time as heresy. For if a new thought regarding God is not consistent with existing orthodoxy, it will, of course, be considered heretical by existing religious establishments. Think of the word "Sanhedrin" of biblical fame, and you will see what I mean. To me, orthodoxy means getting stuck in the mud, theologically speaking.

The Virgin Birth

WAS JESUS BORN OF THE Virgin Mary? Well, he might have been, or he might have not been. Church doctrine says Jesus was both fully human and fully divine at the same time. Being fully human, to me, means that he could not be born of a virgin. But no one knows for sure one way or the other.

If I remember my biblical history correctly, the early Church had to have a doctrine that stated Jesus was born of a virgin, as they had to separate him from another theological construction that popped up after his resurrection: the idea of original sin. You see, the very early Church did not have a doctrine of original sin. So when that doctrine popped up after Jesus's resurrection, the Church needed a way to claim that Jesus was not tainted with original sin—and in their view, making such a claim was not possible unless Jesus was born of a virgin.

You see, the early Church was just sorting out what to believe about Jesus. And in their debate over this issue, the Virgin Birth doctrine won out over other ideas. Can you see now how the Christian traditions we have today are the result of many refinements and changes in theology over the past two thousand years? It is my belief that most of them are products of well intended and loving human minds, but human nonetheless.

Where Did the Bible Really Come From?

Did you know that Christian (or biblical) literature during the times of the early Church was more extensive than what we are exposed to today? Some estimate that there was as many as thirty different gospels circulating in the "Followers of Jesus" community in the 200 years after Jesus's death and resurrection. For example, the first biblical texts included the gospels of Thomas, Judas (yes, that Judas), and Mary, just to name three. The Bible we have today is the result of the early Church's coming together to establish a consistent text for all Christians. Leaders felt they had to come to a common understanding regarding fundamental theological doctrine in order to bring unity to the early Church. As a result, they kept out many books from the final agreed-upon version—and that is the Bible we have today. This is not to say that what they did was wrong. That's just the way it was.

And what if I am wrong, and Jesus was really born of a virgin? I do realize that's possible. But I don't think God will stop loving me if I'm wrong, because regardless, I believe that Jesus is exactly who He said He was—the son of God and the son of man. He is my personal savior, whom I depend on and pray to every evening. Basically, my faith does not depend upon the doctrinal aspects of the Church to be correct. It is sturdier than that. You may believe adamantly in the virgin birth, and that too is just fine. God still loves us both.

Richard Ferguson

The Holy Trinity

WHOLE BOOKS HAVE BEEN WRITTEN about the complex theology that surrounds this idea. Suffice it to say, I do believe in the Holy Trinity, even if it is only the result of our need to think of God in three different ways due to the limitations of our human minds. Again, your understanding of the Holy Trinity might be different than mine, and that is okay too. Very few claim with authority even to understand exactly what the Trinity is anyway; God will not slap your wrists and say you're naughty if you don't get the answer right. More likely the "answer" is beyond our human capacity to understand it anyway.

Original Sin

WHEN YOU RESEARCH THIS IDEA, you run across very complex, highly nuanced arguments over what original sin even is or how it works. Some examples follow:

- Original sin means the transmission of death from parent to child.
- Original sin means the sin committed in imitation of Adam.
- Original sin is the hereditary stain contracted at our birth.
- Original sin is transmitted to all by generation, not by imitation.
- "Original sin is the privation of sanctifying grace in consequence of the sin of Adam."[40]
- "Since Adam transmits death to his children by way of generation when he begets them mortal, it is by generation also that he transmits to them sin, for the Apostle presents these two effects as produced at the same time and by the same causality."[41]

Did you get all that? Take a step back and ask yourself if you think God really intended something to be so hard to understand. I say no. Convoluted concepts are products of the human mind and not the beautiful elegance of God. Compare, for example, the complexity of the

---

[40] For details, visit the Catholic Encyclopedia at http://www.newadvent.org/cathen/11312a.htm

[41] Ibid.

above statements with the beauty and simplicity of what Jesus said about the two most important commandments.

Now, consider the following two points about the story of Adam and Eve:

- All cultures have their creation myths; the Hebrew culture is no different. Thousands of years ago, the Hebrews had to find their own way to explain creation, the existence of evil in the world, and man's free will. For this reason, I believe the Adam and Eve story is not literal. It was written for the benefit of giving many illiterate Hebrews explanations about the universe that they could understand. Today, however, we have a higher understanding of who God is by way of His ongoing self-revelation, so we do not need the story of Adam and Eve to provide an explanation. This is not to say that the existence of evil is not real. It is, in fact, all too pervasive. But I do not think Adam and Eve started the whole thing.

- Are you angry with your grandchildren because of something your kids did? Are your grandparents angry with you for something your parents did? Certainly not! And neither is God angry with you for something a man and woman did thousands of years ago (that is, if they really existed in a literal sense in the first place). When I was just nine years old, I came home from Catholic school one day, bothered by what the sisters had taught us—that we were deserving of hell because of original sin. I said to myself, *I didn't do anything wrong!*

Take from this what you want; research it, and come to your own conclusions.

Open your minds in a prayerful way and ask God for His guidance regarding these things. Don't let anyone tell you that you have to believe in any doctrine. That includes me. I like the following quote. As Bertrand Russell (1872–1970) said, "I think we ought always to entertain our opinions with some measure of doubt. I shouldn't wish people dogmatically to believe any philosophy, not even mine."

Famous spiritual author Sophy Burnham said, "To believe in God or in a guiding force because someone tells you to is the height of stupidity. We are given senses to receive our information within. With our own eyes we see, and with our own skin we feel. With our intelligence, it is intended that we understand. But each person must puzzle it out for himself or herself." Sophy is saying the same thing that Siddhartha Gautama, the Buddha, said about figuring out things for yourself. "Buddha challenged each individual to do his own religious seeking." Do not accept what you hear by report, do not accept tradition, do not accept a statement because it is found in our books, nor because it is in accord with your belief, nor because it is the saying of your teacher. Be lamps unto yourselves."[42]

All that said, I do not believe in original sin for one moment. Look into the eyes of a newborn and tell me she is tainted with sin and deserving of hell. That is a terrible piece of theology in my opinion. And, finally, let's not forget what St. Paul said in 1 Corinthians 6:19: "Do you not know that your body is a temple of the Holy Spirit within you, which you have from God? You are not your own." I do not believe that God's temples are tainted, newborn or not. To me it is as simple as that.

The Crucifixion

THIS ISSUE IS TIED UP with the idea of original sin. If there were no original sin, Jesus would not need to die to save your butt from hell. He would not need to be your substitute on the cross because you inherited sin from Adam and Eve. *However,* I do believe that Jesus was crucified by the Romans and did die on the cross because of His love for all of us.

I believe Jesus died because His teachings were in serious conflict with the existing religious authorities of the time, called the Sanhedrin. His teachings upset their theological apple cart in a way that threatened their existence. In addition, the Sanhedrin worried that Jesus might inflame an uprising against the Roman occupation during Passover week, causing a repeat of the massacre by Romans that had occurred years before under the same circumstances. So the time Jesus threw out the moneychangers in the temple, that was probably the act that sealed His fate.

I believe Jesus knew He would die at the hand of the authorities, due to what He preached and then later did to the moneychangers in the temple. He clearly had a chance to escape the night before His capture just by walking away, over the hill and into the countryside. But He chose not to, because after praying that night, He chose instead to yield to the will of God.

[42] Huston Smith, *The World's Religions* (San Francisco: Harper Collins, 1961), 94.

The bottom line: I believe Jesus died because He loved you and me so very much. He loved us so much that He stood by His teachings in a meeting with the Sanhedrin, hoping to let them see the truth of God. Just think how history would have changed for the better if the Sanhedrin had believed that Jesus was who He said He was and began to teach the people about His gospel of love and compassion.

Here's another thought: do you realize that Jesus was not Christian? Think about that. Jesus was a Jew. The term Christian did not enter into the picture until many years after Christ's death and resurrection.

The Eucharist or Communion

WHAT COMES TO YOUR MIND when you read the following terms: blood sacrifice, human sacrifice, killing an innocent? Sounds a little like throwing virgins into a volcano to appease the gods, doesn't it? Sometimes we forget how it looks to outsiders when we do certain things that are meaningful to us as Christians. Take the Eucharist, or Communion, for example. We say things like "this is his body" about a bread or wafer and "this is his blood" about wine or juice, and then we eat and drink them at a religious ceremony. Yet, the Eucharist is the centerpiece of Mass.

I prefer not to think of the Eucharist this way. To me, the host and wine are not symbolic of the body and blood of Jesus. Instead, they are an invitation to share life with Jesus. Outside of any religious context, breaking bread with another is a statement of brotherhood and closeness and shared experience. So too is it for me at the Eucharist. I am sharing an intimacy with Jesus. I am recognizing what He did for all of us, the sacrifices He made to ensure we heard His gospel message as part of our lives in this modern age.

Jesus gave up His body not because He wanted to appease an angry god, but because He accepted it as the consequence of teaching the controversial truth of God to people. Those who chose to remain blind to His truth were the ones who killed him.

The Resurrection

Was Jesus returned to life after His crucifixion? I believe he was. There are many historical references citing appearances of Him after His death. I believe one account reports He appeared to at least five hundred people before He rose to heaven. (See? A liberal can believe in foundational doctrine.)

Now, if tomorrow, they discovered a body, and had conclusive evidence that it belonged to Jesus, would my faith in God be shattered? No. If they found a full tomb with the inscription, "Here lies the body of Jesus of Nazareth, crucified by Pontus Pilate," would I still be a Christian? Yes. It is because my faith does not hinge on human-given doctrine, but rather on my own personal knowledge of God's character. So to me, the discovery of Jesus's body would simply mean that our understanding of the resurrection process somehow became flawed along the way; for example, that something else happened to make it appear to the ancients as if His body had come back to life.

Here are some questions to get you thinking about where you stand on this topic.

- Do you believe that Jesus was resurrected in His original body—that is, the one that died on the cross and was pierced through the side by a Roman spear?
- Rather, did something else happen that was a product of natural physical laws, which science does not yet understand?
- Will Jesus come back in the future?

My answer to this last question is I hope so, and I hope soon. In fact, tomorrow would be good! However, I don't believe Jesus will judge people and throw them into hell. Jesus is better than that; He is love incarnate.

Heaven

DOES HEAVEN EXIST? HOW COULD it not? And what about hell? I believe, that, too, exists, but not in the sense of fire and brimstone, where a devil keeps poking you with a pitchfork. To me, hell is simply separation from the love of God. Quite simply, people who reject God in this life will be separated from His eternal love in the afterlife. The dark spirits in our world that cause pain and destruction will seek out eternal darkness to avoid God's loving light. Children of the light, on the other hand, will run to God's waiting arms.

The main difference here is that, in my interpretation, it is the dark spirits themselves who will run into the outer darkness because they cannot stand to see themselves in the light of God's eternal love. In other words,

God will not throw them there; they will do it themselves. Considering the current condition of our planet, this is probably part of hell anyway.

Biblical Interpretation: Literal or Not?

DOES THE BIBLE CONTAIN CONTRADICTIONS? Yes! The Bible is full of them. The three synoptic gospels—Mark, Matthew, and Luke—are all very similar, but they do *not* agree on all points; they sometimes say different things about the same event. That is okay with me, however, because my faith in God does not depend on an error-free Bible.

In fact, I think it's a wonder there aren't more inconsistencies, considering how the Bible was written. First, humans wrote it. Even God-inspired humans can make mistakes, can they not? Heck, we all know how two people can look at the very same thing and describe it in very different ways.

Second, as time wore on, more and more humans got their hands on these texts. Scribes added a little text here, reworded or omitted a little more there. In fact, did you know there has been so much human tampering over the years that the world no longer has original copies of any book of the Bible? We have only copies of copies of copies, etc. In addition, we have several different versions of these altered copies. Here are just some of the more popular current Bible translations:

- The King James Version (KJV)
- The New American Standard Bible (NASB)
- The Living Bible (TLB)
- The New International Version (NIV)
- The New King James Version (NKJV)

Each of these translations still expresses sacred truths, but using slightly different wording and styles. Taking into consideration the various nuances that words carry, however, means that even slight difference in wording could impact the reader's understanding of a verse. One good example of this is the Greek word *teleios*. (Much of the Bible [New Testament] was originally written in Greek.) In most Bible versions including the Catholic Study Bible, this word *teleios* as used in Matthew 5:48 was originally translated to mean *perfect*. The resulting verse reads, "You, therefore, must be perfect, as your heavenly Father is perfect." However, later biblical scholars discovered this translation was not exactly correct, as *teleios* can also mean *whole* or *complete*. This slight change in wording causes the verse, now, to read like this: "You therefore, must be complete and whole, as your Father is complete and whole."

Can you see how just one word change affects this verse's implications about our behavior? In the first translation, the reader is likely to interpret the word *perfect* as sinless—without stain or blemish—which is impossible for humans, and we all know it. Essentially, it's saying you suck and will go to hell unless you are perfect, obeying all the Church laws and letting the priest beg God for your forgiveness. This interpretation paints a hopeless picture of guilt; hardly the "good news" that Jesus brought to us in the gospels. (Incidentally, this was the meaning I was given as a kid at St. Tarcissus.) Furthermore the word "gospel" means good news.

The second translation, on the other hand, paints a picture of hope. Being complete and whole is what we all strive for. It brings a deep sense of happiness. Like what Gandhi said: "Happiness is when what you think, what you say, and what you do are in harmony."

This is just one small example of what has led me to the conclusion that taking every word in the Bible literally is dangerous, since, as we've seen, specific words are often subject to human error. In no way does this mean the Bible is not sacred; it just means that humans had a big hand in what we read, therefore contradictions are inevitable. It also means that you shouldn't hang your spiritual hat on just one translation of the Bible, since any given verse in one translation may be expressed differently in another.

A third reason I believe one should not translate the Bible literally: the original writers of the Bible had no idea their works would be included in something called a Bible and considered sacred literature for thousands of years to come. Their main goal in writing was for the benefit of others who were alive at that time. They wrote certain things, within certain circumstances, for a certain purpose, and to a certain audience—not to you and me. Take St. Paul, for example. His "book" is actually just a series of letters that he wrote to church congregations of his time, addressing issues they encountered by sharing his own understanding of basic theology and the teachings of Jesus. St. Paul would be shocked if he saw where his letters wound up and how they are used today.

We need to realize that it was acceptable in biblical times for a disciple to use the name of his master when writing a scripture in order to establish the document's authority. This is one way slightly different meanings and words crept into scripture under the name of religious leaders such as the disciples of Jesus Himself. Books have been written on this topic. This is no conspiracy; rather, just the way it was in the time of Jesus.

The Jesus Seminar

We are not sure even today exactly what Jesus really said and what was attributed to Him by later authors. It was an accepted and understood practice during the times of Jesus and afterward for a disciple of someone with great authority to write something and sign his master's name to it. This alone casts confusion of who wrote what and what was really said. The Jesus Seminar was instituted to attempt to identify just what Jesus really said and did. It comprised about 150 biblical scholars and published authors. The seminar was founded in 1985. It published three reports: the first in 1993, the second in 1998, and the last in 1999. Additionally, it produced a new translation of the New Testament.

Is Jesus the Only Way to Heaven?

Is JESUS THE ONLY WAY to be forgiven of sin? Do you have to accept Jesus as your savior or go to hell? Jesus Christ is indeed my personal savior. He guides me down a wholesome, spiritual path toward God. St. Paul did say that Adam introduced death to the human race, but he also said that, through Jesus Christ, all men are forgiven. Romans 5:18 says: "Consequently, just as the result of one trespass was condemnation for all men, so also the result of one act of righteousness was justification that brings life for all men."

Even those who have never heard of Jesus can be saved by Him. According to the Catholic doctrine of the unconscious Christian, those who live the best they can, just as a Christian would, but do not know Jesus, can still go to heaven. The Aborigines in Australia are perhaps a good example. Members of this isolated tribe may never have heard of Jesus. As long as they live the best they can, they are saved anyway, according to the Catholic Church.

I believe that if you live by the two most important commandments, you will surely go to heaven. Don't let anyone badger you about original sin; Jesus took care of it for you as if it never really existed. Alternately, you might believe, as I do, that the concept of original sin is faulty to begin with. Either way, you will win a place in heaven if you obey the two most important commandments: love God first, and love your neighbor as yourself. That is simple, elegant, and wondrous.

Is the Bible Sufficient?

Does the Bible offer everything you need to know? Again, let us examine the two most important commandments, as identified by Jesus. Luke 10:27: "And he answered, 'You shall love the Lord your God with all your heart, and with all your soul, and with all your strength, and with all your mind; and (love) your neighbor as yourself.'" If you really take these two commandments to heart and really live by them, that is enough.

I have thought long and hard on this; I have meditated on this; and I have come to the conclusion that everything you need to know is derived from these two commandments. Wow, leave it up to Jesus to make it simple, eloquent, and beautiful: anyone can obey these commandments without doctrine from any religious tradition. To me, this is proof that God loves us all—and that heaven is available to us all. Notice that Jesus's words did not contain a hint of any specific religious tradition. As a liberal Christian, I love that.

Think for Yourself—No One Else Will Do It for You

Do you realize that you can have your own opinion about theological ideas? Never believe something just because someone in your past said you were supposed to. You can think differently—and you won't go to hell for it, either, as long as you obey Jesus. If you have an idea that may not sit well with your church, synagogue, or temple, then research it, pray about it, and meditate on it. Diligently pray to God for guidance on what you are thinking. Talk to other believers about what you think and get their viewpoints. After doing this, if you really feel deep in your heart that what you think is right for you, then go with it. You might be wrong, but that is okay. From your mistake, you will learn something about God and yourself. God lets you make mistakes because that is one of our purposes on this planet. For example, I can't imagine God saying, "Rich, you screwed up on what you said about original sin. I have to send you to hell now. Have a nice time ... say hi to Satan for me."

Also, reject people who thump Bibles at you. You have seen them on TV or elsewhere, being loud and boisterous and waving Bibles around over their heads for dramatic effect. God's truth comes as gentle, warm, loving

A Real-Life Christian Spiritual Journey

whispers of peace in your heart; God's truth does not come from loud, bellowing showboats waving Bibles around. Always watch diligently and cautiously for any underlying appeal to fear as a basis to believe something. If someone tells you that you had better believe something or you are going to hell, run—don't walk—away. As "Desiderata," a poem by Max Ehrmann (1872–1945), says, "avoid loud and aggressive persons, they are vexatious to the spirit."

In summary, my personal viewpoint is an open and liberal one. I strive to be open in my spirituality, realizing that I could never put God in a box or define He who is a mystery and transcends all human understanding. I try to consider other religious traditions by looking at the mystical level of their teachings. You would be surprised at how similar other religious traditions are at the mystical level with Christianity; I will cover this in the section about the world's major religions.

Be open, be loving, be yourself, and be true to the teachings of Jesus Christ. Don't confuse those teachings with Church doctrine or dogma. Live out of love and not fear, for Jesus Himself said, "Fear not." Never impose your beliefs on others; instead, state your beliefs respectfully and lovingly.

If you are interested in reading more on the topic of liberal or open Christianity, I recommend an excellent book called Open Christianity by Jim Burklo.[43]

I think the best way to conclude this discussion is a section of "Desiderata." You can purchase the full version of this beautiful poem, engraved on a wooden plaque, at the Web site below.[44]

Beyond a wholesome discipline,
be gentle with yourself.
You are a child of the universe
no less than the trees and the stars;
you have a right to be here.
And whether or not it is clear to you,
no doubt the universe is unfolding as it should.

Therefore be at peace with God,
whatever you conceive Him to be.
And whatever your labors and aspirations,
in the noisy confusion of life,

---

[43] Jim Burklo, *Open Christianity* (Rising Star Press, 2000).
[44] https://www.fleurdelis.com/orderinsights.htm

133

keep peace in your soul.

CHAPTER 11

Roadblocks to Spiritual Growth

Healthy and Unhealthy Spirituality: One Hurts, and the Other Heals

FOR A MOMENT, LET'S DEFINE the word "spirituality." According to the dictionary, spirituality is the quality or fact of being of a spiritual, incorporeal, or immaterial nature; of a predominantly spiritual character, as shown in thought, life, etc.; or a spiritual tendency or tone.[45] Well, that does not help much; it's kind of a circular definition to me.

This word "spirituality" is such an ambiguous term; it means different things to different people. New theology students soon find out that it is not a science. I have a good perspective on this, since I have a degree in chemistry. Boy, theology is nothing like quantum mechanics, that's for sure! The discipline offers no equations or any other kind of mathematics. In theology, it doesn't much matter that $E = MC^2$. During my training in pastoral ministry, I encountered—are you ready for this? —no fewer than fifty-four different definitions for the word "religion." More probably exist; that's just how many definitions I gathered in a class titled Psychological Issues and Spirituality. With that in mind, it is okay for you to have your own prayerful and considered definition for the word "spirituality." Just be open to changing it as you gain knowledge from your life experience.

---

[45] http://dictionary.reference.com/browse/spirituality

My Definition of Spirituality

For me, spirituality is defined as one's personal manner of being—one's own unique perceived existence and the relationship one has with others, God, creation, and oneself. Spirituality is how you perceive your place in creation and the set of values you live by. It is your perception of who you are as a human being, your direction in life, your past, your heritage, your destination, and the meaning of your life. It includes your image of God and His place in your life.

You will find other definitions of spirituality, but this is mine. Hopefully you borrow from it while adding your own unique ideas. Notice that my definition contains no hint of any particular religious tradition—nor should it. Such an inclusion would change my definition into a religious doctrine or dogma.

Are all spiritualities good? No! Spirituality can be healthy, unhealthy, or somewhere in between. Each of us has our own spirituality with its own healthy and unhealthy aspects. That is just part of being human. The important thing is to ask yourself whether your own spirituality could be improved.

But how can you know which attributes of your spirituality are healthy or unhealthy? Let's highlight some characteristics worth paying attention to.

Healthy spirituality is open; unhealthy spirituality is closed. It is just that simple, folks. God made spirituality simple so that everyone on the planet, no matter his or her education or social standing, can understand Him in his or her own way. I find that beautiful. It's magnificent, frankly.

Remember what Jesus said: "Truly, I say to you, unless you turn and become like children, you will never enter the kingdom of heaven" (Matthew 18:3). Now, much theology lies behind that simple statement, but He is speaking about simplicity among other things here. A child cannot understand the nuances of theology, and Jesus says that a childlike approach to life is necessary to enter the kingdom of God. Leave it to Jesus to make something so profound so easy to understand.

What are the characteristics of a healthy and open spirituality? Here is a partial list:

- It expands and enlivens the individual and enhances the fullness of life.
- It is engaged in freely.
- It prompts Christlike behavior and facilitates an ever-increasing closeness to God and other people.
- It remains flexible enough for the complexities of life and all the alternatives and choices that we can make.
- It is consistently exhibited in words and actions driven by the love of others.
- It includes respect for the inherent dignity of others as loved children of God.
- It prompts you to respect the beliefs of others, who love God even as their beliefs differ from your own.
- It allows you to speak your own truth with love and respect while remaining tolerant of others.
- It recognizes that religion is not composed of black-and-white rules.
- It acknowledges that mankind is made in the image of God and His unconditional love for creation.
- It does not burden anyone with threats, such as "you had better do this, or else."
- It respects other religious traditions as adding richness to life and adding perspective on the ineffable mystery we call God.
- It is compassionate, humorous, tolerant, accountable, responsible, whole, humble, moderate, peaceful, just, honest, warm, and loving.
- Lastly, but very importantly, a healthy spirituality is not specific to any particular religious tradition.

Now, an open spirituality has its limits. "Open" does not mean "anything goes." If you adhere to the description above, you can see that the characteristics of a healthy spirituality do not include whatever you want or are tempted to do.

When you inevitably come across situations in life where you are not sure what to do, but you want to exhibit a healthy spirituality in your actions, pray to God for guidance. In a very prayerful manner, look to your conscience, and listen for God's soft whispers from within your inner being. You might make a mistake, but if so, learn from it—and, if necessary, make amends—and go on with life.

What are the characteristics of an unhealthy spirituality?

- It is exclusive, carrying a club atmosphere.
- It refuses to welcome everyone.
- It keeps secrets and denies entry to anyone who does not meet its requirements.
- It is motivated by fear: "Do this, or you will go to hell."
- It operates according to an agenda that is not guided by love for your neighbor.
- It includes words and deeds borne out of self-righteousness.
- It convinces you that you have the answer and others don't. The professional version of such spirituality could be called Bible thumping. We see examples of this on Sunday morning evangelical shows sometimes. If you ever see someone holding a Bible up high, waving it around and bellowing loudly, don't walk, run from people like that. God does not have to yell. His truth is found in loving whispers and loving embraces—no megaphone needed.
- It is elitist and supports the idea that if you know more, that means God loves you more too.
- It focuses on constrained, narrow interpretations of sacred texts, promoting the idea of an official right and wrong way to do anything.
- It induces guilt.
- It seeks control over others.

My feelings are also that you should question everything. Yes—question everything. Question the sermon you hear on Sunday. Question the words of the pope or any other religious authority. Make sure that what you are learning feels right to you in a prayerful way. It is okay to reject what you are told. Question what is in this book too.

Sophy Burnham, the famous spiritual author, said, "To believe in God or in a guiding force because someone tells you to is the height of stupidity. We are given senses to receive our information within. With our own eyes we see, and with our own skin we feel. With our intelligence, it is intended that we understand. But each person must puzzle it out for himself or herself." You should question what you believe as you experience life and look under the surface of things, seeking a higher understanding of creation and of yourself. This means using the brain that God gave you. Do not suspend logical thought just because the topic is theology or something in the spiritual arena; that would be nonsense. You do not want to arrive in heaven and have God ask you, "Why didn't you use the brain I gave you?" Now that would suck!

For an example of words that warrant critical thinking, let's read about Pope Benedict XVI's comments on his trip to Latin America in 2007, as reported by the *Dallas Morning News* on May 22, 2007:

> BUENOS AIRES, Argentina — Pope Benedict XVI's declaration in Brazil that colonial-era evangelization in the New World did not represent "the imposition of a foreign culture" has ignited a firestorm of criticism from indigenous representatives and the governments of Venezuela and Bolivia.

The *Dallas Morning News* also quoted him as saying that the people of the Americas had been "silently longing" for Christ "without realizing it," and thus willingly received a Holy Spirit "who came to make their cultures fruitful, purifying them."[46]

Well, using my brain tells me that the pope was really off base—worse than off base, actually. His words were extremely insensitive and alienated many people from the Church. History tells us that the Spaniards who went to South America brutally killed huge numbers of native people. They hauled tons of gold back to Spain and enriched that country at the bloody expense of the South American people. To say that the arrival of the Spanish in South America was not an imposition of a foreign culture, and that the native people wanted Christ but did not know it, is absurd. The unfortunate use of the word "purify" within this context calls to mind various periods of ethnic cleansing in other areas of the world, such as in Bosnia, where the killing was horrific. Adolf Hitler tried to "purify" Germany during World War II by killing millions of Jews.

By now, you probably get the point that it is okay to reject things that do not fit with your interpretation of Jesus's intended meaning when He said to love God first and to love your neighbor as yourself. A religious statement can be false, even if the pope says it.

---

[46] http://www.dallasnews.com/sharedcontent/dws/dn/religion/ stories/052307dnintpope.364ca54.html

So what does all of this mean in everyday life? How does it affect how you look back at the statements you were told to believe? I guess the best way to describe this examination process is to draw from my own life experience. I will again use some stories from my childhood; after all, what we learn during our formative years affects the way we think for the rest of our lives—that is, unless we make the effort to prayerfully reevaluate those teachings as adults.

The sisters at St. Tarcissus used religion and fear of God on us students in order to control us and influence our eventual behavior as adults. Some would call that brainwashing. For example, we were told as children that what happened in the classroom was none of our parents' business. Yes, you read that correctly: they felt entitled to control their students in such an absolute way that the parents were not and should not be involved. They tried to fragment the relationship between parent and child; this violated a sacred trust.

Regarding other faiths, we were taught in Catholic school that it was a mortal sin to participate in a religious service from other religions. Therefore, if you went to a Jewish temple and died before you got to confession, you would go to hell. Again, the sisters at St. Tarcissus were trying to instill fear and keep us tied to the Church with powerful psychological and emotional weapons.

My advice to you is to reject anyone claiming to have the only answer regarding God and anyone who tries to control you with fear. These people are vexations of the spirit, and they promote unhealthy spirituality. If you want to, go to a Jewish temple—and enjoy it!

Our experiences as small children—and, for that matter, as adults—create stored feelings. When something really affects us, whether positively or negatively, it will affect our feelings regarding any associated events, people, or places. These feelings get tucked away in our subconscious. According to Anne Katherine, author of *Boundaries*,

> Stored feelings control us. They unconsciously influence our values, decisions, perspectives and especially our choice of mates. They determine the types of defenses we'll construct to make up for poor boundaries. We reverse the damage done to us as children by reversing this process—unlocking feelings, meeting basic physical needs, getting dependency and other developmental needs met and building boundaries. The harmed self can then become whole.[47]

---

[47]   Anne Katherine, *Boundaries* (New York: MJF Books, 1991), 111.

Please pay attention to that last thought: you can heal! It will take effort, and it will hurt, but it can be done. I tell you this from my own personal experience; I did it, and so can you.

When I had small children in Catholic school, we had an annual parish fund-raising drive. During Mass one Sunday during that drive, the monsignor gave the homily and talked about tithing. During his comments to us he uttered words that I will never forget: "Do not measure the amount you give to the Church, but measure what it is you have left." What? Did you catch that? His meaning, whether intentional or not, was very clear: "You are being selfish if you keep too much of your hard-earned money"—whatever too much meant. I could not believe my ears, and this was said in the 1990s, not the uptight 1950s.

The monsignor's comments represent an unhealthy spirituality, because it induces guilt in people who are trying to raise families and are nowhere near financially well-off. Give out of love of God, not because someone made you feel obligated, no matter who that someone is.

You may feel differently about this, and that is okay. Healthy spirituality allows for different opinions, and each person should respect the other. Life is full of complexities, but hopefully you are beginning to understand how open spirituality works. Think about this one for a while.

Reflection Exercise: Healthy and Unhealthy Spirituality

As always, prepare for your meditation in the same way as before.

Here are some starting questions to begin with:

- Can you remember an incident where a parishioner said some things that were spiritually unhealthy? (Remember, the absence of love is unhealthy.)
- Has some part of the Church said or done something that you considered spiritually unhealthy?
- What would you have done differently, now that you know the distinction between healthy and unhealthy spirituality?
- Think of some incident where a parishioner said or did something that was spiritually healthy. How did you know it was spiritually healthy?
- What has your parish done recently that you considered spiritually healthy? Why?

You can find a real-life example of healthy spirituality by listening to a wonderful song by Melissa Etheridge called "Silent Legacy." It contains some thoughts that apply to the effects of unhealthy spirituality. Perhaps this will help you put some of your own negative experiences with organized religion into context. In the song, she is very lovingly warning a small child about unhealthy spirituality.

Melissa is speaking of some religious people's intolerance of gay people. Above all, she is advocating pure love for all people. She is advocating the rejection of anything that is based on fear, and she is asking each of us to stop this legacy of intolerance now, to refuse to pass it on to our children. What a wonderful thought! I recommend that you get a copy and give it a listen; you will not be disappointed. Remember, "Love is never wrong."

That song represents open, healthy, God-inspired spirituality at its best. Nothing should ever stand between you and your love for another person, no matter their skin color, religious tradition, position in society, or any other so-called difference. Sadly, some branches of some religious traditions teach that being gay is a sin and so on.

God loves all His creation and every soul in it, no matter how bad that soul seems to us. Yes, dark spirits do reside on earth with us, and they do cause destruction and pain, but they will run from God. God will never run from them or condemn them. If you ever hear statements like "God is on my side" or "my religion is better than yours" or any similar sentiment, just turn away. The truth is not to be found in people who say things like that.

God takes no sides, even if the Hebrews thought otherwise in the Old Testament. This belief in their history was just one point in their ongoing, developing understanding of God. God did not take sides with the Hebrews any more than He took sides in any war humans decided to wage upon one another. He was not on the side of the Catholic crusaders either when they waged war against the Muslims in the Holy Land centuries ago. In God's eyes, everyone is equally loved.

The idea of everyone being equal in God's eyes is fundamental to a healthy spirituality. I know a beggar named Joe who begs every morning at a certain intersection here in Santa Clara, California. He was once shot in the head during a robbery, and the bullet blew away a part of his brain that affected his speech. He is very frail and needs a cane to walk. He has no family. He also has heart problems that make him very weak when the temperature gets too warm for him. The next time you think you have it hard, remember my friend Joe. Think of what it must be like to beg on the street corner almost every day to make ends meet so that he can pay his rent. The help he gets from the state of California doesn't come close to covering even his minimal expenses.

God loves him just as much as He loves you or loves the pope. Giving money to this man out of love for him represents a healthy spirituality. It's just that simple, people. The idea of giving so freely and so lovingly is one of the most wonderful thoughts you could ever have in your head. It is a thought to live by; pray and meditate about this, and ask God whether this is true or not. I know what He will lovingly tell you.

Many years after meeting Joe, I went to graduate school in pastoral ministry at Santa Clara University. There I met a wonderful woman—a classmate. She was a nurse who lived in Santa Cruz, which was about thirty miles to the south, on Monterey Bay. She would take care of her grandmother, who lived in nearby Palo Alto, before coming to class.

My classmate was an openly gay woman. She told me of her plans to minister to other gay people and help them heal from "Bible abuse," as she called it. What a wonderful ministry to have! She intended to help members of the gay community heal from all the Bible thumpers in the world, who had told them they were going to hell for being gay. Many people in that community are very hurt and really do wonder whether God loves them or not.

Folks, the idea that God wouldn't love gays is simply unfounded. No one is going to hell for being gay. Also, AIDS is not some kind of godly revenge upon homosexual people, no matter what you might have heard from some ignoramus TV evangelist. Such intolerant notions are the product of fear—and sometimes hate. Some of the nicest and most loving people on this planet are gay. I wish my friend in pastoral ministry could counsel the gay fellow I had met years earlier at Hewlett Packard—the man who had called the pope a fascist. He would not be carrying so much pain in his heart today. He could benefit from her loving, open spirituality.

Open spirituality can be inspiring. One word of caution: don't try to convert everyone over to what you consider open spirituality. Don't label everything you see as healthy or unhealthy, either, because you might not be getting the whole picture of another person's relationship with God. Speak your truth with respect, and let God do the rest.

God Works in People's Lives ... and They Don't Even Know It

So HOW DID THIS WRITER go from hating the Church and the people in it to writing this book about God and the joy of Christianity? How in the heck did I go from a very unhealthy spirituality to a loving, joyful one? Such a change indeed marks a miracle resulting from God working in my life in ways that I could never imagine. As my story continues, you will witness workings of God that I only became aware of by looking back at my life and observing how turning points in my life seemed to keep me on a spiritual journey ordained by God.

I will describe these turning points to you in a refreshing, unique way that you have probably never experienced before from other Christians. In doing this, I pray that you will see that God has been working in your life in much the same way. Remember, we are all children of God, and He treats us all with kindness and loving tenderness, offering gentle nudges to get us back on track if we need it. I find it amazing that the most powerful force in creation, God Himself, guides us with a touch as gentle and light as a feather. If we are really obstinate and stubborn, God might use a brick instead. I know of that happening to some people.

Can you identify the most powerful force on earth? Think about that for a moment.[48] The answer is at the bottom of the page, in the footnote.

I bet you never thought of that; I didn't for a long time. Water is one of the softest materials on the planet; it takes the shape of whatever container it is held in. But when you think about it, water has the power to change the landscape of the entire earth. Look around you, and you will see the effects of its power in every rock, mountain, and valley. Just as gently flowing water smoothes out the hard, jagged rocks in a stream, so too God gently removes the rough edges in our lives with His caress. He flows through us as we live day to day, unaware of His work within us and within the people around us. Just as rocks will change the tiniest bit each day in response to the flowing water, we slowly develop in our spiritual journey while here on earth. In the New Testament, Jesus spoke of "living water," as you might remember. John 4:10 says: "Jesus answered her, 'If you knew the gift of God, and who it is that is saying to you, "Give me a drink," you would have asked him, and he would have given you living water.'" What a remarkable parallel.

Day to day, the changes within us are so small as to be nearly invisible. Yet when we look back at the events in our lives, we can see how far we have

---

48 The answer is water.

come and be amazed at the extent of our progress. We will be amazed at how we were saved from destructive events and an unhealthy spirituality as we experienced painful circumstances and lessons that allowed us to grow as humans. As we look back, we realize that we all are loved children of God.

God's loving fingerprints are all over my spiritual journey as I look back at the turning points in my life. His fingerprints are on your journey as well. It is only in the prayerful look back that one can see God's influence on one's journey—yet He was invisible and undetectable at the time. Back then, I did not know of His actions within the events and within me, and neither did you. Soren Kierkegaard said it best: "Life can be understood backwards; but it must be lived forwards."

Reflection Exercise: God's Silent Guidance

Prepare for this reflection in the standard way for you. God usually works with us silently although there are times He uses events and other people where something inside you just "clicks." It is in the looking back where you are more likely to detect God's working in your life. That is the purpose of this reflection.

- Look back over your life and try to see where God might have been working within you.
- Start with some of the turning points in your life. Did you have a hunch or a feeling that one way was better than the other? How did it turn out for you and others?
- See where He nudged you to understand more, ponder life more deeply, and take actions that later on would prove very loving and beneficial to not only you, but also others around you.
- Has God ever answered your prayers in some way, improving your situation at a time when life was going terribly for you?
- Continue with personal questions like these, exploring the ways that God has made a real difference in your life.

Prayerfully dwell on these thoughts in a quiet room when you have some time. No hurry but be sure to do this for your spiritual growth.

At one time, my life was an emotional mess. I believe that if He can get me back on track, He can do it for anyone—no matter how far gone they think they may be. All you need is an open heart, a trust in God, and a willingness to follow His gentle nudging. Yes—all you need is to open the door to your heart, and God will walk in. A simple prayer in ordinary English is a wonderful way to get your spiritual journey on the right path.

Spiritual Roadblocks: How Do They Look and Feel?

WE NEED TO UNDERSTAND THE nature of spiritual roadblocks. Just what is it that keeps getting in the way between God and us? Once we examine the characteristics of such roadblocks, we will be able to recognize them, handle them, and recover from the damage they may have already caused. If we understand the nature of these challenges, we already have gone a long way toward overcoming them. The first rule of war is to know your enemy. I learned that in Army ROTC when I was in college; that got drummed into us right from the start. In a sense, we are soldiers as well, waging a spiritual war against all those forces that would derail our spiritual journeys.

The spiritual battleground is the six inches between your ears; that is where all the action is. What goes on there determines the kind of person you become. This area of your physical being serves as the intersection between God, the world, and you. It determines your feelings, your attitudes, your knowledge, what you say, and what you do with your life. It determines your entire existence.

Most of us want to grow closer to God, but sometimes roadblocks seem to be staring us in the face no matter where we turn, with no obvious way around them. We automatically deal with life in a way that can be problematic and results from our life experiences up to that point. Many times, we just don't know any better, and that can be frustrating.

When I was a kid in Chicago, the easiest thing to do was punch someone; that usually ended disagreements instantly. The knuckle sandwich was served up often, and everyone understood the menu. As a solution, violence was quick and definitive, but it was not so good in the spiritual long run. I don't believe that Jesus ever resorted to violence to solve a problem. He did curse a tree once. But when I was a kid, I never heard commandments like, "thou shalt not bloody the nose of thy brethren." No, it was more like, "thou shalt not let thy parents find out." Now, that one, we all obeyed. It was a code among our neighborhood of little future felons. And our entire approach to conflict was one big spiritual roadblock.

What is a spiritual roadblock? My definition is "anything that prevents you from growing into your unique self in the manner that God has planned for you." Spiritual roadblocks prevent a person from growing closer to God and becoming who they really are in the eternal scheme of things. They prevent the fruits of the Holy Spirit from manifesting within our lives. Galatians 5:23–24 mentions some of these fruits: "But the fruit of the Spirit is love, joy, peace, patience, kindness, goodness, faithfulness, gentleness, self-control …"

I have, over the course of my pastoral ministry graduate studies and for a long time afterward, tried to shape everything I know about roadblocks into some understandable, overarching theory. I have always believed that God would not make things so complex that we cannot understand them. No, God would not do that to us.

Conquering such roadblocks leads to a happy state of affairs in your life. Leading contemporary theologian Karl Rahner wrote the following in his book *The Practice of Faith*: "I would like to be a person who is free and can hope, who understands and shows by his actions that he himself is at the mercy of his freedom, a freedom which throughout his life is creating and making him finally what he should be … a person who is faithful, who loves, who is responsible."[49]

Here, Mr. Rahner speaks of a freedom from the influence of spiritual issues and of existing as God made you. Being our true selves and doing those loving things that are generated from our interior beings is how each of us evolve into what God has intended for us. We then exist in harmony with God and the rest of creation. This is how we grow toward our own individual, unique maturity and happiness. But in order to do this, we must learn to be our godly selves. We must be free within this world to be just what and who we are.

But how should an unhindered spiritual life work? From the infinite wellspring of God, deep within the center of our being, comes the light of divine love. From this sacred light of love flows His energy within us. As it makes its way through the layers of our spirit, it mixes with our own unique energy, which reflects our own true selves. These two great lights intermingle and flow outward from the center of our being. Together, they shine outward into the world, and this is what the world

---

[49] Karl Rahner, *The Practice of Faith: A Handbook of Contemporary Spirituality* (Crossroad, 1986).

sees; the great, common divine love shines through each of us. But each of us radiates God's light differently in an expression of our own uniqueness. The world then sees God's light intermingled with our own light, resulting in the beauty that God intended from the beginning of creation. We are like diamonds; no two are exactly the same, but all are brilliant, dazzling the eyes of the beholders. This is what God intended for us; this is how healthy spirituality should work.

If only life allowed all of us to grow spiritually in a paradise of kindred spirits helping each other and dancing around all the flowerbeds! The sky is always blue, and gentle breezes rustle the leaves of the trees, and beautiful music fills the background, as if we are in a romantic movie. Yeah, right—that is not reality on this planet! Unavoidably, each of us runs into spiritual roadblocks that we need to recognize and deal with in a positive manner if we are to succeed in attaining the ideal that Karl Rahner and James Fowler describe. The road to becoming our true selves is beset with obstacles, potholes, and detours. Let's face it: we all need spiritual four-wheel drive and big tires on this road.

The spiritual roadblocks that we encounter throughout our lives originate from many sources. Generally, these can be categorized as naturally occurring, worldly, and religious (or doctrinal).

Natural roadblocks arise within us from our simple humanity. We try to grow spiritually, and in that process encounter a set of challenges barring the way to the next level of spiritual understanding. Natural roadblocks include our emotions, as we are emotional beings.

The worldly roadblocks come from anything outside the six inches between your ears.

Religious or doctrinal roadblocks arise from misinterpretations of religious texts or other doctrine that does not uphold the truth about our loving, tolerant God. The next several sections will examine these types of roadblocks in more detail.

Natural Spiritual Roadblocks

In the previous chapters, I have described the naturally occurring roadblocks that resulted from my mere status as a member of the human race who was growing up through the six stages of faith. James Fowler has done an excellent job of showing us the nature of the roadblocks and what we must remain aware of if we are to continue on our individual spiritual path. At each stage of our spiritual development, life presents us with different challenges that we must overcome if we are to advance to the next stage of spiritual awareness. (The Buddha would probably refer to this as the middle path to enlightenment.) At each level of faith are naturally occurring barriers to our progress; we must pray for God's guidance and make constant efforts to improve our own inner being. Self-awareness is one key.

The spiritual challenges change as we change. When I was a kid, the main challenge was to learn to protect myself and try not to punch too many other kids. However, later in life, the challenge was to realize what my childhood had done to my spirituality, emotions, and view of myself. The challenge was then to repair this damage, so I could become a happier and more fulfilled human being.

Certain challenges are present in each of the six different stages of faith demonstrated by James Fowler and in each of the eight stages of psychological development shown by Erik Erikson. Each challenge carries with it the risk of failure.

In stage one, each child must avoid letting his or her imagination become too influenced by dark images of terror and destructiveness. This is why I rant so much against what I was taught at St. Tarcissus in Chicago; they filled our little brains with images of fire, hell, and damnation, all of which we would supposedly suffer if we did not toe the line and obey every itty-bitty Church law. People become permanently damaged by this stuff unless they somehow realize how wrongheaded these ideas are; they must realize that God will not send you to hell for missing Mass once. The nuns at that school created huge spiritual roadblocks for a huge number of us kids. I wonder how many of them still feel guilty about eating meat on Friday. Heck, go have a steak.

In stage two, children must battle the spiritual roadblock of a rotten self-image. If parents or other authoritative others showed disfavor toward a child by mistreating them, that child could come to feel defective and undeserving of anything good. Parents are responsible for instilling a child's self-worth. A child who has not experienced loving behavior from his parents may soon believe that God does not love him either. This is devastating and it can last an entire lifetime.

In stage three, a person's world extends beyond the immediate family. During these teenage years, the need to conform and be accepted by peers becomes very strong. If a person comes to feel unaccepted among her peers, despair and withdrawal from society can result. If she feels like a misfit in society, she will withdraw to a safe place emotionally, closing down rather than remaining emotionally open—or spiritually open.

In stage four, young adults who have come of age may feel as if they have everything figured out. A sense of confidence ensues. However, overconfidence prompts the closing down of any further spiritual progress, as critical thought ceases when one senses that everything is now known. Pride and overconfidence may stifle one's awareness from expanding into the more transcendent dimensions of existence experienced in stage five.

If, during later adult years, a person has developed into stage five faith, he or she will exhibit an understanding of the transcendent quality of all life and the relationships that exist within creation. However, an understanding of what lies beyond the surface of life can lead to passivity and inaction when injustice is encountered. The feeling that everything is temporary might prompt one to let a rotten thing pass without correcting it.

The last stage is marked by a universal faith that amounts to a radical commitment to peace and justice for all people. This commitment is so strong that a person might put his or her own life at risk in order to bring unjust situations to light. Not many people rise to this level of spirituality. Gandhi and Mother Teresa are examples of individuals who accomplished this stage of faith; their hearts were filled with God's love to the exclusion of everything else.

The Conscious Mind as a Roadblock

THE CONSCIOUS MIND AND ITS attributes represent such an expansive topic. For our purposes, it is sufficient to say that the human mind can distract us from the spiritual life. Our consciousness represents that rational part of us that solves problems and allows us to function in a physical world. We need our minds as the God-given tools they are. However, our minds must not assume complete control. It is then that our hearts are shoved to the side, and it is the heart that is close to God. Our hearts should have pre-eminence over our minds, setting goals for the mind to accomplish.

Our minds are continually working and thinking. If you have ever tried to meditate, you know that the mind constantly generates unwelcome thoughts and distractions during your attempts to commune with God and listen for His whispers. Remember to let your loving heart control your life; never give your mind the steering wheel. It's simple: always choose well-reasoned love over pure logic. Sorry, Mr. Spock.

To hear God, we must tone down the constant clatter and banging in our minds. This does take time, dedication, and desire, but it is nonetheless a natural thing to do, because we are built to commune with God. Do this, and your life will change for the better.

Emotions as Roadblocks

EMOTIONS ARE VERY NATURAL TO human beings. Emotions are so diverse and vast that the entire science of psychology is dedicated to studying them. Emotions, from extreme negativity to blissful positivism, drive our words and actions. Emotions provide us with the energy to get out of bed in the morning and attend to our lives. Emotions form the impetus behind both good and bad deeds.

Because so many different emotions exist, I will just cover those most important to spirituality. One of the big ones is fear. Fear is one of the strongest human emotions, and it can lead us to either really negative or really positive actions. On the negative side, fear is the underlying basis of anger in most situations. For example, when someone cuts you off in traffic, you immediately get angry. Why? Because you fear what could have happened and as a consequence, you feel angry that the other person showed little care regarding your safety. You fear the power the other person has over your own personal well-being and the reckless use of that power.

Once, when I was landing a high-performance, turbo-charged airplane, another aircraft disobeyed the control-tower instructions and flew right in front of me just before I hit the runway. And you thought these things only happened on freeways! Anyway, performing a go-around in a high-performance aircraft is difficult so close to the runway. I did get angry that time, but flying demands a levelheaded pilot, so I contained my anger. All the same, that was the only time I wished I had some machine guns in the wings.

The problem is that anger leads to offensive actions that destroy unity between human beings. Anger separates people, doing just the opposite of what God intended for us. This is true on both the individual and the national level. My father's lifelong anger at life—and, more specifically, at me—caused separation in my family. My story is all too common, which is why wrath is one of the seven deadly sins. (Speaking of the seven deadly sins, the others are lust, greed, gluttony, sloth, envy, and pride—but these sins are not listed as such in the Bible. To see for yourself, read Proverbs 6:16–19 and Galatians 5:19–21.)

Anger and rage manifest themselves in many ways. If you wonder whether you have anger issues, one big tip-off is starting your prayers with, "Dear God, please smite that dirty rat!" Angry people often find fault with others, fantasize about bad things happening to people, distrust people, dislike themselves, and exhibit a short fuse. Anger manifests itself in these ways and many others, but you get the idea.

Fear or anxiety can cause us to resist spiritual change. To some degree or another, we are all habitual creatures who feel threatened by change. We tend to like things as they are. This is true within the spiritual arena as well. Just be aware that you will need to overcome this resistance if you desire spiritual progress.

Fear can prompt good feelings and actions as well. Fear can motivate us to take precautions regarding the safety of loved ones and provide security for them. The recognition of the world as a negative place causes responsible people take good precautions, but these precautions are essentially the result of fear. Thus, fear can be a good emotion. Be careful not to become so protective or afraid that you miss out on life experiences. Out of the dozens of possible outcomes you are worrying about right now, precious few will actually happen. Think about that last sentence.

Many types of emotions arising from issues formed in childhood can poison you spiritually. The root cause of many spiritual and emotional problems can be found in the events, environment, and treatment of children by their parents and other caregivers. I have covered this topic in detail in previous chapters.

"The harm we received as children often sets us up for continued harm as adults. If as children we had to deny our true thoughts or feelings to be safe, as adults we are likely to continue to deny what's true for us. Telling the truth feels very unsafe, a threat to survival."[50] All this is harmful to the spirit and can last a lifetime. Thus emotions as a result of painful experiences can lead to spiritual roadblocks.

Other emotional roadblocks deserve mention as well: elitism can cause you to treat someone as if they are inferior to you; a grudge can

---

[50]   Anne Katherine, *Boundaries* (New York: MJF Books, 1991), 73.

cause you to treat someone unfairly; guilt can keep you from moving on from your past; shyness can disconnect you from others; bitterness and resentment can cause you to find fault in others; conceit can cause you to seek recognition and praise; and so on. These are just a few of the possible emotional issues that can block spiritual progress.

No matter the cause, emotional issues can become large roadblocks to a healthy spiritual relationship with God; the full emergence of your God-given self is harmed. Reflect on the source of any bothersome emotions and look at your spiritual life and attitudes. Stored emotions from long-ago events could be harming your spirit; if you think so, look for help—it's out there. You are to inherit the kingdom of God; let nothing stand in the way. You are a diamond, so go ahead and sparkle with your own personal light of God!

Worldly Spiritual Roadblocks: We Can Overcome These, Too!

WORLDLY SPIRITUAL ROADBLOCKS CAN COME from anywhere outside your head. The world has a profound impact on our thoughts and ideas. It colors our individual experiences of the stages of faith. The manner in which we choose to negotiate our spiritual path, with all its challenges and pitfalls, is the result of the interaction between each of us, the world, and God.

For the purposes of this discussion, the world is set against God. Through each of the six stages of spirituality, the world presents spiritual dangers while God presents us with opportunities to grow closer to Him.

Worldly obstacles are those thrown at us by other people and the physical conditions we experience by just living in this world. These roadblocks can lead to behaviors and thoughts that do not reflect the true person we are on the inside. When muted by worldly obstacles, God's light does not shine through us as well as it should.

When the Apollo astronauts went to the moon and saw the earth, what they saw was only part of what I refer to when I use the word "world." For our purposes in this context of spirituality, "the world" refers to everything that resides outside your head—all that exists outside your own spirit and mind, including your own physical body. This broad definition encapsulates all the influential forces that work upon each of us from the moment our bodies are conceived within our mothers' wombs. These forces influence us right up until we pass away and go back to our heavenly original home. While we are on the earth, the energy of this world will always be upon us.

The world can be a very negative place. If you doubt this, just read the front page .of any big-city newspaper. The world contains many influences that we must overcome on our spiritual journey. The forces of the world promote negative emotions and spiritualities within us—most times without us being aware of it. (The Bible refers to this negative energy as "temptations.") The world affects what goes on inside our heads, therefore affecting what we say and do. We do have free will and can decide how to react to the forces working upon us; we can either follow God's will by taking positive action, or succumb to the negative influences of the world. It's pretty simple, actually: being good in this world is ultimately a choice, albeit a sometimes-difficult one.

Material Wealth

THE RELIGIOUS COMMUNITY ENGAGES IN a lot of discussion about material wealth and its dangers to spiritual health, so I thought I would address this worldly threat to our spirituality first.

Money gets a lot of attention in our spoiled society, but the truth is that it does not matter what kind of house you live in, the kind of car you drive or the clothes you wear or how much money you have in the bank. Spirituality does not depend on wealth. There are kind and loving spiritual rich people ... and rotten rich people too. The same variety exists in poor people, too.

I am aware of the biblical saying that compares a rich man's entry into heaven to the passage of a camel through the eye of a needle. But this verse referred to a love for money above God, not wealth in and of itself. 1 Timothy 6:10 says: "For the love of money is the root of all evils."

Another biblical story about money can be found in Matthew 25:14–29. Servants were given their master's money to invest during his absence. Upon his return, the servants who had done poorly had everything taken away and were cast out; the ones who had acted wisely were rewarded. What matters is not what you have, but how you use it. Remember, what is inside your heart and mind counts for everything—not your bank account, house, clothes, or car. Our culture loves money so much that there is a whole channel, CNBC, devoted to how to get more money and how to spend it. Think about the proper place of money in your life, and strive for balance.

I was once inside the palace of Ferdinand Marcos, ex-dictator of the Philippines—and yes, I was in the basement where Imelda Marcos kept all her clothes. Some of you may remember the headlines from years ago; she really did have three thousand pairs of shoes. I personally saw all of them; it was quite a sight. The extensive array of gowns was absolutely breathtaking; it was like being in Macy's during their big sales events. Wow—now that is too much by a lot.

The bottom line is simple: Ask yourself whether you have enough. If you do, thank God for your abundance and get on with other things. If you dwell on material wealth, your possessions will end up possessing you instead, as in the case of Ferdinand and Imelda Marcos. If you decide you have too much of something, give it away. If you eat too much and are fat, eat less and pray more. If you decide that you need to make a change in the physical area of your life, do that and thank God for the guidance to make that decision.

Books have been written on balancing your desire for material wealth with other priorities in your life. For our purposes, I will just say that wealth can become a spiritual roadblock if you are, as St. Ignatius of Loyola described, inordinately attached to material things.

Any undue attachment can become a roadblock. If you have a nice car, a comfortable home, and some financial security, then I say "good for you." Just don't get obsessed with gaining wealth at the expense of time for prayer and meditation. As for me, I own a high-powered sports car and an airplane. However, if I ever become unwilling to push my shiny, red sports car off a cliff or torch the airplane the day they become spiritual roadblocks, then I am in spiritual danger. If you cannot live without material frivolities, you have a spiritual problem that is blocking you from becoming closer to God. Remember, God comes first.

**Reflection Exercise: Do Material Objects
Interfere with Your Spirituality?**

If you reflect on the above passage, you will develop your own feelings
and opinions on material wealth, and that is a good thing. It's up to
you to decide what moderation means for you.

Use the standard reflection preparation and address the following
questions.

- What drives your spending?
- How much of your budget goes toward necessities and how much
  goes toward discretionary spending?
- Do you save?
- Would you consider yourself frugal or prone to splurges? Do you
  make lots of impulse purchases?
- What can you live without?
- How much money is the minimum to live and what can you cut
  out of the budget?
- Continue with these kinds of questions to determine how
  materialistic you judge yourself to be. Make the changes you feel
  are necessary to your financial and spiritual well-being.

If you discover that the answers to the above questions make you
uncomfortable, that is a good thing. It means that you are growing
spiritually and you have an opportunity to change your life to better
reflect your values.

Attachments

EXCESSIVE ATTACHMENT TO ANYTHING, NOT just money, can become
a spiritual roadblock. It becomes like trying to run a foot race with a
bowling ball attached to your foot. St. Ignatius of Loyola, who founded the
Jesuit religious order, spent a lot of his time pondering Christian decision-
making. He is famous for defining Christian discernment methods that
can be used in everyday life to make good decisions and circumvent
emotional roadblocks that impede spiritual progress.

St. Ignatius recommends a program of spiritual exercises "to order one's life to God without coming to a decision through inordinate attachments."[51] The attachments that St. Ignatius addresses could be to anything, frankly: material possessions, certain emotions, and certain perspectives. You need to get to a state of indifference, where you are not already inclined to a certain decision before self-examination. Be aware of any attachments that might interfere with your ability to determine the best action from a spiritual and godly perspective.

Identifying and Overcoming Cultural Roadblocks

THE CULTURAL VALUES WE LEARNED as kids are a source of strong spiritual influences, both good and bad. As we grow up, we accept these cultural influences without question. In addition, adults are bombarded every day with materialistic messages from our mass media. These messages set a tone for what we think that life should be like. Unfortunately, these values go largely unquestioned and can have adverse spiritual effects.

Cultural values are so much a part of our society that they become invisible to us. A good book titled *American Cultural Baggage*, by Stan Nussbaum, lists the top ten values of our culture.[52] These values exert influence on us every day of our lives. Here is the list, with my comments on the spiritual aspects (in italics):

1. You can't argue with success. This is most likely the highest cultural value. *Is this a spiritual problem or not? Remember the parable of the talents in the New Testament.*
2. Live and let live. *Be tolerant ... but how much should you allow? Are there immutable rules for life or not?*
3. Time flies when you're having fun. *Enjoy yourself ... but to the expense of what else and to what extent?*
4. Shop 'til you drop. *Enjoy your material wealth ... but at what point does this become excessive? Is this point different for each person?*
5. Just do it. *A Nike slogan has made it into our cultural top ten—wow. Have courage ... but at what point do your actions become foolhardy?*

---

[51] George E. Ganss, *The Spiritual Exercises of St. Ignatius* (Loyola Press, 1992).
[52] Stan Nussbaum, *American Cultural Baggage* (Orbis Books, 2005).

6. You are only young once. *Take advantage of your youth … but at what point does this become recklessness? You are old only once too, so how does that fit in?*
7. Enough is enough. *Where do you draw the line?*
8. Rules are made to be broken. *Thinking out of the box is good spiritually, but where do common sense and judgment re-enter the picture?*
9. Time is money. *Is everything in life reducible to the almighty dollar? Where is the proper place for money in your life?*
10. God helps those who help themselves. *God gave us the firewood, and we must chop it … but at what point do we stop ignoring others who need our help?*

Reflection Exercise: Cultural Spiritual Roadblocks

Again, use the standard reflection preparation steps. In this exercise, review each of the ten statements above. To get started, ask yourself the following questions:

- Have I thought about these cultural values?
- Have I accepted at least some of them without consciously thinking about them?
- To what degree do I believe them in my real life?
- On a scale of 1–10, 1 meaning "do not agree at all" and 10 meaning "agree completely," where do I find myself between the extremes of these values?
- How are these values affecting my spirituality?
- Do I want to change some of these values?

For an idea of our cultural mindset and what we hold dear, just turn on your TV. These cultural values affect everyone in our society, either directly or indirectly. Even if you do not own a TV, your life is affected by what other people watch and its influence on their behavior. It's good to take a few steps back and look at what is being broadcast.

I conducted a very small, unscientific survey of what's on the tube these days. My "extensive research"—by which I mean a quick glance at the programming schedule—took me fifteen minutes. Here are just a few of the shows permeating our culture:

Wife Swap: This show takes two opposite dysfunctional families, has them trade wives, and films the resulting conflicts.

Primetime: Crime: New and imaginative ways to kill people are featured and explored in detail.

Criminal Minds: This show details the minds of those who commit social atrocities.

Crime Scene Investigations: New York: This show investigates one murder after another.

America's Next Top Model: Goofy girls hope to be the next Tyra Banks.

American Greed: Viewers are told how to make more money from their couches.

Mad Money: Viewers are told how to get rich on the stock market.

Cold Case: Old, unsolved, gruesome crimes are revisited.

The Unit: This is a paramilitary show depicting violence.

Law and Order: Criminal Intent: See the murder, watch the trial.

America's Most Wanted: This show describes fugitives.

Desperate Housewives: Four insane wives plot all sorts of wicked tactics for our entertainment.

The Military Channel: This entire channel is devoted to how we killed people in the past and what we are developing to do it more efficiently in the future.

I Love Money: The title of this show is pretty self-explanatory.

How to Be a Player: Viewers receive tips on womanizing.

Without a Trace: This show revisits various disappearances.

Poker After Dark: This show depicts gambling, along with other popular gambling shows.

Entertainment Tonight/Access Hollywood: This show gossips about celebrity's private lives, offering a high-school mentality to adults.

Prison Break: The hero of this show gets falsely sent to horrific prison in a foreign country featuring really nasty drug people with the morals of serial killers.

Balancing the above list are the Discovery Channel, National Geographic, the Science Channel, and the Learning Channel, but they are nearly drowned out by all the others, in my opinion. Which conversation would you be more likely to hear at the office: a rundown of the latest National Geographic documentary, or a conversation about which celebrities are sleeping together?

If you want to progress spiritually, pray to God for guidance, ask for help from His angels, and turn off the damned TV. Stare at the walls if you have to; just turn off the TV. Recognize that your life will actually get better. Other cultural roadblocks that deserve mention amount to a multitude of distractions: iPods, computer games, excessive Internet use, and so on.

Music can be a very big cultural roadblock to the extent that it promotes violence, dominating other people, being tough, and other endeavors that appeal to the lower animal instincts of human beings. Sorry to mention it, but rap music has all the wrong elements to it; everyone singing tries to act cool and tough while showing how powerful they think they are. Well, if you groove to the booming sounds of rap music, your spiritual growth is being stunted. You can't get into the spiritual heights by booming on the ground. This music is its own subculture, and it promotes spiritually unhealthy values, in my opinion.

We live in a culture of instant gratification, but God does not grow majestic trees overnight. Someone did not wake up one morning and say, "Wow, where did that Grand Canyon come from? It wasn't there yesterday!" He did not create the universe to work that way, yet our culture promotes the expectation of instant results. The day I recognized this, I prayed to God, "Dear God, please give me patience—and I want it now!" (Get it?)

Our culture is like a large river flowing in a certain direction; we all get caught up in it and must make great efforts against that flow if we are to define ourselves as individuals rather than just another cloned humanoid floating along with the rest of society. Question the cultural values that have nested in your heart. Then have the courage to reject that which you feel is harming your spiritual life.

Think of yourself as a member of the human community; do not overidentify with any one particular group. Avoid tribal thinking, where your identity is totally wrapped up with one culture or group of people defined by race, creed, color, national origin, political stance, or any other artificial dividing line that we humans have created to separate ourselves from one another. You will never ascend higher spiritually than your group if you continue to define yourself by your membership within that group. As they say, you cannot soar with eagles if you always keep company with turkeys. Peer pressure is a true spiritual roadblock that must be overcome if you are to progress on your personal spiritual path.

Physical Life Roadblocks: The Doctor Can't Help Here

THE ANCIENTS REALLY HAD A hard time with the human body, or at least the biblical writers did. Galatians 5:24: "And those who belong to Christ Jesus have crucified the flesh with its passions and desires." The human body can offer many spiritual roadblocks, especially when combined with the world in which we all live. Matthew 18:7: "Woe to the world for temptations to sin! For it is necessary that temptations come, but woe to the man by whom the temptation comes!"

All humans have certain physical needs and desires. These coincide with psychologist Abraham Maslow's first and second levels of his five levels of human need. Maslow was a psychologist and published a paper in 1943 titled "A Theory of Human Motivation." These are biological and physiological needs, such as food, oxygen, water, shelter, warmth, sex, and sleep. The second level is comprised of safety needs: protection from the elements, security, order, law, limits, and social stability. Other needs include the physical desires of pleasure and other forms of gratification. For instance, I enjoy scalp massage or simply having my head scratched.

Now, do you see anything wrong with any of the above needs? Do you see anything particularly sinful in any of the items I mentioned? No? Well, I cannot either. Remember that the body is the temple of the Holy Spirit; by its very nature, it is not a sinful thing. Lots of people will tell you that the body is sinful, but I will tell you it is not. Yes, the Bible does talk about the "sinful flesh," but there is a whole book to be written about that, and it has to do more with the ancients' cultural view of life than the view of God Himself.

Many people will cite Galatians 5:17: "For the desires of the flesh are against the Spirit, and the desires of the Spirit are against the flesh; for these are opposed to each other, to prevent you from doing what you would." St. Paul said this. He also said in Galatians 5:19, "Now the works of the flesh are plain: fornication, impurity, licentiousness." These kinds of thoughts gave birth to the idea of denying the flesh, which meant starving yourself, flagellating yourself, living in a cave, sleeping on rocks, and stuff like that. The more pain you endured, the closer to God you were presumed to be by the ancients.

I should mention that Siddhartha Gautama (the Buddha) tried asceticism (extreme self-denial) and rejected it as not being productive to becoming enlightened. From this experience, he advocated the middle path. This is just like my dear grandmother, who always said, "moderation in all things." (If there ever was a devoted Catholic, my grandmother was it. I think she was a very wise woman—very godly, too.) Just ask yourself if God wants you to be miserable and on the edge of self-inflicted death for your whole life. Pray about this, and God will give you His answer. One last hint about all this: Jesus drank wine. His answer to my own personal prayer about this is an emphatic no.

God has changed the idea of sinful flesh through His ongoing revelation of Himself since the Bible has been written. Remember that God did not shut up two thousand years ago; today's prayerful people do know more about God's character today than the ancients did way back then. It took hundreds of years for the early Church to figure out who Jesus was, and debate continues among different Christian traditions today. But just remember what St. Paul said in 1 Corinthians 6:19: "Do you not know that your body is a temple of the Holy Spirit within you, which you have from God? You are not your own." St. Paul seems to be playing two sides of the same coin regarding the nature of flesh in his writings. I will leave it to the biblical literalists to explain why St. Paul referred to the body as being the temple of the Holy Spirit but referred to the desires of the flesh as being against the Spirit.

If the body is not sinful by its very nature, how can physical desire become a spiritual roadblock? It's a matter of excess—pretty simple, actually. Eating is necessary; gluttony is a problem and a roadblock to God. Too much of most anything physical is not good for you. If you have enough worldly material goods to be healthy, provide for your loved ones, and promote a good measure of security, you have enough. How many pairs of pants does a man need? I guess it depends on individual needs, but I counted mine and I have twelve; that's it. I am not one to have a large wardrobe.

From my own experience, I can identify other problems with the flesh than the ones listed in the Bible. Chronic pain, frequent headaches, asthma, and so on can suck the life out of you. Stuff like this puts thoughts of spirituality as far away as you can imagine. I get headaches that can last for days, and boy, praying is something that can get shoved aside for a while. The last thing that comes to my mind when my head is throbbing from a migraine is prayer, unless it is something like, "I wish this @#$% headache would go away!" After a few days of this, you can get a little cranky; I sure do. Asthma is also a real challenge; breathing as if you are sucking air through soda straws is not fun.

If you do not have chronic health issues like me and so many other people, you might not understand their effects on spirituality. The next time you stub your toe on something, gauge your spirituality immediately afterward; you will get the idea!

The point of this little rant of mine is that chronic pain is a real-life roadblock to spirituality. But its effect is temporary; a bit later, when you get a chance to think about pain and suffering, you can prayerfully put things in their proper perspective and become aware of the role of suffering in spiritual progress. If you suffer, you are more likely to search for the ultimate meaning in pain. It is here that the blessing dwells. Suffering is really an opportunity to grow closer to God, especially after the pain starts to subside and my mind has a chance to clear.

I do consider my infirmities a blessing. When I am not hurting, I can say that God has shown me the blessing in all of it. That blessing is that physical suffering does indeed bring spiritual fruits if you are open to that. That is a big if; you must be open to God first. My compassion, empathy, and love for others has been enhanced by my suffering. There is a feeling that comes with suffering that you are closer to God through the clouds of pain and through your efforts to cope with your afflictions. There is a feeling that suffering has a divine meaning to it, and although we may not be aware of the meaning in its entirety, we will understand within the fullness of time. Those who suffer will know that it has not been in vain. God promised this, and His promises are always kept. But remember, starving or otherwise torturing yourself in the name of God is not spiritually healthy; that is just nuts.

Many years ago, I read about St. Theresa of Lisieux. She said, "I have noticed that the experience of suffering makes us kind and indulgent toward others because it is suffering that draws us near to God. Trials help us detach ourselves from the earth; they make us look higher than this world. Here below nothing can satisfy us."[53] Well, when I first read that, I thought she was out of her mind. I thought she must have been in the convent too long and lost touch with the real world. After years more of my personal trials, I have come to understand the truth of what this saintly woman said.

I guess one question would be whether I would choose to physically and emotionally suffer as I do to continue to obtain the spiritual blessings I have experienced. My answer is yes. I cannot say that I would jump up and down, yelling, "Goody—here comes suffering!" No, that too is nuts.

[53] *Prayers and Meditations of Therese of Lisieux*

But through my trials, God has been ever so good to me. I cannot begin to describe my love for Him and what He has brought to my life through the sufferings I have endured. If God asked me to once again endure what I have endured, it would be more of an, "Okay, if you think it's for the best … ugh." You too are stronger than you think. God will give you the strength; He has given it to me. Open your hearts to my words here, and God will bless you too.

God whispers to us, but we are sometimes deafened by our needs, which fill our ears like a diesel locomotive going by with its horn blaring. Then, after our day is done, we are too pooped, and prayer goes out the window. It's very hard at times to hear God at all, given all the clatter banging around in our heads. All of the time spent on mere survival seems to be a roadblock to spirituality. There just may not be any time to be pious and pray as we think we should.

Is physical life really a spiritual roadblock? I offer the following as something to consider; pray about this when your mind is clear and the tyranny of the urgent has subsided for a while. I ask the following questions: Could it be that working for our survival is also teaching us spiritual lessons, such as perseverance, focus, sacrifice, and dedication? Is this physical life a way to learn about love and selflessness? Could it be that, if we all are in this same survival boat called earth, this situation gives us a chance to rise above ourselves and provide for others too? If we do, this is love in action.

Jesus said that poverty would always exist, giving the rest of us the chance to give charitably to those in need—and, in doing so, participate in the cosmic and loving interrelationships that God has intended for us. If we do get to a world where people regularly sacrifice for others, is this not consistent with how Jesus described the kingdom of God? Does this sharing between people not describe the loving interweaving of kindred spirits in the fabric of the kingdom of God here on earth?

Perhaps our physical suffering is actually intentional, with a divine purpose behind it. We do know one thing for sure: it hurts, and at times it hurts like hell. You can't just read about such suffering; you must experience it to change in a spiritual sense. I guess it is something like watching a linebacker make a huge hit on the guy with the football. We see it, and we hear it, but we are not getting the air knocked out of us firsthand; that would be life changing and memorable. Is that what the physical life is all about?

I do not believe that we are some random cosmic accidents; we are not Shakespearean plays randomly typed out by a roomful of monkeys. There is just too much design to what we observe in the universe for that. I do believe that there is a hidden order to things that remains that way for a damned good reason. The infuriating thing is that we cannot know the meaning of our hardships as we suffer. Only in retrospect will we see the reason for it all and that God was really with us all the time.

If you want more to read on this subject, I highly recommend reading *Man's Search for Meaning* by Viktor E. Frankl. The author found meaning in life while a prisoner in a Nazi concentration camp.[54] This man suffered horribly.

Religious Doctrine Roadblocks

RELIGIOUS TRADITIONS ARE WONDERFUL AS vehicles of worship when they promote love, peace, and justice for all human beings. However, each is limited in its own right; religious traditions are largely a product of man's limited understanding of something infinite. Each religious tradition can be compared to a telescope pointed at a different section of our infinite universe. Each one brings an understanding of the details it sees; each telescope contains some truth of the universe but can never show it all. In addition to the details each telescope shows of some unique part of the universe, it also offers profound hints of the nature of the whole infinite universe as well. This must be so, for any part of the universe shares a deep commonality with the rest of the universe.

The details that any one telescope shows can be compared with the doctrine and dogma of a religious tradition. Each religious tradition asserts specific things about God; this is its doctrine. Just as all parts of the universe share a common thread that hints at the universe's overall character, each religious tradition also points to something of the infinite character of the universe or of God. This, then, corresponds to the mystical level of a religious tradition.

I believe that all religious doctrines are delivering the same message from different perspectives. They all point toward the common ground shared throughout the universe. They all point to the same mysterious, ineffable, transcendent, and unconditionally loving God.

But trouble enters into the picture at the doctrinal and dogmatic level. This is where we get into arguments about who God is and whose telescope is more accurate. It is at this "us versus them" level of religious belief that problems occur.

Let's look at what the word doctrine really means. "Doctrine" refers to a written set of beliefs or body of teachings that has been established

---

[54]   Viktor E. Frankl, *Man's Search for Meaning* (Beacon Press).

to a group as true. In a religious sense, doctrine is a set of assertions that are held as ultimate truth about God. For Catholics, examples include the Trinity, the virgin birth of Jesus Christ, the Immaculate Conception, and original sin. For me, the Nicene Creed summarizes Christian doctrine quite nicely. To a Calvinist, predestination (in which God has preordained all that happens) is a fundamental belief. Islamic doctrine includes a belief in the oneness of God. All of these beliefs can be considered doctrine.

Doctrine is often confused with dogma. For our purposes, dogma can be defined as the core principles that must be upheld by all followers. Dogma is so fundamental to and so well demonstrated in a religious tradition that if a person rejects some dogmatic principle, they are not considered a member of that religion. Within many Christian denominations, dogma is referred to as "doctrine"; hence the confusion. In Christianity, a dogmatic principle would be that Jesus Christ is the son of God; it's really hard to call yourself a Christian if you don't believe that. Islam comprises six dogmatic tenets: a single God (Allah); the prophet Muhammad, of course, but they also consider Jesus a prophet as well; angels; the Koran; the Day of Judgment; and destiny (fate).

The danger with doctrine and dogma is that by their very nature, they are limited. Any doctrine therefore puts God in a box. Within the box is the doctrinal description of God, and outside the box is heresy. This is why religious traditions can become spiritual roadblocks: doctrine necessarily limits a believer to a defined set of godly descriptions that can only describe a small part of God.

You are unique, and so is your spiritual path. One doctrine does not fit all. So let God guide you, follow your prayerful conscience, and become the divine person He intended. All real spiritual progress is born out of heresy—yes, I really said that. If you start to feel the tug of God drawing you toward a more expanded and open understanding of Him, then I say go for it. I am on solid biblical footing when I say this. Just remember that Jesus Christ Himself was accused of heresy and blasphemy. Read the parts of the gospels where He confronts the Sanhedrin the night before His crucifixion. Pray, always pray for God's guidance in these matters, and you will be led in the proper direction for your personal spiritual advancement. If you get some flak from a religious organization, remember the following saying: *Illegitimis nil carborundum*. This is a Latin phrase loosely translated to mean, "Don't let the bastards grind you down," or so it is said. (See? Theology can be fun!) The bottom line is, spread your spiritual wings.

Chapter 12

Suffering

Welcome to Earth ... Expect to Learn, Experience, and Suffer

I REALLY DISLIKE SUFFERING, AND I don't do it too well either. It seems that no matter where you turn, someone is having a really hard time about something. None of us want to suffer, but we all end up doing just that. We are all comrades in suffering; none of us are alone in that part of life. As Woody Allen says, "Life is divided into the horrible and the miserable."

Why must we suffer? This question plagued mankind even before the Bible was written. As Siddhartha Gautama, the Buddha, has said, "All is suffering." It is in overcoming this suffering, however, that we heal, grow, and learn. It is in the overcoming that we come to know God and ourselves. As Helen Keller (1880–1968) said, "Character cannot be developed in ease and quiet. Only through experience of trial and suffering can the soul be strengthened, ambition inspired, and success achieved."

When I entered the graduate pastoral ministry program, I thought that understanding the reasons for suffering might reduce my own. Well ... no, it didn't. If anything, I have become more sensitive to the suffering I see in others. No exemptions from this part of life seem to exist. But learning more about suffering through prayer, meditation, and just plain commonsense thinking will bring a deeper sense of meaning to the pain in your life. Your discernment of the spiritual meaning behind your suffering will give you more strength to endure whatever it may be. Although I cannot claim to have all the answers, I can at least testify that deeper understanding brings with it more strength. It will bring you closer to God, even if it will not eliminate pain. Questions will always remain, however; some of the reasons behind suffering are as mysterious as life itself.

My suffering has probably not been all that different from that of other people. However, people have told me that my family seems to have had more than its share of suffering over the years. Maybe that is true, and maybe not. Regardless, shared life experiences are a true blessing. The sharing of life experiences with others strengthens all of us, for such sharing is an act of love; I found this out in pastoral ministry classes. Within the sacred intermingling of shared experience among kindred spirits, bonds of love are formed. Before realizing this, I always thought that what I went through was unique to me; I could not see the suffering of other people. I really was not exposed to the hardships of others until I listened to their stories in class. Many times, our fellow classmates' stories brought a lot of us to tears. These loving souls strove for understanding, praying to God for strength and a deeper relationship with Him even while they hurt so badly.

Suffering carries a common human denominator, even across different sources, circumstances, and people. Acknowledging other people's suffering gives us the opportunity to see who we really are and what spiritual fiber we are made of.

Why Do We Suffer? Does It Do Any Good?

It seems that people who suffer a lot in this life are spiritually closer to God; at least, that is my opinion. I am speaking very generally, of course, and you could easily find lots of exceptions, but on average it seems to be true for the people I have known. When you read about the lives of the saints, you come away with the understanding that these people suffered a lot, so this idea seems to hold true in their cases as well.

Why must we suffer to become closer to God? Why does it have to be so painful? Why would a loving God do this to us? Humanity has struggled with these questions for all of recorded history. Perhaps suffering is necessary to strip us of our false identities and put our egos back where they belong. My own false identities would include father, husband, computer executive, writer, pilot, golfer, investor, and a host of other roles. Are these identities the real you or me? Well, of course not. Could it be, then, that these false identities form a barrier between God and us? Is suffering the way to strip us of them?

Each of the above identities has limitations; by identifying in those roles, we limit ourselves as well. Perhaps God wills us to understand that our true selves extend far beyond any limited identity that we consider normal. Could it be that He wants to give us far greater gifts than we already have, but must bring us closer to Him spiritually in order to do so? Could it be that one of these gifts is the knowledge that we are far less limited than we think? In the end, it could be that we suffer in order to break out of the false identities that block greater gifts from God. Could this be? I offer these thoughts for your meditation and reflection.

Many of the books I have read on suffering link suffering with transformation. For a variety of reasons, these texts maintain that suffering is necessary to bring about true spiritual transformation into a different and better person. However, none of these books offer a definitive answer. This is not the authors' fault; none of us will know this answer fully until we get to heaven. Like Pope John Paul II said, "innocent suffering must be accepted as a mystery."[55] Certainly, suffering is mysterious, but the pope's suggestion of blind acceptance implies that we should stop thinking about suffering. In contrast, I believe that we can learn something from our experiences in the here and now. I never did like accepting mysteries; I do not want to make the mistake of underestimating what humans are capable of realizing and understanding. There have to be insights on suffering available in this life that point to meanings and reasons.

Is Classic Christian Thought Correct?

CHRISTIANS WOULD SAY THAT SUFFERING is the result of sin; according to Pope John Paul II, suffering is always a trial. In a real sense, any Christian who wishes to grow closer to God must take up his cross, suffer, and through that suffering find harmony with God and all of creation. Something about suffering purifies us and brings us closer to God and the eternal joy in heaven. Remember the words of British scholar C. S. Lewis (1898–1963): "We were promised suffering. That was part of the program. We were even told, 'Blessed are they that mourn.'"

But I would have to add that not all suffering brings us closer to God. Do something stupid, like jumping off the roof of your house, and you will suffer—but I doubt that you will be any closer to God. Wiser, yes. Closer, no.

---

[55]   Donald W. Mitchell and James Wiseman, *Transforming Suffering* (Doubleday, 2003), 28.

There is an excellent book by Fr. Daniel Harrington that reviews the multiple biblical viewpoints on suffering.[56] Yes, there is more than just one. Fr. Harrington says, "I claim no special gift of compassion or pastoral wisdom in dealing with suffering, indeed I am not good at facing the unpleasant realities of life or responding instinctively to the needs of others. Suffering presents as much a problem to me as it does to anyone, perhaps more so." He goes on to say that the Bible itself does not have all the answers either, but it does serve as an excellent starting point for meditation and prayer.

Christian books tend to say that since God is love, our suffering must be either a result of sin, a punishment, a test, or a lesson. Dorothee Soelle, in her book *Suffering*, says, "Every suffering that is experienced as a threat to one's own life touches our relationship to God, if we use this expression in the strict theological sense."[57] Suffering somehow brings up God in our minds, and that relationship becomes immediately important. Could this in and of itself be one of the reasons for our suffering? Dorothee goes on to say that God has chosen us humans to work on the completion of His creation, and therefore God Himself must suffer along with us in order to accomplish this.[58] If you look at the trajectory of the human race, you can see strong hints of just that, in my opinion. God is right there, suffering right along with His children.

Pope John Paul II said, "The interior process in which a person discovers the meaning of suffering often begins and is set in motion with great difficulty. Nevertheless, it takes time, even a long time, for the answer to begin to be interiorly perceived." This is quite a statement. From my personal experience, I can say that I never understood the meaning of my suffering as I was living it. I do not suffer well; I struggle like everyone else. Yet I have found the pope's sentiment to be true. Understanding, accepting, and gaining insight into the major painful events in my life has taken years.

As the ancient Roman poet Horace (65 BC–8 BC) said, "Suffering is but another name for the teaching of experience, which is the parent of instruction and the schoolmaster of life." Looking back into the actual events of your life through the lens of hindsight allows you to perceive the meanings of unpleasant events in your life. For example, I was devastated when my fiancé broke up with me; I loved her deeply. The emotional pain

---

[56]   Fr. Daniel Harrington, *Why Do We Suffer?* (Sheed and Ward, 2000), xi.
[57]   Dorothee Soelle, *Suffering* (Fortress Press, 1975), 85.
[58]   Ibid., 146.

was horrible. A sour torrent of despair would drench me every morning when I woke up and remembered that she was gone. It was all I could do to get up and go to work, where painful feelings of abandonment dogged me. At the time, I did not know that God had another plan waiting for me—another wonderful woman whom I would spend most of my life with. Only a short time later, Marilyn and I started our loving and lasting relationship. Unbeknownst to me in my suffering, joy waited at the end of that dark tunnel of broken love and despair. As it the saying goes, we will know all things in the fullness of time. Looking back, we can see meaning that was invisible to us at the time.

One of my daughters was violently attacked at gunpoint by a man posing as a police officer. At the time, our whole family became numb with shock. We instantly were immersed in a world of police, district attorneys, lawyers, private detectives, and horrible emotional upheaval. Our lives became a whirlwind of chaos, anxiety, fear, and uncertainty about what to do next. We were happy that he had not killed her, as he had told her he would.

Yet now, in the looking back at this miserable event, I can see the fingerprints of God helping my whole family to a better place spiritually. We are much closer as a family than we were before my daughter was attacked. Through our collective suffering, we have become a tighter-knit family—more loving and supportive of each other. That terrible incident brought to us a larger perspective on life and what is really important; our suffering brought spiritual progress and enhanced relationships to all of us.

But none of us understood any of this at the time. None of us could know how this event would change us, but it did—and for the better. We also learned that justice could exist as well. The attacker was caught and will spend the rest of his life behind bars, without any possibility of getting out to harm someone else. I pray that his other victims we met are healing by God's love, as we are. Our difficult experiences will ultimately transform us. Each of us must meet life as it is, as Job finally did. We transcend hard times not by avoiding them, but by going through them and reaching their end.

The pope gives us assurance that the answers are out there; other religious leaders do, too. We simply cannot order up the answer when we want like a Big Mac with fries. I know this firsthand, because I have already tried many times! Only through the tincture of time can we heal and gain understanding of why things happen to us as they do. It is in this slow process that we are transformed spiritually.

Other Christians have had the same experience. Father Daniel Ward said,

> The monastic way of the cross, then, teaches that it is not the cloister or the routine that heals the inner pain but rather the inner journey that a person embarks on through prayer, silence and reading. This journey helps one harmonize God, creation and self. This journey leads through suffering into the harmony. I have found this to be true as I am sustained by the quiet inner way of my journey, the way I come to connect with creation, God and myself.[59]

Simply said, you have to suffer on your way to understanding and spiritual growth. But also notice that you must make a conscious effort to gain this understanding through prayer and reading; lying on the couch won't hack it. To find, you must seek. As Jesus said in Matthew 7:7, "Ask, and it will be given you; seek, and you will find; knock, and it will be opened to you."

Another representative comment comes from Father William Skudlarek. "The paradoxical truth is that we are saved from suffering through suffering. In the patient acceptance of suffering, we find the key to the transformation of suffering into the deeper life we are seeking." Well, here again the idea of transformation and suffering are directly linked. Through patience and acceptance, we are transformed. Somehow, we all must prayerfully do everything we can to alleviate our suffering, but also accept it in our hearts as part of God's plan.

Remaining open to spiritual changes through suffering is very hard to do. This is a personal challenge for all of us. If we fail, our suffering will not yield much spiritual growth. Everything depends on our reaction and openness to God's love for us. Make no mistake: many people get stuck at this point of their personal spiritual journeys. I feel as if I am in danger of that myself at times, for I know that I have a strong will.

The famous theologian Father Thomas Keating said, "It is the radical experience of powerlessness ... in the process of spiritual purification. And it is only a great love of the spiritual journey and of the Ultimate Reality

---

[59]   Donald W. Mitchell and James Wiseman, *Transforming Suffering* (Doubleday, 2003), 39.

(God) that can lead one to put up with this kind of suffering through which on must pass to reach the true goal of the spiritual life."[60]

Could this be the eye of the needle that Jesus spoke of?

Reflection Exercise: Transformation Through Suffering

Since many religious leaders have said the same thing, that suffering brings spiritual transformation, I ask you to reflect upon the sufferings in your life. You can start by addressing these following questions. Start by using our standard meditation steps.

- What have you suffered? How did you react? What were your attitudes and perceptions at the time of suffering?
- Take time to remember your emotions, whether they included anger, fear, delight, or a sense of discovery. Then look at how things turned out.
- If the painful event did not occur, where would you be today spiritually? How does your current situation compare with what would have probably happened without suffering?
- Was the outcome positive or negative? Was the outcome surprising?
- Do you still carry with you those changed attitudes, or have they faded into something different?
- Did your experience bring about more openness and love for others and a sense of greater unity between you and the rest of creation, or did it cause you to close up and become defensive against all of the threats that loom in the outside world?
- Looking back, do you perceive the fingerprints of God in your suffering?
- If so, how has God silently guided you?
- Are you in a better place now because of what happened?
- In terms of your attitudes, emotions, and spiritual thoughts, how did you change as a person?

Whatever you find when you reflect on events in your life, be gentle with yourself. If you feel that your reaction to suffering was not ultimately a positive one, see your mistake, learn, and continue on. Remember, hindsight is always perfect. Remember too that God's love for you will never change.

[60] Ibid., 46.

Some biblical perspectives on suffering include the following thoughts. Suffering is a demonstration of the law of retribution; do something bad, and you get punished. However, in my life experience, this idea does not always hold water. What about all the people killed by natural disasters, plane crashes, or diseases? Surely not all of them are being punished. The Book of Job illustrates innocent suffering. During this time in Hebrew history, people believed that all things came from God, both good and bad; God was the author of all things experienced in life. The Book of Job itself tells that God cooperated with Satan himself to test Job's loyalty to God; God was the cause of Job's suffering. And at the end of the book, some interpretations say that God comes off as a cosmic bully by asserting that He is God, and Job just has to put up with things.

But I believe if you read this book closely, you will see that God is saying that suffering is just part of life, no matter what happens. This is not as arbitrary as it sounds. Suffering does have a purpose behind it, although we would rather decline that offer from God. God is with you and loves you unconditionally. When Job finally accepted life as it is—all of it—his health and wealth were restored. The key point regarding Job is that nothing got better for him until he realized that he needed to accept God's love in all things—not just in the good things, but in the suffering as well. Job began to accept the totality of existence and not just the things he felt pleasure in. Job had to step outside the protective bubble that we all create for ourselves in order to feel safe. Then he began to hold in awe all of creation and the splendor of all that is (Job 42:5–6): "I had heard of you by word of mouth but now my eye has seen you. Therefore I disown what I have said and repent in dust and ashes." Also, the Lord restored the prosperity of Job after he had prayed for his friends; the Lord even gave Job twice as much as he had before (Job VII, Epilogue 10). The message here is that suffering is part of life, but God is there with us as we suffer, and this is what we must accept. Also there is a light at the end of the dark tunnel of suffering we can get into.

All of us, including me, always want to construct a bubble of comfort around ourselves that can protect us from the harsher realities of life. We all do this, and frankly, I find nothing wrong with it as long as we do not go so far as to isolate ourselves from other people and completely lose touch with life's reality. We must live in this reality as it is; that said, providing a level of comfort for our families and ourselves is not wrong.

Consider this important additional thought on suffering: "Our Father never afflicts or badgers His children, although it is His greatest yearning to be known by them in the fullness of existence. It is through challenge, and the survival of suffering that a person grows beyond his protective bubble to experience the love of God in a greater way."[61] It goes on to say, "Whenever you stand firmly in the midst of a hardship, holding and expressing the love that you are, you will witness illusions falling away. Through being the love that you are, you are empowered to transcend your sufferings."[62] In other words, knowing God in only the good times restricts your experience of Him. Suffering helps you experience His love in a more complete way, which is what God desires for us.

Regardless of your situation, God is there for you, and you can experience His unending love for you if you open your heart to Him. Through suffering, God teaches us that not only are we immortal and invincible, but we also have the power to conquer any situation through the love we have within us. We can only learn this truth about ourselves by overcoming adversity. We can learn that we are free forever from illusions that would conquer and misdirect our lives. We can learn that we are more powerful than any situation that this life can throw at us. Through this learning, we can free ourselves from the effects of all afflictions, growing toward God and the person He has meant us to be from the beginning.

The Christian idea of taking up one's cross has a deeper meaning to me now. Suffering appears not to be enough; we must take up our crosses by enduring painful challenges with patience and acceptance. We must remain the love that we are. Thankfully, patience and acceptance do not require us to roll over and do nothing. We should do everything we can to improve the situation, but remember that in the end, we will need to accept the results and learn as much as we can. I do run around and wear myself out trying to fight against what made my wife ill, for example. I do it with all my heart and soul. I get exhausted many times, but this I must do. I also know that I need to patiently accept the facts of this situation. How do I fight and also accept at the same time? I am working on that.

Our Incomplete Perspective: Human Limitations Get In Our Way

No matter how hard we try, we will only get an incomplete perspective on our suffering. We only have one limited point of view. This is why our suffering often seems so unfair, especially when something rotten happens to good people. One of the nurses at Marilyn's cancer center once said that

---

[61]   Love Without End, Jesus Speaks, Glenda Green, Spiritus Publishing, 1992

[62]   Ibid.

life is just unfair, and that everyone in the clinic knew it. Her suggestion was to accept it and go on with our lives as best we can.

The acceptance of reality can be very painful and emotional when accidents or death are involved. It can feel impossible to accept tragedy and still keep on going. But we must recognize that we are subject to forces beyond our control, and we are helpless before them. This form of submission takes a lot of faith. But if we try, we will not just submit; we will also come to understand new meanings and be spiritually changed by the suffering we encounter.

Blank acceptance seems to be stopping short of where God wants us to go, as I said earlier. But no matter how much of your life you spend meditating on the topic of suffering, you will never get to the complete answer. We will never see the complete truth as long as we remain on the planet.

Our perspective is often incomplete even when it comes to simple circumstances, not just deep mystical questions. For example, day and night appear to us to be mutually exclusive; if it is night, then it cannot be day. This is our perspective because we live on the planet. Apollo 8, the first mission to the moon, marked the first time that a human being would be far enough away from Earth to see the entire planet in a single glance. What they saw and photographed was the sun lighting up part of Earth while the other part was in darkness; they saw both the light of day and the darkness of night at the same time. Day and night existed together, despite what we perceived on Earth. If you are interested, a NASA Web site offers hundreds of pictures of Earth taken by astronauts.[63]

In our suffering, we only see part of a much larger picture. If, through prayer and meditation, we are able to rise up to a higher level in our consciousness, we too can gain a new perspective into the deeper meaning of it all. There we may find solace, and perhaps—just perhaps—put one more piece of life's puzzle in its proper place. With God's help, we can heal from and learn from suffering experiences, stripping away our false identities and realizing the unlimited person we actually are.

When Meaning Cannot Be Found

MANY PEOPLE RECOMMEND THAT WE take suffering on faith and do the best we can. Somehow, for me, that is not enough. Faith is great, but I need God to show me some of the divine reasoning behind my suffering. The

---

[63] http://eol.jsc.nasa.gov/sseop/clickmap

word "faith" implies a belief in something without knowledge and laced with some doubt. I would rather have the knowing without the doubt. I want to know God, not just have blind faith. I pray a lot about this.

Sometimes, even if we work really hard at finding meaning in our personal suffering, it will elude us. One Saturday morning, a young sheriff's deputy here in Santa Clara County, California, was driving his patrol car on a very curvy road in the nearby foothills and somehow crossed the double yellow line into oncoming traffic. He struck three bicyclists going the other way on the other side of the road. He killed two of the three, and the third cyclist was severely injured, spending weeks in the hospital recovering. Members of my family know the deputy's parents, and we know him to be a very conscientious and good person; he is very dedicated to police work. Even as a small child, he had wanted to be a police officer.

After the accident, it is said that he was sobbing that his life was over. All of the families involved with the terrible accident are enduring horrific suffering. Yet, as I write this, we only know the direct facts and not the larger context in which the awful event took place. I don't know if we will ever fully understand the meaning behind this terrible accident; perhaps it is only for the cyclists and the sheriff to know within their souls. I do not know. Perhaps we are never meant to know certain things in this life, even if we ask God for answers.

When meditation and prayer do not shed light on your suffering, the time may come to agree with the pope's words after all; sometimes, suffering really is a mystery.

Meanings and the Mystical Approach: Some Surprising Truths

VIKTOR FRANKL SAID, "WE CAN discover this meaning in life in three different ways: (1) by doing a deed; (2) by experiencing a value; (3) by suffering." I have some additional thoughts on how to go about understanding suffering.

To understand more about suffering, we must rise above its physical, emotional, and other aspects. That is the challenge. How do you do that? Over the years, many attempted answers to this question have been published. I tend toward the mystical level of things and try to see that suffering brings about spiritual change in people. I believe that the mystical level of faith and spirituality can provide a measure of meaning to suffering and the other parts of life as well. Mysticism basically bypasses all religious doctrine and attempts to look at God directly. Think of mysticism as the most basic common denominator between all the major religions on earth. Think of it as the most deeply held yearning for God that exists within the center of our souls. This desire for God does not concern itself with the details of any one specific religious tradition. The mystical approach opens up more possibilities regarding our entire understanding of God and existence itself.

From this mystical perspective, I believe that each of us is on our own unique path to God. Each of us is different; no two people are the same. Therefore, our journeys to God cannot be the same either. Each person's path is different, with different challenges, joys, and sufferings. Thus, in a sense, we must all find our own answers and our own way with God's guidance to rise above our suffering.

I end this section with some questions. Could it be that we really are immortal spiritual beings? If we are immortal, wouldn't that mean that we are also indestructible in an eternal sense? Wouldn't that mean that the suffering we experience here will not permanently damage us? Wouldn't this be especially true if God did love us unconditionally and we really were made in His image as His children? This would lead us to the conclusion that all the suffering that we experience here on the earth does have a purpose and will not damage the eternal us. If this is true, God certainly knows it, which perhaps is why He allows his children to suffer. In this scenario, suffering is the way we learn about our true selves and our true relationships with both each other and God Himself. Could this be accurate?

Perhaps this suffering will allow us to experience the love of God and how it can reach us no matter what our conditions. Could it be that God's love for us permeates every situation, no matter how bad off we think we are? Could it be that the act of suffering gives us the opportunity to experience the love of God in a fuller way? Could that be?

I think yes.

But if the answers to the above questions are anywhere near yes, then we have answered the question of how God can let bad things happen to good people. We will have explained why there is so much suffering in this world. Could the above thoughts be true? Think about it. Pray about it. In doing so, you will certainly come closer to our loving Father in heaven.

Loving Brings Joy ... But Pain Comes with It Too—Damn!

IF YOU LOVE SOMEONE, YOU are very blessed. If you are loved, you are twice blessed. Love forms the fabric of God's kingdom and brings us happiness here on earth. Joy becomes a shared experience for those who love each other; this bond will carry our relationships into eternity. Love brings fulfillment; it gives us life. As we love, we also share in the experiences of those we love. Watching your children play baseball and seeing the joy in their faces brings that joy into your heart as well. What a blessing it is to experience the joys of another human being!

Love, however, is more than attachment and bonding with another human being. Love has a power intrinsic to it. Love actually runs the universe and powers every right action in this world. If love drives your intentions in this world, rest assured that you are inexorably connected with our Father. Thus, love is far more than just a sweet emotion that we express on Valentine's Day or Mother's Day. It is the powerhouse of creation, and its author is God Himself. If we truly are children of God, then it is His love that empowers us to create good things through our actions—and in a sense become co-creators of the future according to His will.

When we love someone, we share in their joys and accomplishments as they walk the path of their personal spiritual journey. However, when someone you love hurts, so do you. At times, this empathy might be almost unbearable because something serious is happening to a person you love.

The pain of this empathy may become very intense. Injury, death, deep financial problems, or a serious illness could strike our loved ones. The love between my wife, Marilyn, and me runs deep through our souls; we are eternally connected through our love. When Marilyn got sick with cancer and passed away early this year, I cannot begin to describe the intensity of the emotional anguish I experienced. I still cry at least once every day of my life.

During these difficult times, many of us turn to God for answers and relief, even if we were not in the habit of doing so before. Even if a tragedy had to happen before you turned to God, He will be there for you; He always has, and He always will. When you feel overwhelmed during these times, you might consider the following prayer.

A Prayer of Suffering

Oh, Lord, I hurt terribly; there is an arrow in my heart.
I bleed from my heart of hearts, because this event has crashed into
my life.
From whence it came, I do not know—
the why of it is a mystery to me, but I know of its strife.
The wreckage of my emotions, my dreams lie
lifeless like a corpse frozen dead in the snow.
The ache and pain of anxiety, fear, and numbness
run through me like a freight train rumbling me into pieces.
My feeble attempt to block its track to my anguish is not heard.
It can't hear my suffering whispers to stop;
it can't hear my spirit above the roar of my jangled nerves.
I feel alone; I feel isolated from others. I have no one but you, dear
Lord.
Yet I cannot feel even you, Lord—where are you?
No one on this earth can understand my anguish. They are blind and
deaf.
They sleep in Gethsemane.
Hear my prayer, dear Lord.
Feel my agony, dear Lord, and share my pain.
Share with me my cross and my darkness, dear Lord
I cannot bear this without you, Lord.
All else will pass away, yet my pain feels eternal.
Share my agony, and give me your strength to endure.
I pray for your strength for just one more day;
I pray for strength for just one more hour, just one more minute, just
one more breath.
I pray for strength until we see each other again in paradise.

Amen.

During times of intense suffering for a loved one, your mind will generate unwelcome thoughts of doom and despair. Its predictions of the future will take the worst case and multiply that by ten; this fear will be so powerful that you can get wrapped up in it and forget what you are doing that instant. These terrifying thoughts just come on their own; we do not have to dredge them up.

Each time such thoughts arrive on our doorstep, we must take realistic stock of things and remind ourselves that the reality of a situation is usually not as bad as our imaginations tell us when they run away with our minds. Take a deep breath, and pray to God for His peace. Take a moment to look around you and realize that millions of people have experienced similar tragedies.

Here is a little coping mechanism that I use: I tap my forehead between my eyes and slightly above my eyebrows. This is where your sixth chaka, normally called "the third eye," is located. Tap it gently for a minute with your eyes open, looking at what is really before you. Look at reality as it really is. This works for me; it stops the wild negative imaginings and brings me back to reality as it exists.

Countless times during Marilyn's battle with cancer, my imagination had taken hold of my conscious thoughts without warning, filling my brain with painful and unlikely scenarios. I would catch myself thinking the worst and then feel guilty about the whole thing.

Compassion can make our hearts ache. If you are like me and have strong healing instincts, you can feel the pain of others. One time, when I drove by a beggar that I know and give money to, I just started crying for him, as I knew and felt his daily suffering. We must realize, however, that our emotional resources are limited; we should not allow ourselves to feel the pain of everyone we come into contact with. That would destroy us, which is not what God wants for anybody. Our hearts contain great amounts of empathy and compassion, but we need to manage it.

"Because the heart is singular and committed to perceptions of unity, it does not always discern the difference between the experiences of self and others. Through the exercise of compassion, the heart often accepts or confuses the pain and distress of others as its own. From such feelings it can develop guilt, remorse, fear and grief."[64] Those of us who are blessed with a compassionate heart must guard against such negative side effects, or we ourselves might become too sick to help anyone. I speak from experience here, as I hit bottom caring for my wife during her cancer. I finally got smart and asked for help. That made a great difference.

I must make one final point: you do not love the suffering person any less if you realize that they are indeed on a different spiritual path, and you do not have to experience their sufferings as they do. "It is up to our

---

[64]   *Love Without End: Jesus Speaks* (Spiritis Publishing, 1999), 22.

souls (us) to effectively manage his own heart and to maintain its purity. Negative feelings that have permeated the sacred center may generate negative beliefs and attitudes."[65] What good is suffering along with a loved one if it causes you to conclude, "Life is a bitch, and then you die"?

My spiritual director and many others with mystical insight say that suffering born out of loving marks a new beginning. Whether or not we can feel it at the time, our spirits are expanding and opening, gaining additional capacity to love, experience life, and appreciate the joy that our suffering will bring us. My spiritual advisor continues to tell me my suffering will lead to more joy if my spirit remains open to what God will provide in the future. It is up to each of us not to close down and put ourselves in an emotional cave; then the joy will not reach us, because God will honor our free will. However, if our hearts remain open to the wonder of all that is, God's joy will be waiting for us on the other side of our suffering.

You Are Never Alone

As MARILYN STRUGGLED FOR YEARS through her illness, all who knew her suffered with her. Beyond her immediate family, friends and others have suffered to a surprising degree of intensity. All of these people loved and cared for my wife, and because of that, they too suffered with her. They have expressed this to me many times. They felt as I did: helpless, frustrated, worried, and eager to do something but unsure of how. Countless people told me that they prayed for her every day. My wife was aware of all this support, and I think it brought her comfort. When God gave her healing energy through me as a Reiki practitioner, she said it gave her peace and comfort. This statement was a big deal for me, as it is direct evidence of a triune connection with God at the center.

My mother-in-law is a wonderful and spiritual person. She is eighty-six years old and is struggling with pain and immobility. Recently, she was talking to my wife on the phone. Knowing that they both had a short time left on earth, she said these words: "Let's both of us let God's love wash over us." What a beautiful way to express the ultimate reality of everything: *Let God's love wash over us.* If you suffer, try to remember this simple, yet profound thought; it will bring you peace and point your soul in the right direction. At the end of things, the boundless joy we will feel will be far

---

[65] Ibid., 22.

beyond any suffering we may have endured to gain it. This is what Jesus Himself promised.

Caregiving: A Noble Form of Suffering

I CAN SAY THAT MY suffering as a cancer caregiver has changed me in profound ways. Being a caregiver has made me more understanding, open, and loving toward other people. It has shown me what is important in life and what is not. It has made me realize that in the end, we have nothing except our spiritual existence, our unique love we bring to the world, our relationships with others, and our relationship with God. We own nothing.

Do these realizations mark the birth of a new me that God intended? If so, it is an excruciatingly painful process. Some days, I just prayed to make it through until bedtime. I guess that I will not know the reasons behind my suffering until my time is done on this planet, but the changes within myself are evident to me even now. I know they would not have happened without the suffering I endured and continue to endure for the sake of my wife. The pain of a caregiver can be deep and agonizing.

The books I have read on suffering never really describe the mental process of intense suffering. But suffering is best understood in the trenches, where our emotions and minds meet the reality we deal with. I wrote the following during a time of despair. This was written at about three in the morning, after I had tended to Marilyn's needs all day and found myself unable to sleep. I was totally exhausted and had these thoughts. I wrote these from brain to pen.

Thoughts of a Cancer Patient Caregiver

My mind is filled with clouds of pain.
They rain down needles of agony on every part of my being.
Nothing is left whole; I shatter like glass, my shredded body on the ground,
Writhing with sorrow for my dear loving wife.
Acid anxiety of what will be washes over me, burning every particle of my existence.
My life has stopped, suspended in pain on a cross of darkness.
I feel no warmth of God. If God whispers love, I cannot hear.
The stampede of dire thoughts blares inside my head; they blot out all that was good.
I am numb to joy; there is none in my veins.
There is no time except of giving medications, support, and what love I can bring.
A touch, a caress, and a kiss of devotion from my heart that lays shattered in the mud,
trampled by the cruelty of disease that tortures my darling.
The birds sing, but I cannot hear them.
The sky is blue, but I cannot see it.
The world has stopped dead in its tracks, yet it goes on.
My soul shudders, moans the deepest of sorrow for what is and what is to come.
The crushing cancer vise wrapped its steely fingers of torture around Marilyn.
Her body groans, fighting disease, bent over in wretched waves as toxic organs desperately pant for life.
The agony of love abounds, helplessness, watching, cringing with each wince of pain from someone you love.
Fighting a disease that curses mankind, it blows apart all that we think we are.
Cancer: assassin of human dignity that you are.

I mentioned earlier that the suffering of others can drag us down, sap our energy, and remove our ability to do much good for anyone. There is a term for this: compassion fatigue.[66] This real phenomenon carries with it serious emotional dangers. Somehow, when we are a caregiver of

---

[66] http://www.compassionfatigue.org

a loved one, we need to establish emotional boundaries that will preserve our own health. This is not being selfish; rather, keeping control over our compassionate selves will allow us to be more useful in the long run. It is a recognition that we are limited in what we can do.

But what about the spirit? Could the pain that caregivers experience out of love be the pain that brings about spiritual progress and changes souls forever? Is this the pain that Mary experienced at the foot of the cross as she helplessly watched her child suffer and die? Do these experiences strengthen our ability to love—and endure suffering while still being able to love? Does this increase our ability to love no matter what? When tasks like caregiving get so very painful, is God bringing us closer to the ability to love unconditionally? Could that be the divine intent behind suffering that knits together families of kindred loving spirits for our lives in eternity? Could that be?

Becoming a loving caregiver will involve giving up your own life for a time; almost every action you take will be for your loved one. Meanwhile, scary thoughts will assault you with the force of a bullet. Yet, no matter how you feel, you must get up and tend to the needs of your love. This you will do—I know you will.

Why Did This Rotten Thing Happen to Me?

ALL OF THE LITERATURE I have seen on the topic of suffering is either philosophical or theological in nature; they explain suffering in terms that most of us have a hard time relating to. For example, saying that you broke your leg to balance your karma because you did something bad in your past life really doesn't do much good, does it? Nor does the idea that your financial situation stinks because you are a sinner and deserving of hell due to Adam and Eve's fall from the Garden of Eden. No, other explanations must exist that do more to satisfy our sense of reason and our inner sense of what God is. Explanations of suffering need to conform to what we know of the universe and how it works.

Ideological explanations just do not do justice to an experience as central to the human experience as suffering. Everyone suffers, so there must be a divine reason for it—and if God does love us, there must be something that we gain that will make it well worth the pain. If this is not true, then all of Christian theology is called into question. Suffering is part of being human. As Aristotle (384 BC–322 BC) said, "To perceive is to suffer."

We need to understand suffering within the context of normal, everyday living. Let's bring theological, psychological, and philosophical thought down to earth in a manner that we all can understand. We can then use these ideas to improve our lives for our own benefit and the benefit of those people around us.

Each of the major religious traditions has been forced to deal with the question of human suffering. Each has its own explanation, but I see a fundamental commonality in their teachings. Basically, everyone agrees that suffering is unavoidable; the reasons for suffering vary, but the cause is not as important as your reaction. Does suffering bring out the good in you or the bad?

My personal experience has allowed me to make a list of the temporal reasons behind suffering. ("Temporal" means "pertaining to or concerned with the present life on this world.") These reasons exist apart from the purely theological or mystical. This list purposely avoids ideas like karma and original sin. I am sure that you can add something of your own to my top ten.

My Top-Ten List of Why People Suffer

1. Your free will: The consequences of choices you made with your own free will can include unintended results. What have you learned from the choices you have made in your life?
2. Other people's free will: The consequences of choices other people made with their own free will can include negative outcomes—and not just for the person who originally made the choice. This is a manifestation of how united we all are, like it or not. Each of us has power over all others; we need to learn how to use that power for the benefit of others. Have you realized that you are equally connected to both the people you like and to those you don't?
3. Natural disasters: The upheavals of natural forces include disease. Earthquakes, tornadoes, hurricanes, and other natural disasters show that we cannot control our own lives; we are subject to much larger forces in the universe. For example, malaria killed 990,000 people in Africa in 1995. Is this a test of our ability to persevere and accept that which we cannot avoid?

4. God's mysterious plan for us: God ordained some events before you were born, according to His plan for you. I believe certain goals for each of our lives are determined before we are born. Somehow, God allows certain things to happen to us in order for us to accomplish those spiritual goals. This is not predestination, but rather a plan that gives us certain choices to make at the time of a particular event in our lives. Ask yourself the following question: Where you were five years before you were born? What did you decide about the life you live now? Is this an odd question for a Christian to ask? If so, why?

5. Our imperfect world: The imperfections of this earthly existence can cause things to go wrong—like when your car gets a flat tire out in the desert, and you realize that your relative borrowed your tire iron and didn't put it back. Einstein said that God does not play dice with the universe. But recent cosmological evidence even points to an unevenness in the cosmic background noise following the big bang where the universe was created. Things are uneven in the universe, not just on earth.

6. Random occurrences: Some events are just unpredictable. What do you think are the odds of being hit by a meteorite while going about your business? In 1946, in Zvezvan, Yugoslavia, a meteorite came screaming in from outer space and hit a bridal party, killing one person and injuring others. I can only imagine the scene afterward. Random things just seem to happen. What random thing has happened to you recently? Some people deny any randomness in the universe.

7. The oxymoron of constant change: Life perpetually changes, and as humans, we naturally resist such change. As we age, we go through involuntary transitions. What life changes have you experienced lately? Greek philosopher Heracleitus of Ephesus said in 500 BC that the paradox is that change is a universal constant caused by unseen laws. The constant of change has been with us from the beginning.

8. Ignorance and stupidity: Ignorance is a source of suffering; that which you don't know can and will hurt you. Sometimes, when something bad happens, you'll think to yourself, *If I had only known ...* Unfortunate consequences can arise from

the ignorance of any laws that govern this reality, including physical, moral, ethical, and spiritual.

9. Loving another person: If you love, you will have great joy, but you will suffer too. I have devoted a whole section to this idea.

10. Fear: Science would say that fear is the single strongest emotion we have. They have measured brain activity and singled out the amygdala as the organic source. Our organic brains appear to devote more space and energy to fear than to any other emotion. I guess this is why we suffer so much when something really rotten happens; we fear that the future could hold even more suffering. When we experience fear, we suffer physiological responses, such as sweating, heart palpitations, and nervousness. Also, uncertainty in and of itself can be a source of fear, and hence suffering. In a real sense, we must battle our own brains in order to keep our emotional balance.

These are many of the temporal reasons that we suffer in this life. But the overwhelming question remains: is there a higher purpose to our pain?

Responding to Suffering

As Helen Keller said, "The world is full of suffering, it is also filled with overcoming it."

Overcoming suffering is easy to talk about, but hard to do! Extremely intense emotions can overrule your internal spiritual guidance. Even Jesus cried out to God on the cross, "Why have you forsaken me?" I think that tells us that God is not expecting perfection from us as we do our best to cope with suffering.

Open yourself up to others that you trust. You would be surprised at that commonalities shared by your experiences. One day, my friend and I were playing golf. I asked him about the emotional impact of his sister's sudden death on him and his wife. He recounted some private thoughts and philosophies that represented positive reactions to that tragedy. What he said helped me cope with what I was dealing with.

When you are suffering, seek a place of beauty and solitude. Make this effort to remind yourself that life is beautiful. In this place, pray to God for healing. It will not come instantly, but come it will.

There is message to us in the beauty we see. I read a wonderful commentary on the beauty of a solar eclipse by Kent Nurburn. As he saw the full eclipse, he said,

> In the moment, something momentous happened. I lost my fear of death … I can't put a name to what was shown me in that moment. It was too far beyond the human for me to understand. But I do know that it had to do with death, and that I was swept up into the greatest peace that I have ever known, a peace that surpassed all understanding. I accepted it like the tranquil embrace of a long-sought sleep.[67]

Suffering and grief will come and go; nothing is constant in this life. While praying to heal every day, be gentle with yourself. Avoid looking back and thinking of what you could have done, should have done, or would have done. That will just tear you down. Things happen for a reason; remember, we each have an incomplete perspective of these events, no matter how close to them we think we are.

It is okay to cry. Men, this means you too. Do this privately, and pray as the tears fall from your eyes. Crying is a healthy thing to do; it has brought relief to me more times than I care to admit. Realize that your suffering is happening for a reason, even if you haven't the slightest idea why. Dig for meaning, but if it escapes you, then pray that one day God will reveal all to you. God knows when you will be ready for the answers you seek.

Distract yourself with activities that bring good to others. This allows you to help others while keeping your mind from becoming paralyzed with grief. But even as you distract yourself, realize that one day, you will need to face whatever pain happened. Do so prayerfully and confide in others that you trust. As you tell your story, relief and meaning may come to you. Seek out others who have already gone through what you have. Listen to what they have to say. I was repeatedly advised to take one day at a time and make the best of it. Friends who had grieved loved ones advised me to avoid anticipating the future. I have a hard time with this, but therein lies wisdom. Everything exists in the eternal moment of now, not what

---

[67] Kent Nurburn, *Simple Truths* (New World Library, 1996), 102.

the future may bring. Our minds always anticipate the worst; we need to resist this natural tendency and be gentle with ourselves. Some people will come to you and offer to listen to what you have to say. Accept this offer, for these people are your true friends.

Realize that if you have lost a loved one, they are with God. They are with all the loved ones who went before them as well. They will be waiting for you to join them when the time is right for you, too. This is not just something nice to say; it is reality. They are doing better than you are now, for all has been revealed to them, including why things happened the way they did. Remember that you will see them again. They are not lost in the emptiness of space. They do not only live in your heart, but also continue to exist separately and objectively, as they always did, even before they were born. They are closer to you than you think. The love the two of you shared is not lost. It is eternal, for love is eternal.

I have thought and prayed long and hard about suffering. One question keeps coming back to me. What if you absolutely knew that everything would turn out just great 100 percent of the time? What if, during your suffering, you knew without a doubt that everything would turn out wonderfully for everyone involved? What if you knew that your painful event had a purpose and meaning? What if you knew that your suffering would cause a better outcome for everyone in the future? How would you feel? You probably would still suffer, but you would also be able to see the light at the end of the tunnel.

Basically, this is what the Christian message is all about. In fact, all the major religions of the world have this fundamental message in common: a better existence awaits those who suffer this life on earth. This shared central idea cannot be a coincidence. Could it be that God has infused this message into all the people of the world, and the different religions just express this basic thought in different ways?

When I say that reacting to suffering in a constructive way will bring you closer to God, I defer to the quotation that I offered earlier from St. Therese of Lisieux. It bears repeating: "I have noticed that the experience of suffering makes us kind and indulgent toward others because it is suffering that draws us near to God. Trials help us detach ourselves from the earth; they make us look higher than this world. Here below nothing can satisfy us."[68] In the end, we all will be shown the meanings and reasons, and we all will be fulfilled beyond what we can imagine.

---

[68] *Prayers and Meditations of Therese of Lisieux*

I will end this chapter with a well-known story. It's a story about a man who invited Jesus Christ into his life. He thought that doing so would bring him peace and happiness, while ridding his life of difficulty and all negative experiences. He was wrong. In fact, his life after was no less than a mess at times, which made him wonder whether believing in Christ was just a waste of time. After many trials and tribulations, he died. When he met Jesus in heaven, he complained that his life had seemed even harder after his profession of faith than before. Jesus said to him, "Look back at your life, and see where I was walking with you each step of the way." The man looked back and saw two sets of footprints in the sand, walking together. However, sometimes, often during the times of greatest pain in his life, he saw only one set of footprints. He asked Jesus, "Why did you abandon me during the most anguish-filled times of my life?" Jesus put his hand on the man's shoulder and said, "Dear child, those were the times I carried you."

CHAPTER 13

The World's Religions and What They Teach

Different Religions, Same God?

THROUGHOUT LIFE'S JOURNEY, NO MATTER where we were born, we usually are raised up in one religious tradition or another. As I have mentioned earlier, I was raised Roman Catholic. Being raised in a single tradition limits our general knowledge of other traditions in the world; big misunderstandings can result from our fragmented knowledge. These ill-informed ideas can carry on well into adulthood. In Catholic school, I was taught that I would go to hell if I attended a non-Catholic church service.

This chapter will offer some of the important truths of the major religious traditions in our world. The similarities between existing religious may come as a shock to many people—well, good. All of us in the world are much closer to each other than we think. This makes sense, as godly truth is by its divine nature beautiful and simple. Mankind demonstrates a unity across these religions; each person is given the divine responsibility to take care of others.

Mahatma Gandhi said,
For me, the different religions are
beautiful flowers from the same garden,
or they are branches of the same majestic tree.

Therefore, they are equally true,
though being received and interpreted
through human instruments equally imperfect.

I find Gandhi's words to be beautiful and absolutely true. The differences we see in religious traditions occur in the individual doctrine, dogmatic rituals, ways of worship, symbols, celebrations, and descriptions of God. Religious doctrine is a body of written teachings that is generally accepted as divine truth. Many people were killed during the Inquisition for the slightest infraction of the doctrinal rules. Dogma, on the other hand, is an established belief determined to be authoritative and not to be disputed, doubted, or diverged from. These beliefs are foundational to the religious tradition. Established traditions dealt harshly with so-called heretics who challenged existing doctrine and dogma. Disagreeing with dogma like not believing Jesus was crucified and resurrected is a dogmatic violation and calls into question if that person is a Christian at all.

Over the course of human history, many people have been accused of heresy and killed for disagreeing with the dogma of the Catholic Church. Galileo was almost executed for refusing the flat-earth dogma of the Church based on his direct celestial observations with his new telescope. In that time period, Catholic authorities behaved like kids on the schoolyard in Oakland: "How dare you say that about my dogma!" To save his life, Galileo recanted his claims but spent the rest of his life under house arrest.

As reviled as it may be in some religious circles, heresy is the fountain of religious progress in our age. God's ongoing revelation of Himself continually gives us new information that must be dealt with to keep the Church a viable and living body of God on this earth.

Christianity, Buddhism, Hinduism, Islam, and Judaism all seem so very different from each other, don't they? Each has its own specific beliefs, practices, rituals, and view of what humans are and who God is. The rules of each tradition seem so very different.

Their doctrines and dogmas are different, yes, but not quite as much as you might think. Underlying all the dogma, rituals, celebrations, and different ways of worship, I see many commonalities among the major religious traditions. If you look beneath the surface of rituals, practices, and doctrine and get to the foundational core of what is believed, these religions are similar in some ways.

Why So Many Different Religious Traditions, Anyway?

HUMANITY COMPRISES MANY INDIVIDUAL JOURNEYS; so too does faith. Each faith tradition is born out of the cauldron of desire for God and the already existing connection between God and the human heart across the world. Faith expresses itself outwardly into this world and reflects God's light into the world through the lenses of the human hearts that it graces with its divine beauty. God's love transcends all religious traditions, expressing its divine beauty in a rainbow of different colors as it beams its peace to us in so many different and rich ways. The different traditions are born out of a divine love and are expressed and evolved via the hearts and minds of people in different cultures and different geographies. Differences in perceptions of God will always emerge because of cultural, geographical, and political factors. For instance, the Jewish people had a history of enslavement with the Romans. This caused them to look for a Messiah who would deliver them from bondage. This became a central theme in Judaism.

Faith itself changes as time passes, for nothing in the universe remains static. After the seeds of faith were lovingly planted across ancient history into the hearts of a few people, these seeds flourished in the hearts of others who heard the sacred truth and formulated a religious tradition. A connection then grew between God and those whose hearts inwardly understood the divinity of their newly blossoming faith. In this way, the truth of God spreads across the world as more and more people respond to the sacred truths that resonate within their heart of hearts.

Yet even within each faith, evolution occurs as man's capacity to understand and accept God's truth has increased. This is especially true for those with open and loving hearts who have the courage to look past established tradition and gaze directly into the eyes of our loving Creator. Their reward is great as their hearts expand to love more deeply than before.

Driving this force of change within the human heart and within the religious traditions themselves is none other than God Himself, for it is He who impels us on our spiritual journeys. It is He who impels the expressions of faith itself to change. As He does so, we all grow ever closer to Him and our own appointed destiny in the kingdom of God to love, to behold, and to sparkle His light in our own unique ways for all of eternity.

Within God's creation are an infinite number of ways to worship Him and pray to Him. No sincere, loving prayer is ever wrong, no matter how it is expressed or which culture it arises from. Who is to say his or her path to God is the only one? There is no single anointed way of worship. If God is infinite and transcends human understanding, it is unavoidable that different peoples of different cultures from different parts of the earth will express their deepest longings for God in unique ways that enrich all human love toward God. This has been part of God's plan from the beginning. I ask you to open your heart and mind to embrace all of God's children and their different ways of showing adoration to God.

In the following pages, let's take an adventure of understanding and discovery. Let's observe the variety and richness among the various paths toward God. Let's see the beauty of others' hearts and revel in the common yearning we all share. Let's absorb in wonderment the creativity of other loving souls in their understandings of God and how to best live and love others on our planet, as God has intended from the beginning.

Let's open our minds to understand how similar Judaism, Islam, and Christianity really are in their core teachings and their common roots. These three great religious traditions are truly brothers in the worship of God. Let's also begin to understand that Eastern religious traditions are at their core really much the same as the Western religious traditions, adding more color to our human rainbow of worship.

Could it be that God continues to reveal Himself to everyone in the world over time, and this is reflected in the evolution of religious traditions? Could it be that God fully participates in all religious traditions on earth, gently nudging them in a certain direction according to His purposes?

So with open minds and open, loving hearts, let's explore the beliefs and perceptions of the other major religious traditions on earth. Let's allow them teach us about God. If we are open and do this, we become closer to God, as He lives in the hearts of other people of other traditions as well as ours. An expanded perception of God will be our reward if we can free our minds from the implanted shackles of doctrine that we have been raised in. Release yourself, and ask for God's guidance in this, as in all things. Dare to know God through the eyes of another.

A Prayer of the Loving, Open Heart

My dear God in heaven,
I pray to You this day that You guide me.
Guide me in my thoughts and heart of hearts
that I may discern the truth of all things,
that I may open my heart to all Your creation,
that I may release myself from all fear—
fear that I may violate some religious doctrine
and violate what I have been taught,
fear that I may overstep some imaginary boundary
in my pursuit of You, dear God.
Help me release the dogmatic shackles of my mind.
Help me be open to Your truth within the different
traditions, so that I may discern Your magnificent truth,
which abounds throughout the entire world.

Amen.

Islam

ISLAMIC BELIEFS CENTER AROUND THE teachings of one person, Muhammad. He was born around 570 AD in Mecca. His spiritual life propelled him to believe in one God, Allah. In his forties, he began to describe religious visions, along with messages or revelations from the angel Gabriel. One can only imagine what spiritual event happened within Muhammad to bring this about. The messages he received are contained in the Koran.

The word "Islam" can be translated as "submission to the will of God." Other translations include the word "peace," such as "being in peace committing oneself to God." There is a parallel to be seen here with the two greatest commandments as identified by Jesus: to love God first with all your heart, mind, and soul; and to love your neighbor as yourself. Pursuing peace is loving your neighbor, and committing yourself to God is loving God. Islam and Christianity appear to be born out of the same central, mystical relationship with God (Allah), the core of their teachings. To a Muslim, Islam is a way of life, and actions are a form of prayer; Allah looks at the whole person, not just his or her participation in ritualistic prayer. Jesus said much the same thing when referring to the Pharisees as whitewashed tombs.

In the time of Muhammad, both the Christian and Hebrew faiths were well established in the region. Christianity as an organized religion had been around for about five hundred years; the Torah of the Hebrews had been around for far longer than that. It is not surprising, then, that Muhammad accepted the Hebrew prophets of the Old Testament and the gospels of Jesus Christ. Islam purports, as Christianity does, that God sent many prophets to earth. Islam also maintains that Adam was God's first prophet; he repented of his sin and was forgiven by God. This is not so strange, considering that Christians believe that God does forgive sin and that His love is unconditional. Therefore, Muslims do not believe in original sin. How about that—I am part Muslim, because I agree with their belief about original sin. Islam recognizes the prophets of the Bible; it acknowledges that the Torah was given to Abraham, the Old Testament was given to Moses, and the gospels were given to Jesus. Muslims perceive Jesus as an honored prophet of God, but not the only son of God. Muslims also believe that Muhammad is the last of the prophets.

Muhammad did not intend to preach a unique and new faith in the Middle East of his time. Instead, Muhammad wanted to preach a religious tradition that Muslims believe was intended by God from the very beginning. Muslims believe that the teachings of the earlier prophets were genuine and divinely inspired; these teachings are considered the revealed word of God. But, according to the Muslims, errors crept into these texts over time due to imperfect oral traditions and language translation issues. Muslims believe that the Koran remedies this situation, since Muhammad wrote it, and it still exists today in its original language. It is considered the final and correct record of the divine messages given to Abraham, Moses, Jesus, and the earlier prophets. Remember, the Koran is the last major divinely inspired sacred book in history, not counting the Book of Mormon.

Unlike the Bible, the Koran is read today in the same language it was written, classical Arabic. In comparison, the Old Testament was written in Hebrew, and the New Testament was written in Greek for the most part, with some chapters in Aramaic. What we read in our Bibles today are translations determined by scholars who strove to find the most correct meaning as intended from the original authors. Different versions have different wordings; you can see this by comparing a King James Bible with other versions. The words will be different, and the subsequent meanings altered as well. It is interesting to note that we have no original copies of any original biblical texts written by the original authors; they are lost in antiquity. We only have copies of copies of copies, and so on. The texts in these copies do not always agree with others we have. Thus, scholars have searched for the most likely intended meanings.

Unlike Christianity, where Jesus chose twelve apostles and named Peter as the rock of His church, Muhammad did not choose a successor. As a result, different groups believed their individual method of establishing a successor was the best. Over time, this dissension resulted in the different groups in Islam we see today. The main body of Islam is known as the Sunnis. Other minority sects include the Shi'a and Sufis. What started out as a unified teaching fractured over time into differing groups believing slightly different theologies; the same evolution occurred in Christianity, yielding many denominations.

The Nature of Allah

MUSLIMS BELIEVE THAT GOD (ALLAH) is perfect. There is only one God, and that God is all-powerful and perfect in all ways. Allah is omnipotent and merciful; He knows all things about all people. Allah created the heavens and the earth. One day, Allah will judge all people for their deeds while on earth. He is infinite, and His essence is unknowable. He transcends all human understanding. God is merciful, and everything depends on God, including all of nature and the heavens. God created man out of clay. Allah's followers must strive for good and reject evil at every turn. The Book of Genesis says the same things in the Old Testament about the nature of God and how He created humankind.

Koran Problematic Texts

AS IN THE BIBLE, SOME problematic texts appear in the Koran. In the chapter titled "The Women," here are a few for consideration. These texts imply that Allah does not love every person on earth.

4.36: ... surely Allah does not love him who is proud, boastful;

4.52: Those are they whom Allah has cursed, and whomever Allah curses you shall not find any helper for him.

4.107: And do not plead on behalf of those who act unfaithfully to their souls; surely Allah does not love him who is treacherous, sinful;

Biblical Problematic Texts

EXODUS 20:5: I THE LORD your God am a jealous God, visiting the iniquity of the fathers upon the children to the third and the fourth generation of those who hate me.

Deuteronomy 4:24: For the LORD your God is a devouring fire, a jealous God.

These texts offer the idea that God will curse certain people and does not love every person on earth. This is in contrast to the Christian concept of hating the sin but loving the sinner unconditionally, in spite of the above texts from the Bible. Similar problematic texts can be found in the Koran chapter 4 called "The Women":

4.99: So these, it may be, Allah will pardon them, and Allah is pardoning, forgiving.

And from the chapter "The Disbelievers":

109.6: You shall have your religion and I shall have my religion. This is religious tolerance for other beliefs.

Here the Koran describes a God like the Christian God, who loves unconditionally.

Angels in Islam

IN THE KORAN, ANGELS PLAY an active role in the lives of human beings and influence all of us within our hearts, guiding us to succeed in doing good deeds. They strive to encourage humans to pursue good and resist evil. I strongly believe that each of us does indeed have a personal spirit guide (or, in Islamic and Catholic terminology, a guardian angel) that is with us 100 percent of the time.

I know the name of my spirit guide; he is called Theo. He has lived on earth before and is a prim and proper gentleman who is slightly miffed that I have not included him in more of my activities. I have promised him that I will in the future. Additionally, some of us can have more than one protective real angel in addition to our spirit guide. Spirit guides and angels are two different spiritual entities with different jobs. The spirit guide closest to us is also called a guardian angel, but spirit guides are are not angels. They are spirit beings that have lived on earth before. Real angels have never been human and are here to protect us from evil forces. I have five real angels, but I do not know their names. Yes, we all have typically one spirit guide or guardian angel. But we can have multiple angels here to protect us and bring to us God's word. After all, they primarily are messengers. It was the angel Gabriel who revealed the Koran to Muhammad.

Beliefs vs. Works

WITHIN ISLAM, IT IS STRESSED that belief in God is not enough; we must make efforts to do good in practice in this world.

Koran 5:5 The Dinner Table: But as for him who rejects belief [in God]—in vain will be all his works: for in the life to come he shall be among the lost.

This is very similar to James 2:17: "So faith by itself, if it has no works, is dead."

The Presence of Prophets

THE KORAN SAYS THAT GOD has sent many prophets to earth. He has spoken through these prophets to the people of history. Prophets and messengers of God were sent to all the nations of the world; these special people taught about God and led virtuous lives as high moral examples. Twenty-five prophets are named in the Koran, including Noah, Abraham, Moses, David, and Jesus, to name a few. Jesus is revered as the greatest prophet before Muhammad, though he is not believed by the Muslims to be the only son of God. Muhammad summed up all previous revelations and is therefore the Last Prophet for all humanity. In Christianity, we demonstrate that same finality in the Nicene Creed when we say, "He has spoken through the prophets."

Islam and Other Scriptures

ISLAM DOES NOT CLAIM THAT the Koran is the only Holy Scripture. Muslims recognize that other books, such as the Bible, have also revealed divine truths. Islam recognizes that all the books of God contain guidance to mankind on God's truth, how we should live, and how we should conduct our affairs on earth. Islam gives Jews and Christians special status in the Koran as "people of the book." Muhammad believed that the Bible and the Torah were both divinely inspired, even though these books are said to contain distortions that the Koran corrects one last time. I find Muhammad's attitude toward other religious traditions to be open and loving. It takes a great man to realize no one has all the answers, even when receiving divine messages from the angel Gabriel.

Islam and the Afterlife

MUSLIMS BELIEVE THERE IS AN afterlife, as Christians do. In the afterlife, everyone shall see the effects of all their deeds while on earth, both good and bad. It is also then where we all shall face the consequences of what we have done. In Christianity, we would call this the Day of Judgment. The Day of Resurrection and Judgment is the day when God will hold every person accountable for his or her actions while on earth. Each person will either go to heaven or burn in the eternal fires of punishment.

The Five Pillars of Islam

THE FIVE PILLARS OF ISLAM are religious practices that every Muslim is expected to perform.

The Creed: Each Muslim must declare the Creed publicly at least once in his or her lifetime. Most Muslims do this privately every day. The Creed contains twenty-one verses and is fairly long. It seems to me that the Christian equivalent of this would be reciting the Nicene Creed every day, especially at Mass. If you like, you can read this creed online.[69]

Prayers: Prayers must be performed five times in Arabic every day—at dawn, noon, midafternoon, sunset, and nightfall. They do this while facing Mecca. It is through prayer that a person directly connects with God. In Christianity, you may pray at any other time of day as well, if you wish; Christian prayer is not so formalized. Most Christians pray in the morning after rising and before going to bed.

Purification: Purification deals with wealth. As in Christianity, Muslims believe that everything belongs to God. We are just stewards of God's possessions while we are here on earth. Therefore, wealth should be distributed throughout the community of believers through what the Muslims call a "purifying tax." The usual amount is about 2.5 percent of a person's wealth to be distributed to the poor. This is very similar to the Christian concept of tithing.

Fasting: During the Islam holiday of Ramadan, Muslims fast between dawn and dusk. Ramadan celebrates the month when the Koran was revealed to Muhammad. This fasting is seen as another way of purification.

---

69   http://www.bible.ca/islam/islam-creed.htm

Of course, the Christian celebration of this order would be the Lenten season.

Pilgrimage: All Muslims are required to make one pilgrimage to Mecca in their lifetimes. This pilgrimage is called the Hajj. Making a trip to Vatican City and Jerusalem would be the equivalent in Christianity.

Spiritually, the purpose of these practices is to bring a Muslim closer to God. As with any other rituals in any other religious tradition, if one performs the practices without a love for God and a commitment to improve spiritually, the practices themselves will not do much good. This had occurred in Christianity when Jesus scolded the Pharisees for being like whitewashed tombs—religious on the outside, but rotten on the inside.

Other Philosophical and Cultural Aspects

HUMAN LIFE ON THIS PLANET Earth is basically a test for each of us to choose between good and evil. This is the purpose and meaning of our lives. How we respond to this test will determine how we spend eternity. Satan is real to the Muslims and is always tempting them to stray away from the straight path.

Islam places great emphasis on family and is foundational to the society that Muhammad envisioned. Much of the Koran deals with fairness in society from both an economic and social perspective. It is interesting to note that marriage is not considered a religious sacrament, as in Christianity. Rather, it is more of a legal agreement in which either party can specify certain conditions.

Regarding women, the Koran indicates that women are equal to men; neither gender is greater than the other. By my count, seventy-two verses in the Koran discuss the status of women and how to have proper relationships with them. Two examples that show equality are from the chapter titled "The Women."

4.7: Men shall have a portion of what the parents and the near relatives leave, and women shall have a portion of what the parents and the near relatives leave.

4.32: ... women shall have the benefit of what they earn.

Women are free to choose their own husbands, maintain their own names after marriage, and manage their own financial assets, including property they can own separately. They are entitled to their fair share of inheritance as well.

Some texts are problematic, however, when viewed from a modern cultural perspective. In the chapter titled "The Women," verse 34 says that good women are obedient to their husbands—and that, if necessary, a husband may beat his wife. The actual word used in the text is "scourge."

Women in Christian areas did not fare much better; that whole area of the world was very patriarchal. Thomas Aquinas said, "Since man is said to be the image of God by reason of his intellectual nature, he is the most perfectly like God according as his intellectual nature can most imitate God."[70] Much of this thought can be traced to Aristotle. He ascribed to the Pythagoreans, femaleness is associated with darkness, badness and irregularity, the opposite of maleness, clarity and goodness.

St. Paul continued this hostile attitude toward women in the New Testament when he said that he doesn't allow women to speak in church (1 Corinthians 14 or 1 Timothy 2).

Remarkably, and in contradiction to the images of Islamic society we see in modern-day news media, the Koran is very tolerant of other religions. Remember that Islam accepts both the Torah and New Testament as divinely revealed from Allah. In the chapter titled "The Council," verse 42.8, it is said, "And if Allah had pleased He would surely have made them a single community, but He makes whom He pleases enter into His mercy ..." This speaks of the different religious traditions and associated communities, maintaining that if God wanted only one religious tradition on earth, He would have made it that way in the beginning.

The hatred, war, and turmoil we see today in the Mideast are not the result of Islamic religious belief. I recoil from the media term "Islamic terrorist." Terrorists are just plain evil people driven by political aspirations while they ignore the basic peaceful theology of the Koran. Any religious tradition will include a few people with extreme interpretations meant to justify hidden political agendas and aggression against other people on the planet.

As it has been many times in the past, the people in political power have not always permitted rights granted by the Koran. Christian, Jewish, Hindu, or other traditions have not always carried out their theological teachings into real life, either. The Christian Crusades of the twelfth century are a good example of a failure to uphold Christian ideals in the real world. I end this thought with a quote from French mathematician

---

[70]   Grace M. Jantzen, *Power, Gender, and Christian Mysticism* (Cambridge University Press, 1995).

and physicist Blaise Pascal (1623–1662): "Men never do evil so completely and cheerfully as when they do it from a religious conviction."

A Common Theme

IT IS MY PRAYER THAT in reading this section, we can realize just how much in common Christians have with the people of the Islamic faith. There are differences for sure, but if you strip away all the doctrine, dogma, politicos posing as religious leaders, and forms of the rituals in any religious tradition, you will find that the mystical essence of the various religious traditions are more similar than different. We can see that, at its essence, Islam has much in common with Christianity.

This commonality of belief indicates the existence of one transcendent author who has infused His truth into the minds of godly men and women. Certain teachings have a beauty and consistency about them no matter where in the world they surface. Magnificent, isn't it? Pray and meditate about this, and ask God to guide you to the truth. Do this with an open heart, and God will show you what is true.

Judaism

IF YOU LIVE IN ANY Western culture, you have been exposed to the teachings of Judaism, no matter what religious tradition you identify with. Judaism traces its roots back to the times of Abraham and the Hebrews, about four thousand years ago. Judaism has certainly stood the test of time. No religious tradition or system of belief could thrive this long unless it spoke the truth about God—and, in my opinion, had blessings from God as well. Other religions that have stood the test of time include Daoism, Buddhism, and Hinduism, to name a few. I believe that each must contain elements of God's truth, or they would have disappeared from the history of humankind.

History is of utmost importance in Judaism. Whereas the sacred texts of most ancient religions focus on values, ideals, and philosophical concepts, the Jewish Bible is centered on a historical narrative. This in turn centers on the evolving Hebrew understanding of and relationship with God. Jewish history begins with Abraham and his encounter with God; Abraham is considered to be the founder of Judaism. God sought out Abraham, not vice versa.

The Jewish Bible

THE JEWISH TANAKH (HEBREW BIBLE) is the same set of books that Christianity calls the Old Testament. Even in the Christian Bible, the Old Testament is a record of Jewish history; the New Testament is a record of the teachings of Jesus Christ and the newly forming Christian Church.

The Tanakh tells the religious history of the Hebrews, beginning with creation and ending with the last of the prophets in the fourth century BC. It tells the stories of how and when the Hebrew nation experienced periods of favor and then discipline from God, and it lists all the different covenants that God established. It describes a set of laws through Moses, who set apart the Hebrews as God's chosen people. When the Hebrews stray, God sends prophets and invading armies to bring them back to their senses and to God.

This belief that God is directly involved with the events of humankind is unique to Jewish religious thought. The timeline and sequence of events points to a spiritual destination for the Hebrew nation; this concept is unique among the religious traditions of antiquity. At Mount Sinai, God established the nation of Israel and made another covenant with them: the Israelites were to be God's chosen people. This designation did not indicate their superiority over other peoples. Rather, it meant that the Israelites were to receive the Torah and worship the one and only true God.

Once established in the Promised Land, a united monarchy was necessary under Saul, David, and Solomon. This kingdom lasted for many years. It is said in 1 Kings 11:3 that Solomon had 700 wives. Hugh Hefner must be very jealous, huh?

After Solomon died, the nation split up into two kingdoms, with Israel in the north and Judah in the south. The Babylonian army later conquered Judah, and many Hebrew tribes were lost to antiquity. The land of Israel is at an important crossroads between the east and Europe, so many tribes wanted to claim it as their own. The Romans occupied this land during the time of Jesus Christ. The Romans were cruel taskmasters, and the Jewish people revolted in 66 AD, only to have their temple destroyed and many people killed by Roman soldiers.

Rabbinical Judaism and the Articles of Faith

RABBINICAL JUDAISM DEVELOPED FROM THE Pharisaic movement after the destruction of the temple. This form of Judaism dominated Jewish religious practice for 1,800 years. In Judaism, there is no official creed or doctrine, as there is in Christianity. But back in the twelfth century, a rabbi named Maimonides assembled a number of articles of faith that he believed every Jew should believe and live his or her life according to. Over time, these articles of faith have been accepted as central to Jewish life, even to this day. But as in Christianity, not every single Jew fully and blindly accepts exactly everything put forth by the Jewish articles of faith.

The Jewish God

THE FACT THAT GOD EXISTS is a given in Judaism. He is eternal, He is unique, and He transcends the physical world. God is incorporeal and eternal. There are no gods above Him. God is indescribable; He cannot be divided into parts or described by attributes. This is different from Christianity, in which God is viewed as a Trinity; Judaism is more similar to Islam in this regard. God created everything; everything comes from God, including evil (Isaiah 45:6–7). God has no form and should never be depicted with one, just as in Islam. (Christianity, on the other hand, believes that Jesus Christ was both fully God and man, as decided at the Council of Nicaea in the year 325. Thus, depictions of Jesus can be considered to be God incarnate.) In Judaism, God is omnipresent, omnipotent, and omniscient. God is just and merciful. God knows all the thoughts and actions of everyone.

Unlike in Catholicism, where we pray to the saints, Judaism dictates that prayer be directed to God alone and no one else. Like Christians, the Jews believe that the prophets taught the truth of God, but Jews consider Moses to have been the greatest prophet; the Torah (the first five books of the Old Testament) and the Talmud were given to Moses.

The Ten Commandments and the Torah

THE TEN COMMANDMENTS WERE GIVEN to Moses, which is one of the reasons he is considered the greatest prophet of Judaism. These are the same commandments adopted by Christians. For the Jews, the Torah defines how to act, how to think, and even how to feel about life and death. Each of the many stories in the Torah can be considered to be a lesson about God and His relationship with the Jewish people. The Torah actually contains 613 commandments, not just the ten we are familiar with. However, the Ten Commandments are considered to be the most important.

Richard Ferguson

The Jewish Messiah

ACCORDING TO JUDAISM, A TIME will come when the good will be rewarded and the evil punished. The Messiah will come, and all the dead will be resurrected. Jewish belief says that the Messiah will be a descendant of King David (2 Samuel 7:12–13; Jeremiah 23:5), observant of Jewish law (Isaiah 11:2–5), a righteous judge (Jeremiah 33:15), and a great military leader. This is basically the fundamental belief of Judaism. Christians believe the Messiah has come in the person of Jesus Christ; Jews definitely do not believe this. Rather, according to them, the Messiah has yet to come to this earth.

Original Sin and Free Will

UNLIKE CHRISTIANS AND SIMILAR TO the Muslims, Jews reject the concept of original sin. According to Judaism, every person has the ability to choose good or evil; the idea of human free will is fundamental. Humans are considered basically good, since they are made in the image of God. People who choose evil will be cast down to hell after the judgment; good people will ascend to heaven. All this is generally very much like Christianity. The Jewish texts don't say much about the nature of heaven and hell. Rather, they focus on the actions and deeds that must be done while here on earth. For Jews, actions lead to belief. Christians maintain that belief leads to actions.

Jewish Sects

THE TORAH HAS MANY VERSES that address how life is to be conducted in various sectors: economic, social, and so on. The Book of Leviticus lays down the regulations for daily life in the Jewish community. Jewish belief is not monolithic; rather, Judaism has different sects, just as in Christianity. Judaism has six or seven branches ranging from the Ultra-Orthodox to the Humanistic to the Flexidox branch. Each has its own interpretations of the Torah and emphasizes rules on living as a Jew.

Christianity

CHRISTIANITY IS THE WORLD'S LARGEST religion, with 2.1 billion believers; Islam comes in second, with 1.5 billion. About 20 million people practice Judaism.

Christianity came from Judaism by way of Jesus Christ. Many people are surprised to hear that Jesus was not a Christian—but he wasn't. He was a Jew. Jesus was born a Jew, lived as a Jew, and died as a Jew. If fact, Jesus never used the term "Christian" in his ministry—ever. The term "Christian" was not used until many years after Jesus's death and resurrection. It appears for the first time in the Book of Acts 11:26, which was written long after Jesus died—arguably at least seventy years after the fact.

It was St. Paul who reached out to the Gentiles about the Jewish Christian movement, as it was known as during that time. He traveled extensively, establishing churches as he went. The books of Galatians, Corinthians, Ephesians, Colossians, and Thessalonians all comprise letters from St. Paul addressing the issues that each of these early churches had. If it were not for St. Paul, I doubt that the Christian movement would have spread worldwide; it would probably have remained a Jewish sect of some sort.

Christianity, like other religious traditions, was born of the politics and culture of the biblical writers, along with existing religious influences. We tend to forget the cultural, religious and political situation from which religious traditions come. The time of Jesus was very turbulent due to the Roman occupation. The Romans ruled with an iron fist and taxed the Jews heavily. This is the reason that the Hebrew nation was looking for the prophecy of a messiah that would come to free the Hebrews from bondage. They thought this messiah would come from the line of David and be a military-type leader who would throw out the Romans and other enemies.

It is not generally known within the Christian community that rival teachers of Jesus are alleged to have existed during His time on earth. These teachers offered gospels that were similar to Jesus's gospel in many ways, with some major differences. One of Jesus's alleged rivals is Apollonius of Tyana, who was reputed to have healed the sick, worked miracles, and raised the dead. Another alleged rival is Simon Magus, who is actually mentioned in the Bible. Acts of the Apostles 8:9–11: "But there was a man named Simon who had previously practiced magic in the city and amazed the nation of Samaria, saying that he himself was somebody great. They all gave heed to him, from the least to the greatest, saying, 'This man is that power of God which is called Great.' And they gave heed to him, because for a long time he had amazed them with his magic."

No, Jesus was not the only rabbi preaching the word of God within the Jewish nation at that time. Yet, through the divine workings of God, it is He who has influenced the entire world for thousands of years—in spite of the fact that He never wrote anything down.

Today, many different branches of Christianity exist, ranging from the literalist conservatives who believe the Bible is totally inerrant to the more liberal branches that take the Bible as a document that is to be interpreted according to modern needs.

The Nicene Creed

THE BEST SUMMARY OF CORE Christian beliefs is the Nicene Creed, the first version of which was adopted by the First Council of Nicaea in 325 AD.

We believe in one God, the Father, the Almighty,
maker of heaven and earth, of all that is, seen and unseen.
We believe in one Lord, Jesus Christ, the only Son of God,
eternally begotten of the Father, God from God, light from light,
true God from true God, begotten, not made,
of one Being with the Father; through Him all things were made.
For us and for our salvation He came down from heaven,
was incarnate of the Holy Spirit and the Virgin Mary
and became truly human. For our sake He was crucified under Pontius
Pilate;
He suffered death and was buried. On the third day He rose again
in accordance with the Scriptures; He ascended into heaven
and is seated at the right hand of the Father.
He will come again in glory to judge the living and the dead,
and His kingdom will have no end.
We believe in the Holy Spirit, the Lord, the giver of life,
who proceeds from the Father [and the Son],
who with the Father and the Son is worshiped and glorified,
who has spoken through the prophets.
We believe in one holy catholic and apostolic Church.
We acknowledge one baptism for the forgiveness of sins.
We look for the resurrection of the dead, and the life of the world to
come.

Amen.

In this creed, we see that Christians believe that God can be thought of as three entities that comprise the whole—and yet they are indivisible from each other. God created the universe and man. Jesus Christ is the only Son of God, and He died because of original sin and the sinful nature of all humanity. The Holy Spirit is with us always and gives us life. God has spoken through the prophets. There is only one true Apostolic Church, and we look for the resurrection of all those who have died in anticipation of the kingdom of God, which is at hand, as Jesus taught.

God is active in the events of the world and can be prayed to directly. In some sects of Christianity, like Catholicism, praying to the saints is allowed as well. Christians believe, as do the Jews and Muslims, that world history is headed toward a climax where all people will be judged for their actions and be rewarded or punished appropriately.

Original Sin

Christians believe that humanity fell in the Garden of Eden because of the sin of Adam and Eve. This original sin stains all people and necessitates salvation. Because of this, Jesus Christ was crucified to atone for our collective sins and allow for our salvation. Born of a virgin, Jesus was not stained with original sin; thus He was the perfect sacrificial Lamb of God to save humanity.

Our Visit to the Vatican

Marilyn and I visited the Vatican in 2002. Our tour guide was an expert in Roman history; he had a degree in the history of Rome and the Catholic Church. As we toured St. Peter's Basilica, we encountered a tomb of Pope Alexander VII close to the main altar on the left side. Above the entrance of this tomb, I was shocked to see a statue of a menacing-looking skeleton holding an hourglass. I was amazed to see something like this right inside St. Peter's. I asked our tour guide about this sight.

Our guide explained that in the mid 1600s, Pope Alexander VII was fighting against the rise of Anglicism in England and the fact that many people were leaving the Church. People were fed up with rampant nepotism and corruption in the papacy. The Church was sliding downhill in terms of size, influence, and power. Well, the pope commissioned many artisans to create sculptures, paintings, and mosaics that reminded the people that they better come back to the Catholic Church, because the Angel of Death was stalking them, their time was limited, and the threat of going to hell was real. This was very frightening to the people, who were mostly illiterate. Although the pope lost his battle against Anglicism, his commissioned artwork frightened many people, who then returned to the Church and resumed their financial support of the papacy.

If you look closely at a photo of this pope's tomb, you will see the skeleton holding an hourglass in his right hand and emerging from a shroud. On the right stands an angelic-looking woman with her foot on top of a globe of the world. Well, her left big toe is resting on top of a spike that has been driven into the globe right where England should be—right where all those Anglicans live. The Church played rough back in those days, or so it seems. You can find these photos at the Vatican Web site.

According to this tour guide, a sea change of emphasis occurred within the Church when it started to preach that the Church was the only way to heaven—that hell awaited those who were not Catholic. Those of you who were growing up during the 1950s and 1960s will remember this kind of teaching. Have you ever wondered why, in the New Testament, Jesus never mentions God sending people to hell— yet that is something that the Church talks about? Now you know the origin of this. It was never part of the teachings of Jesus, who taught love, forgiveness, and compassion. According to our Vatican guide, the looming threat of hell is the work of a pope who used fear against the people to scare them back into the Church. It worked; to this day, according to the more conservative branches of Christianity, you will be sent to hell unless you profess faith in God and Jesus Christ.

This idea of original sin is not adhered to by the other two traditions from the Mideast, Islam or Judaism. But some Christians argue to this day that you are destined for hell unless you do certain things, like go to confession. If you don't go to Mass, God will punish you. As a kid in Catholic school, I was taught this. But God's supposed plans to smite me did not represent teachings of the early Church; this idea came much later.

The Greatest Commandments

ONE OF THE CENTRAL CHRISTIAN beliefs is contained in the answer Jesus gave to His disciples when they asked Him which was the greatest commandment. This is found in the gospel of Matthew 22:37–40: "And he said to him, 'you shall love the Lord your God with all your heart, and with all your soul, and with all your mind. This is the great and first commandment. And a second is like it, you shall love your neighbor as yourself. On these two commandments depend all the law and the prophets.'"

If a person were to fully understand the meaning and depth of this simple, beautiful, and elegant response, then they would understand the essence of the entire gospel message as far as human conduct and our relationship with God are concerned. This verse in Matthew specifies God's place above all else. It specifies how you are to behave regarding other people and how you are to consider yourself. Jesus's words cover everything, in a sense: God, you, and others.

Jesus went on to say that we should forgive those who hurt us not seven times, but seven times seventy. Regarding enemies, Jesus said in Matthew 5:44, "But I say to you, love your enemies and pray for those who persecute you." It's pretty clear that Jesus is emphasizing love under almost all conditions. Even on the cross, He said to God, "Father, forgive them, for they know not what they do."

Differences and Commonalities Between Denominations

THE PRECEDING TENETS REPRESENT THE bare basics of the Christian faith. Like Islam and Judaism, Christianity is not a monolithic faith; many different denominations call themselves Christian. Some of the differences in biblical interpretation between denominations are quite large. However there is general agreement that belief in the following points is a requirement to be considered a Christian:

The Trinity
The deity of Jesus
Jesus's physical resurrection after His crucifixion
Atonement as a result of the life, and particularly the death, of Jesus
Personal salvation by the grace of God
God's inspiration of the Bible's authors

The virgin birth of Jesus of Nazareth
The anticipated second coming of Jesus

Buddhism

THE BUDDHIST RELIGIOUS TRADITION WAS largely shaped by the personal experiences of one man within a culture suffering problems of poverty. Siddhartha Gautama was born sometime in the early 600s BC. According to legend, he was born a prince in his clan, as his father was the king. He lived a luxurious existence early in his life—that is, until he made some journeys out into the world, away from the palace. Then he saw the reality of life for the first time. He saw the poverty, sickness, and death of people who were suffering greatly. He was shocked and horrified to see what life was really like. During one of his trips away from the palace, he saw a religious man who seemed to be serene and calm among all the pain of the people. This, too, affected him deeply, and he wondered how peacefulness could exist among such suffering. He subsequently decided to become religious and leave his privileged life, his wife, and his child. There is a parallel here with Jesus, who said that whoever wanted to follow Him must leave his family behind. But instead of following Jesus (who had not yet been born, after all), he chose to search for the peacefulness and serenity that he had seen in that religious man.

Siddhartha Gautama spent many years pursuing spiritual enlightenment. One day, he sat under the Bodhi tree; only then did he begin to have strong spiritual experiences. It is said that he began to recall all his past lives; he also began to see the past lives of other people and how their conduct in one life determined what they would experience in the next. Lastly, he began to understand that he had progressed beyond "spiritual defilements" and his desires for worldly things; he had attained nirvana. Siddhartha and his monks began to travel and preach his teachings regarding enlightenment to anyone who would receive them. His teachings formed the belief system known as Buddhism. Siddhartha Gautama became the Buddha, also known as "the man who woke up."

An Unusual Religion

EARLY IN ITS HISTORY, BUDDHISM purposely did not include all the elements of a religion like Christianity. In his book *The World's Religions*, Huston Smith explains that a religion has six major features: authority, ritual, tradition, speculation, mystery, and grace. These six different elements, when taken together, form a complete religious tradition. However, the Buddha purposely preached a religion without these features; he eliminated these traditional elements on purpose as a reaction to the structure and practices of Hinduism and what he saw as the Brahmins strong control over the people.

The Buddha instituted no rituals in Buddhism and made no speculations regarding where we come from or the meaning of life. Buddhism had no traditions to hand down to future generations, in contrast to the other world religions. The Buddha said, "Do not go by what is handed down, nor on the authority of your traditions."[71] Instead, he preached intense self-effort to achieve spiritual enlightenment. Everyone was to make the effort to progress spiritually on his or her own. This teaching contrasts starkly with the Christian belief that the saving grace of God is required to bring us to heaven. (John 3:17: "For God sent the Son into the world, not to condemn the world, but that the world might be saved through him.")

After the Buddha's death, however, the rituals and features of a more typical religious tradition made their way into the lives of Buddhist followers; humans seem to need these kinds of things. This is not stated overtly, but the content of Buddhist teachings bear a strong core resemblance to Christian teachings. Follow Buddhist teachings and the eightfold path in general, and you will become a spiritual person, just as a Christian strives to do in order to save himself from judgment.

Buddha said nothing about the supernatural; he preached a "religion" where God was completely missing. Regarding the supernatural, he perceived a danger in the practice of mystical powers that we would call today paranormal. I suspect he felt this way not because he did not believe there was a God, but because the character and illiteracy of the people of his time may have promoted misinformation and confusion. I believe the Buddha felt that the population could not handle any discussion of the supernatural.[72]

---

[71] Huston Smith, *The World's Religions* (San Francisco: Harper, 1991).

[72] This is the most common story of the Buddha in the literature. However, other versions exist as well. This version of the life of the Buddha can be found in: Osho, *Buddha: His Life and Teachings* (Bridgewater Book Company, 2004) and Huston Smith's *The World's Religions* (San Francisco: Harper, 1961).

Buddhist Beliefs: The Four Noble Truths

THE FIRST NOBLE TRUTH IS "All is suffering."[73] Life itself is suffering. In Buddhism, suffering does refer exclusively to emotional or physical pain. Suffering also includes the loss of pleasure. There is nothing wrong with the pursuit of joy and pleasure, a Buddhist would say. But since everything in life is impermanent, pleasure can never be permanent either, and when it is lost, suffering results. The greater a person's attachment to pleasure, the greater his or her pain will be at the loss of that pleasure. Thus, the First Noble Truth identifies suffering as the lot of human beings in this life.

In Christianity, suffering is a way to perfect the soul, become more Christlike, and gain entrance into the kingdom. 2 Timothy 2:3 says: "Share in suffering as a good soldier of Christ Jesus." Suffering will lead to a far greater glory in heaven, according to St. Paul, who wrote in Romans 8:18, "I consider that the sufferings of this present time are not worth comparing with the glory that is to be revealed to us." Within Christianity, suffering can be embraced as a way of spiritual purification and becoming closer to God. But the Buddhist beliefs regarding suffering are quite different.

Buddhism states that the causes of suffering can be eliminated, and Buddhism is the method or path for eliminating those causes. Part of the goal of the Buddhist tradition, then, is to eliminate human suffering. Buddhism offers a path toward a mental and emotional state of human existence that prevents the enlightened person from suffering. You can live in this life, taking full part in earthly activities yet remain peaceful in your heart, no matter what ill wind blows pain into your life.

The cause of human suffering is addressed in the Second Noble Truth. This truth states that the causes of suffering are desire and ignorance.[74] St. Ignatius of Loyola would certainly agree. He just used a different word: "attachments." We desire much in this life that we do not have: material wealth, a better relationship, an improvement in our health, and so on. There is also much in this life that we do not know; this is ignorance. Sometimes, the word "ignorance" is considered insulting, but in the Buddhist context, ignorance is simply a state of not knowing.

What is meant by desire in Buddhism? Desire is the craving for pleasure, material wealth, and immortality. Christianity also warns about such cravings and worldly temptations, as such cravings can never be completely satisfied. (Mark 8:36: "For what does it profit a man, to gain

---

[73] Huston Smith, *The World's Religions* (San Francisco: Harper, 1991).
[74] Ibid.

the whole world and forfeit his life?") Buddha goes on to say that even if a person obtains pleasure from something, that pleasure will inevitably be lost, causing suffering and frustration. The world cannot satisfy a human being completely or for very long.

Buddhism purports that if you extinguish your desire for worldly things, you eliminate this as a cause of suffering. Jesus Christ said much the same thing in Matthew 6:19-20: "Do not lay up for yourselves treasures on earth, where moth and rust consume and where thieves break in and steal, but lay up for yourselves treasures in heaven, where neither moth nor rust consumes and where thieves do not break in and steal."

Buddhism defines ignorance as the inability to see the world as it really is. If one does not have the ability to concentrate or gain insight, then one's mind is not developed and therefore unable to understand the true nature of this reality. Nasty human traits, such as greed, envy, hatred, anger, and dishonesty, all are a result of ignorance. In Christianity, these thoughts can be related to the seven deadly sins: lust, gluttony, greed, sloth, wrath (anger), envy, and pride. A Buddhist would say these sins are the result of ignorance of how the world really works or a failure to see reality as it really is.

With the Third Noble Truth, Buddhism offers a way to avoid human suffering. This truth states that achieving nirvana will put an end to our suffering. This can occur either during our physical life on earth or during our spiritual lives. When a person achieves nirvana, he or she arrives at a transcendent state free from suffering and our cycle of birth and rebirth; this is much the same as in Hinduism. The person who reaches spiritual enlightenment will be freed from desires and ignorance. Nirvana can be achieved through individual effort. This differs from Christianity, where we are saved not through our own efforts but through Jesus's atonement on the cross for our sins and through the grace of God.

What is nirvana? It is the enlightened state that describes a perfectly peaceful mind free from suffering, cravings, anger, greed, and so on. Christians could describe nirvana as an absence of any temptation toward the seven deadly sins. Nirvana could be with the term of *teleios*, which is a Greek word for "wholeness" or "brought to completion." This Greek word was used in the Bible in the gospel of Matthew before it was translated into English.

The Fourth Noble Truth specifies the Eightfold Path. One must take this path to achieve enlightenment and avoid suffering. There are eight steps in this path: Right Understanding or Beliefs, Right Intent, Right

Speech, Right Action, Right Livelihood, Right Effort, Right Mindfulness, and Right Concentration. In addition to these eight steps are three themes: good moral conduct (Understanding, Thought, Speech); meditation (Action, Livelihood, Effort), and insightful wisdom (Mindfulness and Concentration).[75] If a person masters these eight steps, enlightenment will follow and nirvana will be achieved. Notice that the Eightfold Path mainly addresses the manner in which a person thinks; a practicing Buddhist is in charge of changing his or her thinking. Similar to the Ten Commandments, the tenets of the Eightfold Path originate in the mind and are then manifested in the physical world.

Sects in Buddhism

As do most religions, Buddhism divided into sects after the death of its header. These various factions usually wish to emphasize different aspects of the original teachings. This happened in Christianity, Judaism, and Islam, for example. Members of the early Christian Church engaged in many disagreements regarding the contents of the canon and other issues; over time, different sects of Christianity appeared accordingly. This same thing happened to Buddhism.

Many different types of Buddhism exist today: Tendai, Shingon, Jodo, Jodo-Shinshu, and Nichiren, just to name a few. Zen is the most well-known from of Buddhism in the Western world. Many festivals have come into being to celebrate things like the enlightenment of Buddha, the day of Buddha's teachings, the spiritual community of Buddhism, and the death of the Buddha. Rituals have also made their way into the lives of the Buddhist.

Buddha did not discuss the existence of God. However, over the years, a host of deities have emerged. These include Avalokitesvara, the Lord Who Looks in Every Direction; Manjusri, the Gentle Holy One; Ksitigarbha, the Womb of the Earth; and Maitreya, the Loving One. Lastly but very prominent is Tara, the Goddess of Compassion and Virtuous Righteous Action. Before Buddhism adopted Tara, she was worshipped in Hinduism as a manifestation of the goddess Parvati. Each of these deities has a different role in the spiritual life of Buddhists as they help people attain enlightenment. These gods all demonstrate attributes of the Christian God.

---

[75]   Ibid.

An Evolved Religion

THE BUDDHA COULD NOT HAVE imagined all of these practices, deities, and festivals. His teachings were simple and practical, characterized by reason and sincere spirituality. The things he purposely left out of his teachings have managed to appear in the lives of Buddhist believers of today. I think it is fair to say that Buddhism, like most other religious traditions that became exposed to different cultures, has evolved within each culture in different ways to meet the spiritual needs of the people. This is also true with Christianity, which is why many different forms of Christianity exist today in various parts of the world. If you want to see an extreme example, go to New Orleans.

According to the Buddha, all human suffering originates within the human mind. Buddhist philosophy centers on those six inches between everyone's ears. Get those six inches right, Buddha taught, and all external action and relationships will be healthy, constructive, and filled with peace. Certainly, many psychologists would agree with the Buddha on this point. If we can fix the human mind by recognizing the Four Noble Truths and follow the Eightfold Path, we will reach a point where we are basically incapable of committing evil acts.

Other Traits of Buddhism

IN BUDDHISM, THE UNIVERSE IS timeless. It always existed and always will. In a sense, it is static. In Christianity, as in Judaism, history has a direction to it; it begins with the creation story in Genesis. Time is viewed differently in Christianity, Islam, and Judaism, where events have a sequence that are leading to a conclusion.

Other differences are seen in what is missing. Buddhism has no formal creed like the Nicene Creed, no God, no angels, no designated spiritual descendants of Buddha (the Dalai Lama cannot define doctrine), no prayers to God, no saints, no sacraments, no regular worship services (though there are regular holidays and festivals), no emphasis on doing good works (although charity is discussed), no faith in a single creator, no sin, and no judgment. Lastly, the Buddha said that humans also have no soul, since nothing in this world has any substance. Rather, our personal identities are like a flame that gets passed from candle to candle. Regarding this, the Buddhist metaphorical question is whether or not the flame on the next candle can be considered the same flame as the one on the last candle. I will let you meditate on that one.

Buddhism and the Christian Tradition

IT IS VERY GOOD FOR Christians to be aware of the Buddhist way. In a sense, this tradition compliments Christianity because of its focus on the inner self and meditation as a way to attain the highest potential for human life. Although the Buddha could not describe nirvana, saying it is "incomprehensible, indescribable, unutterable, and inconceivable," we cannot really describe heaven, either.

In the end, good Buddhists are very much like good Christians in a very fundamental sense: striving to understand themselves, do the right things, and make a positive contribution to this world. Between the two traditions, the rituals, concept of the divine, and other theological concepts are very different. But the miraculous thing is that each tradition points toward the same goal: living a proper life where peace and justice reigns supreme. Attaining such a life is a wondrous act of responding to God's tug of love for all humans, whether Christian or Buddhist. At the core of it all, Buddhists are responding to the same God we are, no matter what they may or may not call Him.

I hope that you take away from this discussion that we are all more alike than not. We should not fear the surface differences in our religious traditions. Under the surface of any religious tradition is a group of wonderful human beings who are doing the best they can. I believe that these other religions are wholly acceptable to our God, who shows unconditional love to all His creations, no matter what religious tradition they are born into. If you still have doubts about this, just think about what you would believe in if you had been born in Tibet, Thailand, or China; I bet you would be Buddhist. If you were born in Japan, you might believe in Shinto. Think about that.

Hinduism

HINDUISM IS THE THIRD-LARGEST RELIGIOUS tradition in the world today, with almost one billion believers. Unlike most other world religions, Hinduism cannot be traced back to a particular person in history. Unlike Christianity, which can be traced back to Jesus Christ, Hinduism is so old that no clear beginning can be defined. This religion of the people in India and beyond has evolved over the last four thousand years. According to a Web site offering religion facts, "Although today's Hinduism differs significantly from earlier forms of Indian religion ... the early history of Hinduism is unclear. The most ancient writings have yet to be deciphered."[76]

The sacred texts of Hinduism are the Upanisads, Smrutis, Ramayana, Mahabharata, and the Puranashave. Authors that are unknown today wrote these sacred texts. These authors' names have been lost in its long history, if they were ever known in the first place; this is not unusual. Christians are not completely sure of the identities of the authors of many books in the Bible. For example, our tradition says that Moses wrote the five books of the Pentateuch. Modern textual criticism studies shed doubt on that due to variations in writing styles in the texts and other factors. Not all of the authors of the New Testament are known for sure, either.

Over the many years, Hinduism evolved from what it was four thousand years ago into today's set of traditions. Hinduism is not monolithic; rather, it encompasses a wide variety of beliefs, gods, and practices—more so than the other major religious traditions, though all religions tend to evolve along with cultures and values. The Christian traditions of today are different from what the early Christian Church believed.

A Vast Religion

ACCORDING TO HUSTON SMITH'S BOOK *The World's Religions*, if one were to summarize the vast expanse of Hindu literature into one sentence, it would be, "You can have what you want."[77] Sounds good—but this idea comes with great responsibility for your own actions. In a sense, you are in charge of what a Christian would call salvation. But Hinduism is a free-flowing, flexible religion. It does not include the complex doctrine or dogma found in Christian traditions.

Hindus believe in one supreme reality; this reality has different names, such as the One, Purusha, or Brahman. The Hindus I have met simply say "God." Most Hindus are followers of one of the principal gods: Shiva, Vishnu, and Shakti. Other gods can be followed as well. All these gods are considered to be manifestations of the one reality. So, in a sense, Hinduism is more monotheistic than it might initially appear.

Today, Hinduism has no central leader, like a pope or other authority figure, but it is generally agreed to be made up of four devotional sects.

---

[76] http://www.religionfacts.com/hinduism/history.htm
[77] Huston Smith, *The World's Religions* (San Francisco: Harper, 1991).

Three of them are monotheistic, believing in one God.[78] Consider these sects much like the different branches of Christianity. They center on the ultimate reality being Brahmin or the Self, which must be attained by one of the four paths in order to attain liberation from the cycles of birth and death. The devotional sects generally regard the other sects as complimentary, freely borrowing their beliefs and practices.

General Hindu Traits

ALTHOUGH IT MAY SEEM TO a Christian that Hindu beliefs are scattered all over the place with many gods and paths, some beliefs are common to almost all forms of Hinduism.

Hinduism supports the idea of an enduring human soul that survives death, as in Christianity. However, the Hindus believe that the soul is reincarnated into another body at death. This is to provide the soul more opportunity to attain liberation from the birth-and-death cycle. What one does in a life follows to the next life; the law of karma determines a person's destiny in both this life and the next one too.

Hindus believe in the authority of the Vedas, Upanishads, Sutras, and the Bhagavad-Gita, which are the oldest sacred texts. They feel about the Vedas as Christians do about the Bible. The One, or Brahmin, inspired different people across many years to write the Vedas.

Hindus also believe in the authority of the Brahmans, or priests, over spiritual matters. The Brahmans are a caste of Hindus demonstrating purity and spiritual supremacy by birth. The Brahmans perform rituals, such as weddings and funerals, and they also teach the scriptures. The Hindu ultimate reality can be imagined as either a personal or transpersonal God; this would depend on the spiritual needs of the devotee. Either view is acceptable. Hinduism recognizes that there is more than one way to God. In fact, Hinduism is probably the most open-minded tradition when it comes to accepting other traditions as valid paths toward the same God.

One God, Many Paths

ONE FAMOUS NINETEENTH-CENTURY HINDU SAINT, Sri Ramakrishna, proclaimed that any religion was just another means for achieving union with God. Sri Ramakrishna actually spent periods of his life practicing his own understandings of Islam, Christianity, and various Yogic and Tantric

---

[78] http://www.religionfacts.com/hinduism/sects.htm

sects within Hinduism. He reported that in each instance, he found the same God: incarnate in Christ, speaking through Muhammad, and in the guise of Vishnu the Preserver or Shiva the Completer.

This Hindu saint has spoken an ultimate truth: Many paths lead to God, but no matter what path you choose, if you are diligent and persevere, you are going in the right direction and will achieve the close relationship with God that all others pursue, no matter what they call Him. I don't think God really cares what name you use for Him. I'm the same way: call me what you want; just don't call me late for dinner.

I wish I could have met Sri Ramakrishna when he was alive. He summarized his point by saying, "Truth is one, but sages call it by many names."[79] What a beautiful way to say an eternal truth in so few words. Those people who thump Bibles and preach hell and damnation should read what Sri Ramakrishna has said.

The Ten Commitments

Hinduism uses ten commitments instead of commandments.

1. Ahimsa: do no harm.
2. Satya: do not lie.
3. Asteya: do not steal.
4. Brahmacharya: do not overindulge.
5. Aparigraha: do not be greedy.
6. Saucha: be clean.
7. Santosha: be content.
8. Tapas: be self-disciplined.
9. Svadhyaya: study.
10. Ishvara Pranidhana: surrender to God.

Interestingly, Hindus feel that the source of these commitments can be identified as the human heart or inner being. In contrast, Christianity uses commandments that have an external, enforced character to them. Hinduism comes from within, while Christianity comes from external factors that produce an inner commitment.

---

[79] Rig Veda, Mandala 1, Sukta 164, Mantra 46.

Four Purposes, Four Paths

HINDUISM SAYS THERE ARE FOUR purposes in life: to fulfill moral, social, and religious duties; to attain financial and worldly success; to satisfy human desires in moderation; and to attain freedom from the cycle of reincarnation through enlightenment.

Additionally, the Hindus believe in three different paths to God, depending on the personality of the person: the path of works and action; the path of knowledge; and the path of devotion to God. One size does not fit all, as many Christians have been taught. Different people are at different points on their spiritual journey; thus, they have different needs. Humans are considered to be in bondage to ignorance and illusion, but able to escape through meditation and enlightenment by walking one of these paths to the truth of Brahmin.

The Three Desires

THE BASIC VIEW OF MANKIND in Hinduism is that we want three things—actually, four, but the first three are dominant in most people's lives. The first thing we want is pleasure, and the Hindus see nothing wrong with that. Your search for pleasure is a marker for where you are on your spiritual journey. The second thing we want is power, via knowledge, success, and so on. The world offers such forms of power to us. Again, Hinduism sees nothing wrong with these pursuits; they point out, however, that pleasure, success, and power are ephemeral and temporary. The Buddha has said the same thing.

These first two pursuits of people are driven by desire—the desire is to feel good, have money, enjoy authority over others, and so on. The accomplishment of these pursuits lends a certain feeling of security and satisfies the ego. This is the Path of Desire.

The Path of Desire for worldly offerings may take many lifetimes to satisfy, according to Hinduism. These offerings are not bad, but they do not satisfy completely the whole needs of mankind. The objects of the world are considered as toys. There will come a point in the life of each Hindu where they realize they have had enough of these toys and start looking for more. They will ask, "Is that all there is?" It is at this time that a person enters the Path of Renunciation. Satisfaction of the ego will no longer be the driving force in that person's life. Huston Smith puts it this way: "Myriads have transformed the will to get into the will to give, the will to win into the will to serve."[80]

Is there more? According to the Hindu tradition, definitely. Life offers many other potentials or possibilities. Since the toys of the Path of Desire fail to satisfy, we must look deeper within our being to discern our true human needs. What are they? The first thing we really want is just "to be," to exist. The second is "to know"; we want knowledge. The third thing is joy. We want no more suffering, pain, or ill feelings. We are limited beings and therefore have limited amounts of these three inner needs. What we really want deep down inside is infinite amounts of being, knowledge, and joy. Our desire for these things marks the third Hindu pursuit.

Surprisingly, Hinduism maintains that we already have these things. Every human being already has infinite being, infinite knowledge, and infinite joy; they exist at the center of our being already. This center is referred to as the Atman or the Godhead itself. We are part of God, in other words. This idea is actually quite biblical. Luke 17:21: "for behold, the kingdom of God is in the midst of you." Christian doctrine also states that man is made in the likeness of God.

The Challenge of Hinduism

THE PROBLEM IS THAT THIS eternal, all-knowing, blissful part of us exists beneath almost impenetrable layers of distraction, emotion, assumptions, incorrect ideas, and so on. According to Hinduism, we suffer from illusions and ignorance. (The Buddha would agree.) All these problems exist in the third layer of our being, so the issue for the Hindu is whether we can get past these barriers and to the Godhead in the center of our being. Famous German psychologist Carl Jung would certainly agree, for his model of the essence of the human being follows the Hindu construct.

According to Hinduism, ignorance allows our ego to control our actions; every action we take to satisfy our ego takes us farther away from God. Every selfless action brings us closer to God. Each action a person takes has consequences that they are responsible for. Enter the concept of karma as the universal scorekeeper. In Christianity, God Himself does this, in the form of Jesus Christ. (John 5:22: "The Father judges no one, but has given all judgment to the Son.")

---

[80]   Huston Smith, *The World's Religions* (San Francisco: Harper, 1991), 19.

Karma: The Universal Scorekeeper

ROUGHLY TRANSLATED, "KARMA" REFERS TO the moral law of cause and effect. This is certainly true in the physical world: an effect can never be its own cause, and for every cause, there will be an effect, either good or bad. Christianity agrees with this in Galatians 6:7: "for whatever a man sows, that he will also reap." See also Proverbs 22:8: "He who sows injustice will reap calamity, and the rod of his fury will fail."

Yet Hinduism takes karma to the point where it says that everything that happens in the affairs of mankind is a result of human action. Everybody gets exactly what they deserve; there is no such thing as randomness. We live in a world without chance or accident. Words like "randomness" just cover up our own ignorance of the true nature of the world.

Hindus also view the world as a training ground where we have the opportunity to develop our highest potentialities. It would seem, then, that a suffering person might learn from the law of karma and correct his or her ways in the future.

Summary

IN THIS SECTION, WE DARED to know God through the eyes of other religious traditions.

What did we find by looking at God in these ways? First, we found out that the differences we see in religious traditions occur in the areas of individual doctrine, dogmatic rituals, ways of worship, symbols, celebrations, and descriptions of God. All this stuff is on the surface of tradition, not in the core of our beliefs and our relationship with God.

If you look beneath the surface of rituals, practices, and doctrine and get to the foundational core of what is believed, these religions are similar in many ways, saying very much the same thing. When you think about it, this would have to be the case if there were indeed, as we Catholics call it, "one true God." Now, the little investigation in this section could be labeled as heresy, stepping out of our religious tradition and its orthodoxy. Well, so what? God cannot be contained in any one tradition. Each religious tradition is limited and therefore has its own version of the "God in the box" syndrome.

As reviled as it may be by some people, heresy is a new frontier to be explored for new understandings of our loving God of all creation, seen and unseen. Heresy is the fountain of religious progress in our age, in my opinion. I think I should send a copy of this book to the pope. Maybe I'll get a free trip to Rome.

We learned just how similar Judaism, Islam, and Christianity really are in their core teachings and their common roots. These three great religious traditions are truly brothers in the worship of God, for they all worship the very same God. All the surface stuff is very different, but beneath all that are the same God, the same core values, and so on.

We learned that all religions preach peace and love, and that the word "Islam" can be translated as "submission to the will of God." Other translations include the word "peace," such as "being in peace, committing oneself to God." There is a parallel to be seen here with the two greatest commandments, as identified by Jesus: to love God first with all your heart, mind, and soul; and to love your neighbor as yourself. Look for these similarities and you will find very many of them.

Buddha preached a tradition that addressed the human condition and how to eliminate suffering. He did not worship a God. But he did acknowledge a higher power. All the things he said, our God could have said too. He said nothing incompatible with Christianity if you look under the surface and get past the terminology.

Throughout this section, I pointed out where all the other religious traditions were saying the same thing by including specific biblical references and what the other tradition had to say. The Hindus have many gods and paths. That doesn't seem very Christian, but consider that the multiple gods could be interpreted as just the different aspects of our ineffable and mysterious infinite Christian God.

So, finally, human beings are all united, as we will see in Chapter 14 (the science chapter), and we are all united far more than we think in our religious traditions. Isn't that wonderful? Leave it to God to unify us humans without us really realizing it. But God is guiding all of us to this conclusion, and what a happy day that will be.

CHAPTER 14

Science and God: Friends or Enemies?

Science and God: Two Sides of the Same Coin?

IN OUR SOCIETY TODAY, MOST people view religion and science as completely separate from each other. At times, open conflict emerges between the two when a new discovery challenges a previous scientific or religious belief. But the main theme that I propose here is that science and religion are in reality two sides of the same coin.

Science is the study of the laws that govern our physical universe. By examining the universe, you can learn a lot about its creator. Science requires that its observations be expressed in measurements. If you cannot measure an attribute, it does not fit into the scientific paradigm. On the other hand, few ideas in religion are measurable. Yet science and religion both are inexorably related in ways that we are just beginning to understand. As Albert Einstein said, "Science without religion is lame. Religion without science is blind."

The word "theology" refers to the study of God. If God created the universe, it reflects His design and plan for all things physical and spiritual. Science can only study the physical part, but I believe that unity exists between the physical world, the spiritual world, and God. God does transcend our universe; He is unlimited and ineffable. But I believe that God participates in the physical world, continually speaking to us through it. I believe He also uses the spiritual world to guide us within our inner being. So in this sense, God is as much a part of the physical universe as we are, while also existing in the spiritual world and far beyond.

Therefore, we should coin a new word that combines the study of God, the study of our spirit, and the study of the physical world. Think of these three as a sort of continuum, all related in ways that we do not yet understand.

This new word that I propose is *"existentology."*

Existentology: The study of all existence, including the study of the relationships of all things physical; the human psyche; religion; the relationship between God and man; the spiritual; man's place within all creation; and so on.

Today, the line between science and the mystical or spiritual is starting to blur. Two distinct spheres of study no longer exist. The previous antagonism between the two disciplines is weakening with each discovery by leading astrophysicists and cosmologists.

For hundreds of years, the debate has raged between science and theology. Science says it cannot prove the existence of God; well, of course not. Science does not address God or define Him in measurable ways. There is nothing to measure against, just as fish cannot know they are wet. But God created the physical laws that govern the physical universe, and He actively participates within His creation. To say otherwise would mean that God could never answer prayer, for example. I say that this ongoing battle between God and science is obsolete.

The study of science is merely the study of one aspect of God and His participation in the universe as creator and designer of the physical laws science pursues. Stephen Hawking and other leading physicists are pursuing the Theory of Everything. (The documentary *The Elegant Universe* offers more information on the study of everything, if you are interested in learning more.[81]) It is said that if we can produce a mathematical model of everything, we will know the mind of God. Well, I disagree; God transcends everything man can study and understand. But as a person with a scientific background, I know that the study of science is a very worthy endeavor. To me, such efforts are part of existentology. As we learn more about quantum physics, for example, we can learn more about the underlying intentions of God.

[81]   "The Elegant Universe," NOVA, 2003. Can be purchased through Amazon or other sources.

For example, why does God allow a particle to be in two places at the same time? Yes, this does happen. (I have provided a complete reference section at the back of the book. For more on this scientific concept, read *What The Bleep Do We Know?!*) What is the theology behind it? If we study both science and theology from the perspective that both influence our lives, I think we will discover that they are deeply related. At this point, however, mankind has just begun to ask the right questions.

Man Cannot Perceive the Universe as It Really Is—How Can That Be?

WE ALL KNOW WE LIVE on Earth. It's the third planet from the sun, and there are nine planets (unless you agree that poor Pluto is no longer a planet, as the International Astronomical Union concluded in 2008). We revolve around the sun once a year, and we experience four seasons because the axis of Earth is tilted 23.5 degrees from our orbital plane around the sun. This planet includes all sorts of biological life, including us. We know that our solar system is only one of many in our galaxy, which is called the Milky Way. We know that each galaxy contains billions of stars, and the universe contains billions of galaxies; it's a big universe. Out in space is a vacuum with nothing in it at all—just empty nothingness ... but not really. Some people know that the universe is expanding and that our sun will become a red giant and consume Earth before dying in about five billion years. If humanity hasn't escaped Earth by then, I can only imagine that the sunblock industry will take off. Actually, our ionosphere would go first, Earth would heat up to levels that would kill all life on the planet, and the oceans would evaporate into space, leaving a dead, dry planet. As the sun approached, it would begin to envelop Earth in the outer reaches of its gases, eroding Earth away into nothing. The sun will have already consumed Mercury and Venus before consuming Earth. Mars will also be consumed.

Experience tells us that we live in a solid world; if I drop a computer on my foot, it will hurt. We know that matter can exist in three states (if you don't include plasma): solid, liquid, and gas. We have all heard that matter is made of things called atoms, which are very small and combine in many different ways to give us all the different substances we find on Earth.

To get an idea about the relative sizes of objects in our universe, I recommend the mind-boggling "Powers of 10" Web page.[82] I suggest you click on the manual button on the site, as it goes too fast for my taste.

---

[82] http://micro.magnet.fsu.edu/primer/java/scienceopticsu/powersof10/

Sir Isaac Newton gave us the three laws of motion. A body at rest will stay at rest; that certainly describes me on the couch. The second law states that if you give me a shove, I will resist the force you apply. Give me a harder shove, and I will resist more. Overcome my resistance, and I will accelerate to a certain speed. Shove me harder, and I will accelerate faster and attain a higher speed. Mathematically, it's simple: $F = MA$, or "force equals mass times acceleration." The third law says that I will resist your force with an amount of my own force that is exactly equal to the force you apply to me to get going and cut the lawn. These laws are the ones we live with every day; they are so natural to us that we hardly think about them.

Reality May Seem That Way … But It Isn't

WE LIVE IN A WEIRD universe. What we see around us is not what actually is—we cannot perceive physical reality, as it actually exists! What? Yes, we perceive only a small part of the picture. How can that be?

We are limited by our five senses. In our daily lives, we become so accustomed to using our senses that we accept reality as being the itty-bitty picture painted by our senses. We rely on this understanding for everything we do. What you see, hear, smell, taste, and touch has many more characteristics than our senses lead us to believe, but that's okay—it works, and God meant it to be this way for our benefit.

We do not directly perceive the world. Most people have never heard this before, but it is true. Rather, our brains interpret information sent from our limited senses. For example, when we open our eyes, we can only see a very small range of wavelengths in the electromagnetic spectrum. Our eyes can perceive the rainbow of colors and the intensity of light, but that is it! Uncountable wavelengths exist beyond our perception, including infrared light. For that matter, did you know that the image that gets focused on our retinas is upside down? Yes, upside down. Our brain flips the image, making the world right side up again. It does this 100 percent of the time without us even noticing.

Think for a moment what life would be like if our eyes were sensitive to infrared wavelengths, where heat is detected. We would be able to see just as well at night as we do in the daylight; our cars would not need headlights. The lightbulb industry would not exist, and we would clearly see the expulsion of other people's bodily gases—no more blaming the dog! This is probably why God did not allow infrared vision in us.

Our other four senses are limited as well, and our failure to accurately perceive reality does not stop there. Our life experiences and culture also play a role in how we interpret information. Our scientific analysis is certainly affected by these limitations, although scientists do make heroic efforts to take objective measurements using what is called the scientific method.

If you are not a mystic or scientist, you will be amazed at what I am going to tell you next about creation and man's latest understandings of what creation is really like, both from a religious perspective and a scientific perspective. But first, let's briefly review what the major religious traditions say about the physical universe and how it got started.

The Creation Story Across the Major Religions

THE WORLD'S DIFFERENT RELIGIONS EXPLAIN the universe and where it came from in seven main ways. All but two of these invoke the concept of a Creator or God that got the whole thing started. After that, differences arise regarding God's relationship to His creation. The seven understandings, culled from at least twenty-six different religious traditions, are as follows:

1. The universe was always here and is uncreated at any point in time.
2. God created the universe out of nothing.
3. God created the universe, but it is separate from Him.
4. God created the universe, and He is the source of life in it.
5. God created the universe from a pre-existing substance.
6. God created the universe as it came out of Him, therefore it is divine.
7. The universe is the result of causal actions. [83]

Now we can argue all day long regarding the above seven understandings, but the truth is that no one on this planet really knows for sure. When someone says the universe is one big illusion, that is a fair statement. But when people get into arguments about creation and what started it all, they are saying, "My illusion is better than your illusion." Even the pope doesn't know for sure—besides, there is probably an eighth idea out there that is closer to the truth of God than these seven. Who knows?

---

[83] http://www.thetruelight.net/pillars/pillar1.htm

Also, does anyone really accept that if you believe one way but turn out to be wrong, God will deny you His unconditional love? When you stand at the gates of heaven, will St. Peter tell you, "Boy, did you ever screw things up regarding where the universe came from. Off to hell you go! Heaven calling Satan: I got another one for you!" Of course not! Stretch your spiritual wings and be open to new ideas regarding creation. If you want, accept the proposition that all of these ideas have some truth to them.

Someone might think you are a heretic. So what? The Church branded people who realized the earth is not flat as heretics, but they were right. I personally believe that God is real and that He created the universe, both seen and unseen, in some manner that we do not yet understand. Frankly, we will never know all there is to know, for then we would be God. However, God is always willing to guide all of us toward His truths, including the creation of the universe. Ask Him in prayer; you won't get any mathematical equations in return, but He may infuse you with subtle feelings about where everything came from.

Say this little prayer:

> Dear Father and Mother in heaven,
> I do not have a clue where the universe came from.
> I think You were involved but do not know how.
> Guide me to Your truth, for I open my heart to you.
> Amen.

This little prayer will please God our Father and Mother immensely. Why? Because it shows that you are seeking truth and looking to Them for guidance. This is the most God can expect from any of us. Don't ever feel bound to one doctrine about creation, for nobody knows for sure.

I think I should mention that our astrophysicists have created solid mathematical models of the universe going back to when it was only a small fraction of a second old. However, at the instant of creation, the models break down. We have excellent ideas of what the universe was like just after creation, but not during—and certainly not before. However, the very latest advances in cosmology have introduced the idea of M Theory, where M stands for membrane. Each membrane is infinitely long, but only 10^{-20} millimeters thin. That is billions of times thinner than a human hair. According to M Theory, the pre-existing "branes" sometimes collide—

possibly creating the big bang. But this theory has not been proven, so the seven theories of universal creation remain.

Let's take a look at a few of the main religious traditions and their approach to the creation of the universe.

Buddhism

BUDDHA AVOIDED THE CONCEPT OF a creator. His theology centered on his Four Noble Truths and the Eightfold Path to nirvana. Thus, Buddhism as it was originally conceived maintains that there is no God as we know it. Three things determine the nature of reality: impermanence, suffering, and insubstantiality; nothing has an enduring essence. The universe was not created, but it is not permanent, either. All things in reality are empty of lasting value and are empty of anything substantive. All things are only appearances to our five senses; all things are only temporary illusions. We will find out later in this chapter that the Buddha was closer to the truth than you might have suspected. As Albert Einstein agreed, "Reality is merely an illusion, albeit a very persistent one."

Christianity

GOD THE FATHER CREATED ALL things out of nothing by speaking commands, such as "Let there be light." This creation process is recounted the book of Genesis. The universe that we see as humans is a result of God's creative powers. God transcends His creation and is not limited by it, yet God can also dwell within creation. Our universe is very big, but limited—unlike God, who is infinite and goes beyond anything humans can perceive. The universe is not an emanation of His being, but exists separately from Him. The physical world is not an illusion, but a gift to humankind to be enjoyed and used for our spiritual advancement.

Some Christian mystics, such as St. Teresa of Avila, have said that reality is an illusion, just like the Buddha. Christians in general, however, would say that the world is real and that we must obey its laws or pay the consequences. Experience tells us that this is correct. However, our universe is constantly changing. Nothing is static, no matter where you look; everything is somewhat different today than it was yesterday. Christianity recognizes that reality does change and that nothing is permanent; in this way, it concurs with Buddhism. Both traditions are closer in belief than the words being used would indicate on the surface.

Hinduism

DIFFERENT CREATION STORIES EXIST SIDE-BY-SIDE in Hinduism, all with different gods playing different roles.

Hindu belief states that creation came from a primordial substance, and that all things in the universe are of one essential substance. This is closer to the truth than most people think; today, scientists in the field of quantum physics are coming to the conclusion that all of the universe can be reduced to one basic building block.

Brahma, the first god in the Hindu triad, created the universe by opening his eyes. When he closes his eyes at the end of each eon, creation ceases to exist; then another cycle begins. Remember, Hindus believe that everything has its cycles. However, not all Hindus believe that Brahma created the universe. Of the three gods in the triad, Brahma, Vishnu, and Shiva, many Hindus believe that Vishnu is the creator.

Hindus believe that there is no absolute beginning point to creation; rather, an infinite number of cycles of creation and dissolution have occurred.

Islam

SIMPLY PUT, MUSLIMS ACCEPT THE first five books of the Bible, including Genesis. Therefore, they believe that God brought creation into existence by the power of the spoken word, just as Christians and Jews do.

Judaism

THE CREATION BELIEFS OF JEWS are basically identical to the Genesis account. I find it extremely interesting that Christianity, Islam, and Judaism all share the same creation story and agree on the vast majority of their stated core theology—yet such hatred exists between members of these religions.

What Does Science Say About Creation?

WE HAVE ALL ASKED WHERE the universe came from; I think that almost everyone has heard of the big bang theory of the creation of the universe. By the way, contrary to its name, the big bang would have been silent; the state of the universe did not allow for sound.

At any rate, according to the big bang theory, an unknown something smaller than an atom burst in order to kick things off.

Discoveries in astronomy and physics have shown us that our universe did actually have a beginning. The latest observations and some really beautiful calculus all point to the universe being about 14 billion years old. Prior to the moment of the big bang, nothing existed—no energy, no space, no matter, no light … nothing at all. (I guess that you and I were somewhere else, enjoying ourselves.) Millions of years later, particles started to form, and for the first time, temperatures cooled enough for light to be possible.

The universe we live in did in fact have a definite starting point, before which it just did not exist. We know this to be true because of the existence of cosmic background radiation in the microwave region of the spectrum. Tune your radio so that the dial is between stations. One percent of that static you hear on your radio is caused by this cosmic background radiation in the microwave portion of the electromagnetic spectrum. Yes, it really does exist, and you can see and hear it for yourself.

Billions of years later, we have the universe as we know it today. The big "bang" was actually a fast inflation in which space itself expanded faster than the speed of light. Why? At that time, light would not exist for millions of years. Galaxies started to form even as they constantly moved farther and farther away from each other. Edwin Hubble (1889–1953) discovered this continual movement back in 1929. To this day, all galaxies are moving away from each other, without traveling from an identifiable central point. Want to see what this is like for yourself? Take a balloon and an ink pen. Put dots all over the balloon; these dots represent the galaxies. Blow up the balloon, and notice that all the dots are moving away from all the other dots. The galaxies in our universe are behaving in much the same way.

These galaxies aren't just moving away from each other; they are actually accelerating away from each other at a faster and faster pace. How is this possible? The culprit appears to be dark energy, which has a repulsive property to it. This gives all celestial bodies the energy to distance themselves from each other at an accelerating rate. Dark energy constitutes about 74 percent of the entire universe.

An Empty Reality

LOOK AROUND YOU. WHAT DO you see? Whatever it is—trees, chairs, walls, desks, your spouse, flowers, or anything physical—it is actually 99.99999999999 percent empty space.

Yep—what appears to be very solid is in fact not even close. The reality we know is almost entirely made of the empty space between atomic particles, such as neutrons and electrons. If that's the case, why can't I walk through walls? Why does it hurt to drop something on my foot? These properties exist because the strong nuclear force of the atoms at the surface of an object repels whatever comes into contact with it.

Think of the north poles of two magnets repelling each other. Now multiply the strength of that force a few billion times and make it work across a very, very short distance—like the width of one or two atoms. When one object comes really close to another, the strong nuclear force repels the surface atoms of the other object with a massive strength that makes both objects seem solid ... but they are definitely not. They are almost all empty space.

This notion applies to our bodies, too. If you removed the empty space from your body, arranging your atomic particles so that no space existed between them, you would fit onto the head of a pin many times. You, like everything else, are almost entirely made up of empty space.

So what is the real nature of the physical stuff around us, including our own bodies? Let's look at a simple hydrogen atom. Its nucleus contains one proton and one neutron, and that nucleus is orbited by one electron. If that nucleus were slightly larger than a major-league baseball, its electron (which is 1,836 times smaller than the nucleus) would then be approximately 15 football fields away—that's 1,500 yards, or slightly less than one mile. That's a lot of empty space between two very small objects; solidarity really is an illusion.

Such an illusion works for us in everyday life, but we now know the truth. Mystics from many religious traditions have been on the right track for thousands of years.

At least protons and neutrons are solid objects, right? No such luck. Protons and neutrons are made up of smaller particles called quarks. Quarks are made in turn by strings, which are unfathomably small. They have different frequencies of vibration and charge. This gives the quark its properties. Quarks combine to form composite particles, like protons and neutrons; the electron that we all learned about in school is actually a quark.

Quarks can be categorized into six different oddly named types of quarks: up, down, charm, strange, top … and, of course, the bottom quark. Quarks have various properties, such as electric charge, color charge, spin, and mass. We can create quarks in our particle accelerators around the world. So the world is made up of quarks, right? Well … not really, if we ask what are quarks made up of. For the sake of brevity, I will attempt to simplify that mathematical explanation, which is called string theory and involves one-dimensional lines vibrating at different frequencies.

So how does all this stuff fit together? Starting at the smallest and least understood level, different combinations of strings vibrating at different frequencies give the quark its properties. Combinations of quarks give subatomic particles, such as the proton, their properties. Different combinations of subatomic particles give the elements their properties. Different combinations of the elements give us molecules. Molecules give matter its properties. The strings of string theory also give us the strong nuclear force, which makes matter solid. Different arrangements of molecules then give us material that we can shape into objects and serves as the basis for all biological organisms, including you and me. The great question is, then, what gives our human molecules life? If, at the basis of everything seen in creation lies nothing but complex arrangements of one-dimensional strings of vibrating energy, how do we end up with life? I will let you ponder that one for a while. You know already that my answer is "God."

Additionally, string theory might explain the four basic forces in the universe: gravitation, strong nuclear force, weak nuclear force, and electromagnetism. This would mean that the universe actually has eleven dimensions, rather than the four we usually think of. As far as we know today, these strings are made of energy and are the foundation of the entire universe that we know. Everything is a form of energy, including the chair you are sitting on—and you, too!

If I am made up of mostly empty space that is an arranged bundle of energy, then why do I find it so hard to lift my butt off the couch? Perhaps this is for our philosophers to answer.

Strings are too small to be observed. Even at the subatomic level, they appear as points to our most powerful scientific instruments, yet they possess the root causes of all properties of matter, including mass and the four basic forces in the universe. Perhaps these strings amount to the primordial substance the Hindus hit upon thousands of years ago.

When we get to the bottom of our physical world, we see that everything made of matter is really not solid; it is mostly empty space, and its most fundamental particle is an infinitesimally small, vibrating line of energy. Einstein once said that matter is just energy waves slowed down. This is the real world as best science can describe it: matter is just another form of energy that vibrates at different frequencies; it only appears solid because of strong nuclear force.

The next time you drop something heavy on your foot, just remember that the falling object is 99.999999 percent empty space. Unfortunately, some of those nasty one-dimensional strings are vibrating a certain way in order to create a particle called the Higgs particle, which gives atoms their mass. When combined with the strong nuclear force that will lend an illusion of solidarity to that falling object, all of this guarantees that your foot will, in fact, hurt.

This explanation is about as weird as it gets; the next time you pick up your coffee cup, what you are actually doing is lifting a formed, large group of stable strings vibrating at different frequencies that give the cup its visible properties. In other words, our perceptions do not amount to underlying reality. Using our five senses alone, without the benefit of mathematical formulas, we certain couldn't have come up with something as bizarre as string theory.

So what is the conclusion of all this? Simply put, God's creation is actually much different and expanded than we perceive. The Buddha was mostly right: all is an illusion. Even Christian mystics say the same thing; this is nothing new. Back in the eighteenth century, Immanuel Kant, a German philosopher, pointed out that we could never truly know the nature of reality as it really is. When one person says to another, "Your reality is not mine," they are not kidding—it's true!

The Universe: Weirder than You Thought

THE UNIVERSE IS NOT ANY less weird on a cosmic scale. In fact, when we zoom out and view the universe as a whole, there seems to have been a robbery. 96 percent of the entire universe is missing. Yes, it actually is missing! We cannot find it even with the most modern astronomical instruments. Many of our smartest scientists have tried to find it and failed. Scientists definitely know it's there, but in no way can we observe it or make any measure of it. Yipes! Who took it? Where is it hiding? That is the big question these days in cosmology or astrophysics. This question has theological implications as well; this is heavy stuff.

What led us to discover that 96 percent of the universe is missing?

Given the amount of matter we could see in the universe, scientists realized that galaxies could not retain their spiral shapes without flying apart. An additional source of gravity had to exist. In the process of that investigation, scientists discovered that we can see only about 4 percent of the universe. About 22 percent of the universe is now thought to be composed of dark matter. The other 74 percent is thought to consist of some kind of dark energy. All this stuff is diffused throughout all of space, and we cannot directly observe it. The scientific hunt is on, but we have not found either the dark energy or dark matter; we call it dark because we cannot see or measure it.

The So-Called Vacuum of Space … Is Full

AND THE WEIRDNESS CONTINUES. WE have all been taught that once you leave Earth's atmosphere, you enter the vacuum of space; nothing at all is there. Recent advances in cosmology and astrophysics have discredited this idea. Throughout the entire universe is something called zero-point energy. Is all the "empty space" between atomic particles really empty? As it turns out, no—this space is clogged with particles and energy.

"Empty space" actually contains enormous quantities of very subtle, very powerful energy. We know that energy increases as we go to subtler levels of matter; nuclear energy is a million times more powerful than chemical energy, for example. Scientists now say there is more energy in one cubic centimeter of empty space (about the size of a marble) than is needed to boil all the oceans of the earth. Although scientists have not been able to measure this sea of immense energy directly, they have seen its effects.[84] Other scientists have estimated that one cubic centimeter of empty space contains the energy equivalent of 10^{94} grams of matter. Compare this to our sun, which radiates the energy equivalent of only 10^{12} grams of matter each second to provide us with heat.[85] Empty space beats out the sun by a large margin … but empty space's energy cancels itself, disappearing quickly, whereas the sun's energy does not.

---

[84]   William Arntz, Betsy Chasse, and Mark Vincente, *What the Bleep Do We Know!?* (Heath Communications, 2005).

[85]   Fred Alan Wolf, *The Spiritual Universe* (Moment Point Press, 1996).

This energy results from a very dense sea of particles coming into existence in space, then disappearing again so quickly that they cannot be measured. The next time you look into the night sky, realize that you are not seeing empty space, as your senses tell you. Rather, you are looking at a sea of high-energy particles coming into and out of existence.

What you thought the universe to be is not even close to the way things really are. Remember what Einstein said: "Reality is merely an illusion, albeit a very persistent one."

Everything is Connected … Surprise?

MORE WEIRDNESS STILL. ALL OF creation is unified. Everything affects everything else, and distance does not matter too much. Now, you would think that if the distances between galaxies are increasing each day at a faster and faster rate, we would be getting more and more out of touch with other parts of the universe. Not so fast—it appears that at the subatomic or quantum level, at least, every part of the universe seems to know what other parts of the universe are doing. Somehow, every particle in the universe is linked in a way that supersedes our understanding of space and time. Something is going on that the scientific community cannot explain.

Quantum entanglement has been proven scientifically to be true. Quantum entanglement refers to the idea that subatomic particles, like electrons, are connected in a manner that scientists do not understand. Some particles are intertwined in some way such that if something happens to one particle, the other will somehow know that and adjust itself instantly—no matter how far away these particles are from one another. In the laboratory, "You arrange to have two particles created at the same time, which means they would be entangled. Then you shoot them off to opposite sides of the universe. Then you do something to one particle to change its state (spin perhaps); the other particle instantaneously changes to adopt a corresponding state that rebalances things. Instantaneously!"[86] Somehow, both particles remain linked, and each particle knows the state of the other. When one particle changes, that information travels to the other particle infinitely faster than the speed of light—yes, faster than the speed of light. This really irritated Albert Einstein, who referred to

[86]   William Arntz, Betsy Chasse, and Mark Vicente, *What the Bleep Do We Know!?* (Heath Communications, 2005).

quantum entanglement as "spooky action at a distance." He meant this as an insult.

Human Entanglement

I BELIEVE THAT THE PRINCIPLES of quantum entanglement apply to human beings as well. I have been involved in it. So many stories exist in which people sense events happening far away, even when normal physics says that this cannot be possible. I believe that all human beings are connected in deep ways that we are yet to discover. A union between all of us lies at the deepest level of human existence.

We enter the mystical realm when discussing premonitions and other gut feelings. Physical law is not being violated when mystical things happen; rather, the laws of the universe are working, but we just do not understand them yet. We do not have to understand something for it to exist; nor does something have to seem rational or believable to us in order to exist.

The following is a true story of human entanglement. I was there; I actually was part of it.

During a hospital visit near the end of her life, my beloved Marilyn got so upset about her hospitalization that she stopped acting rationally. As the doctors arrived early in the morning, she started to rip out her intravenous tubes. Since I was sleeping overnight in her room, I woke up to witness the whole thing. We got her calmed down after about ten minutes.

About twenty minutes later, my cell phone rang; it was my mother calling. She was upset, as she had just had a vision of a very agitated Marilyn ripping out her tubes. Oh, how right she was! My mother's vision had played out in reality at the exact same time. My mother lives ten miles away from the hospital, but a change in Marilyn's state of existence caused my mother to have a vision of what was happening. Human entanglement is a common phenomenon in our world.

Going beyond this little story, I believe that every human being on the planet is entangled in some fashion with every other human being. Our actions affect everyone else in ways we cannot fathom right now.

I can tell you that I remain wonderfully entangled with Marilyn even though she passed away some time ago. I have experienced too many mystical events to pretend otherwise.

The Unity of the Universe

ACCORDING TO TIMOTHY FREKE IN his book *The Wisdom of the Christian Mystics,*

> Mysticism is the spiritual essence of Christianity. The great Christian mystics, however, have often found themselves horribly persecuted as heretics by the established Churches for their outrageous claims and idiosyncratic ways. The mystics are not content to have a relationship with God via priests and institutions, but look inside themselves to know God directly. When they do, God is revealed as an all-embracing love that unites the universe into one indivisible whole. In communion with God, the mystics no longer experience themselves as separate individuals but as expressions of the Oneness. God is the only reality. God is everything. God does everything. This mystical vision is not a psychological anomaly: it is the natural state. Human beings fail to experience it only because they believe themselves to be separate from God, when in fact He is their very essence. All mystical practices are designed to dispel this pernicious illusion of separateness.[87]

Over the history of mankind, we have always assumed that mankind lives in the universe, separate from it but dependent on it. Our connection with the universe and earth was considered a physical one. But over the last twenty years, scientific experiments point to a much deeper connection between mankind, the physical universe, and God.

Okay, fasten your seatbelts, and unleash your imaginations. We are going for a short ride through quantum physics in order to examine how human beings are central players in the universe as we know it.

First, let's consider poor Erwin Schroedinger's cat. Erwin was a German physicist in the 1920s. In 1924, he described the following experiment: Put the cat and lots of food into a box along with a vial of poison attached to a mechanism that may or may not release it. A radioactive particle that has a half life of a thousand years will do nicely along with a detector hooked up to the mechanism that will release the poison. Keep the box closed, so no one knows whether the cat is dead or alive.

---

[87] The Wisdom of the Christian Mystics, Journey Editions, April 15, 1998.

From a quantum perspective, the cat occupies two states of existence at the same time: dead and alive. The cat will stay in these two states until an observer opens the box to see whether the cat was poisoned; the act of opening the box collapses the two possibilities into one certainty. Without the observer, the reality of one state for the cat will not occur. Thus, the human observer becomes a critical participant in the creation of the reality of whether the cat is dead or alive. Fortunately for the cat in question, this experiment was never actually carried out.

The same concept holds true in the world of atomic particles. Since electrons exist in a probability cloud around the nucleus of the atom, we have no idea where an electron is at any given moment in time. Think of a baseball surrounded by a dense fog; the baseball is the nucleus of the atom, and the electron could be anywhere in that fog. But as soon as an observer measures the location of the electron, all other probabilities fall away, and the electron becomes a negatively charged point of matter in one position. An observer is required to create this reality; again, humans are necessary to this process.

"In this view," writes Brian Breen in *The Fabric of the Cosmos*, "when we measure the electron's position we are not measuring an objective preexisting feature of reality. Rather the act of measurement is deeply enmeshed in creating the very reality it is measuring."[88] This is heavy stuff; by observing things, humans participate in the creation of them. Fritjof Capra concludes, "The electron does not have objective properties independent of my mind."[89]

In other words, our human minds are inexorably intertwined with the creation of reality from a blur of possibilities. Our minds set reality in stone. Before we get to the theological implications of all this stuff, I will end this section with the following experiment, which has been performed hundreds of times around the world and prompted the same results in each case.

A certain random-number experiment that has been conducted hundreds of times over the past four decades. A random number generator is used that only produces sequences of random bits of ones and zeros, like flipping a coin. The experiment is that you simply ask somebody to press a button on the generator that produces two hundred bits of random ones and zeros, but you ask them to try to make it produce more one bits than zero bits. This establishes human intention.

---

[88] The Fabric of the Cosmos, Brian Greene, Vintage, February 8, 2005
[89] Ibid.

Did this human intention affect the outcome? Overall, the answer is yes, it does matter. Somehow, human intention is correlated with the operation of the output of the random-number generators. If you wish for more ones, somehow, the generators will produce more ones.

The odds are fifty thousand to one that pure chance caused the appearance of a correlation between human intention and outcome where no correlation actually exists.[90] Now, don't get too excited, as the effect is small and would not help you one bit in Las Vegas. But if the existence of this effect does not weird you out, we can take this discussion to the next level.

During the O. J. Simpson trial, scientists decided to measure the effect, if any, of the shared simultaneous coherence of millions of minds. These researchers set up random number generators to operate during the highly publicized event. As it turned out, these number generators twice showed significant aberrations in statistical probability. Twice, the generators produced a spike away from the ordinary 50/50 odds. The first occurred when the camera in the courtroom was turned on; that produced a spike that had one thousand-to-one odds of being random. The second was when the verdict was read; this was a much larger spike, and all five generators around the world recorded it. For some reason beyond what we understand, when millions of people focused on the same thing, the generators deviated greatly away from their typical behavior at the precise time that everyone was focused on the same thing. Does this not point to the universe being connected in ways that we do not understand? Is there not a unity among everything, including people and devices, that we just do not understand?[91]

Because of experiments like these, the Global Consciousness Project was started. To learn more, visit http://noosphere.princeton.edu.

Carl Jung

CARL JUNG WAS A SWISS psychiatrist who founded analytical psychology. He is now believed to be the first modern psychologist to state that the human psyche is "by nature religious" and to study this concept at length. Such an idea was unheard-of during his time and not well received by his peers.

---

[90] Ibid.
[91] Ibid.

Regarding the preceding discussion about mind over matter, Jung coined the idea of a collective unconscious or subconscious. The idea is that, at the deepest level of our subconscious, we are all connected in some manner that science does not yet understand. Now we are getting into the realm of theology and metaphysics. Jung distinguished the collective unconscious from the personal subconscious particular to each human being. The collective unconscious is also known as "a reservoir of the experiences of our species." The peoples of a society and humanity share collective experiences in general. Carl Jung, a student of Freud, discussed these ideas in the 1920s and early 1930s.

What Conclusions Can We Make about Science and God?

AFTER MANY YEARS OF STUDY, I've received my bachelor's degree in chemistry, a master's degree in business, and a master's degree in pastoral ministry; I have become a Reiki master; and I have arrived at the following conclusions as a result of these studies.

The physical universe is far different than our senses lead us to believe, and we can never know the universe as it really is. Neither Buddha nor Immanuel Kant used scientific instruments of any kind to conclude that reality is an illusion. Yet they described what modern science is just beginning to prove. My question is, how did these two people come to this conclusion? How many of their realizations were guided by God? The Christian answer would be that these men arrived at their conclusions through God's ongoing revelation of Himself.

Another question is, why would the God of truth create a reality that presents itself to us in a false way? If you look around you, the answer is staring back at you: this reality that we perceive with our five humble senses has been created for us—and for a purpose. Thing are the way they are supposed to be, made perfectly for us so that we might come here and experience various lessons in order to advance spiritually.

The universe is a school of sorts that has been constructed for us so we can take actions, make decisions, and live through the good or bad result. Physical creation also limits us so we must learn to be resourceful—and, through the scarcity of the world and all its upheavals, learn that we must help others. This realization forms a bond between people.

The challenges of physical existence are full of lessons for us individually and as members of a society. Yes, God knew exactly what He was doing when He created a universe that hides its true character from us and thus can teach us what we need to know, so we can become spiritually strong and develop a love for our fellow man across the world. All this is in front of everyone; sadly, few people realize it.

Additionally, the physical universe cannot eternally hurt us. If we are immortal beings as God has said, we will not be destroyed or eternally damaged, no matter what happens here. We will certainly suffer while here; everyone does. (In fact, that is the First Noble Truth in Buddhism: all is suffering.) But it is through suffering that we really learn; suffering has the power to change us in a positive manner. The construction of this physical illusion gives it the power to teach us lessons that we will carry back to heaven with us.

Heaven is hidden from us for a reason; it is so beautiful and filled with joy that it would distract us from the lessons we are to learn on earth. My wife is waiting for me there right now; this she promised before she passed away early in 2009. Now, if you really screw up in this life (and we all know a few people who have), you will be sent right back here to try again.

Do the physical world and heaven overlap sometimes? Is the veil that prevents us from seeing heaven like a concrete wall that offers us no chance to sense what is on the other side? The answer is no. Certain people have gifts from God that allow them to see certain aspects of heaven and its spiritual residents. I personally know three people who have such gifts, the specifics of which are unique to each one. God has given these gifts to a few people so they can help the rest of us. God has also given us spirit guides; Christians call these spirits guardian angels.

Even if we are not one of the especially gifted people who can gain great insight into heaven, each and every one of us can communicate with the other side. Love is the most powerful force in the universe, and it flows through the veil unrestricted. I dearly love my wife, Marilyn; I talk to her every day, and I can tell you from my personal experience that she visits me fairly often. I can actually feel her feelings and understand what she says to me. Our ability to do this is based on the deep love we share. Most people don't believe such things are possible, because they have allowed this mystical gift to become dormant within them, but that gift can always be reactivated. If you use your gift, it will grow stronger and become easier to use. If you are interested in developing your spiritual gifts, a very good book to start with is *Contacting Your Spirit Guide* by Sylvia Browne.

Science has educated all of us to believe the universe exists in four dimensions, the fourth being time. More recently, science has advanced the idea that at least eleven dimensions might exist. These extra seven dimensions are hidden from us; is this where heaven is hiding? I will let you ponder that one.

Not only do humans observe the universe, but we unavoidably affect what matter does. It seems we are inexorably part of the overall cosmic picture, whether we know that or not. Physical laws will operate even if we are not aware of them. We are ingrained within a seamless universe that we previously considered separate from us.

We humans are immortal sparkles of light who are here to learn and love as part of our God the Father and God the Mother. We are only starting to understand that which has been true before the universe was even created 14 billion years ago. So, let your light sparkle brightly, and pursue as much knowledge about creation and God as you can. Your spiritual life will be enhanced, and your knowledge of this universe and God's place in it will deepen.

PART III

Hope for All of Us

CHAPTER 15

Prayer: What Good Is It?

Just What Is Prayer?

IF YOU ARE TALKING TO God, then you are praying; it's just about that simple. Prayer is a sacred act of love for God—no matter what form it takes; no matter how long or short it is; no matter how simple it is; and no matter its content. If you hold God in your thoughts, that too is a form of prayer, for you are in communion with Him. One published definition of prayer reads as follows: "Prayer is responding to God by thought and deeds, with or without words." It goes on to say that Christian prayer is a response to God the Father through Jesus Christ in the power of the Holy Spirit.[92]

Prayer is probably the most powerful thing you can do while on this earth. It affects not only you and your life, but also other people's lives in ways that you may not even anticipate. You must pray seriously and reverently, with great love for God, yourself, and all other people. Prayer acknowledges that you are indeed not alone—that there is a God and He does hear your prayers, along with the prayers of every other human being on the planet. In this and many other ways, all of humanity is deeply connected.

---

[92] Thomas Keating and Basil Pennington, *Centering Prayer* (Continuum Publishing Company, 1998), 52.

In general, though, what does prayer say about God and about us? First, we see the immediacy of God. He is here right now—always has been and always will be. God knows all about us already. Matthew 10:30 says: "But even the hairs of your head are all numbered." God even knows the number of hairs on our head. He loves us unconditionally and knows each of us better than we know ourselves. Regardless of your feelings about your relationship with God, He always welcomes prayer.

You can pray anywhere and in any way you choose; God is everywhere. Prayer reveals an apparent duality: God is both within us and is also separate from us. This so-called duality actually represents the uninterrupted continuum of God's presence. We, His children, are actually part of this sacred continuum; we have eternal life within God, and nothing can change that. Yes, you and I are immortal. But how you spend eternity depends on you—your thoughts, intentions, and actions.

As I have mentioned, I was raised a Roman Catholic. As a kid, I thought that praying meant dragging out my Sunday Missal and reading the ritualistic prayers in it. Praying was what I did at Sunday Mass or in school while wearing my little blue tie and white shirt. Prayer could also serve as penance for the naughty. In other words, prayer was what I did when I was told, whether because it was simply rote behavior or because I had been bad.

Oh, how wrong all that was! Prayer is never a punishment, and it is not just for Sunday. Prayer can happen anytime at all and serves as a priceless form of divine communication with God. God has made it simple to communicate with Him—no little blue tie required. All you have to do is to simply clear your mind of worldly distractions, settle down in a peaceful state of mind, and speak to God from your heart.

The first time I heard this, I was surprised. But the more I think about the simplicity of prayer, the more sense it makes. Prayer is actually a response to God; He is seeking you. Your felt need to talk to God is the result of Him reaching out to you, inviting you into communication and communion with Him.

Within each of us is our sacred heart. Carl Jung said that God lives at the center of our spiritual being. Our sacred heart is a very sacred place within us; there, we are inexorably connected to God as one of his children. This will never change. True prayer takes place in the holy chamber of our sacred heart. It is a place of peace and solitude—a place so powerfully connected to God that all you have to do is enter there for prayer to occur. It does not matter what you say, if you say anything at all. Entering your holy chamber is a sacred act, and your presence there with your Father is the prayer.

Prayer begins with the silencing of our busy minds and acknowledges the felt awareness of God. The intellectual mind we all use for day-to-day activities can never become aware of God; our minds were not designed for that.

Our true self exists within our sacred heart, stripped of all the false identities we use in this world: father, husband, chemist, pilot, flight instructor, computer marketing executive, mentor, investor, Reiki practitioner, and so on. All of these identities are false; they do not represent the true me, which can only be found in my sacred heart. Jesus suggested that his apostles to go into a closet or another quiet place of solitude and silence in order to pray. This can help a person enter his or her sacred heart. This sacred heart "is a very special place within your beingness and you can know when you have entered it by the complete stillness therein. Within your Sacred Heart there is a sacredness and purity like a blanket of new fallen snow."[93]

Through prayer, you will discover that all of God's children are connected through one Holy Spirit:

> The One Holy Spirit is a living intelligence beyond all comprehension, which retains all memory and holds all potential. Through prayer and meditation in which you acknowledge the oneness of spirit you can receive great ideas and wondrous messages about your life and your future. All you have to do is ask … In communing with the One Spirit the key is to surrender and to listen. In that mode of receptivity, The Holiness of the Spirit will descend upon you and give you nourishment and guidance.[94]

I can, from personal experience, testify to you that the above is true. During the five years of my wife's battle with cancer, we struggled with four major surgeries, five minor surgeries, twelve one-day hospital procedures, four years of chemotherapy, and literally hundreds of doctor and hospital visits. My sweetie almost died on three separate occasions last year. She entered hospice, but lived long enough to resume treatments. It has taken

---

[93] Glenda Green, *Love Without End: Jesus Speaks* (Spiritus Publishing, 1999), 95.
[94] Ibid., 229.

a terrible emotional toll on both of us. But I have persevered out of love for Marilyn; somehow, I know that God put me in this situation for a reason.

One day, the whole family was gone. Marilyn was feeling well enough for my daughters to take her to the mall in the wheelchair. I stayed home alone, feeling rotten emotionally. I went to my favorite chair by the window and bathed in the sun's warmth. Somehow, to me, the sun has a divine feel to it. I began to pray, lying on my side and looking out the window. Anxiety and panic threatened to overwhelm me; such feelings haunted me. After a number of years as a caregiver, your ability to withstand the stress begins to wear thin, or at least this was true in my case. My emotions that day were off the scale; tears flooded from my eyes, and I cried out to God to please "just hug me. Just hug me, dear God, so I don't feel so alone, isolated, and abandoned. Oh, God, I know you are here, but I cannot feel you!" I always felt the worst when I could not sense the presence of God.

But then, after a few minutes of shivering and crying, I sensed the presence of a divine being descending from above and to my right. The divine being slowly descended onto my right shoulder; I could feel it inside of me as well as on my shoulder. I could not see anything with my eyes, but I could see this formless being with my mind. I asked this being if I could see it with my eyes, but I received no response. The being stayed with me for a little while, then dissolved away from me.

After this visit, I regained some emotional stability. My crying stopped, and I felt well enough to pray normally while enjoying the warmth of the sun. After a while, I felt strong enough to go do other things in our home. Was this the Holy Spirit? I do not know. But I do know without reservation that God answered my prayer for a hug that day, and for that I am forever thankful to our Lord. He does hear us when we pray. His response just depends on what we need, not what we want.

Healing Prayers and the Holy Spirit

EACH OF US SHOULD HAVE a daily prayer practice, no matter how long it may be and no matter what its contents. While Marilyn was ill, one hour each evening before I went to bed, I'd turn out all the lights, and light a single candle in my bedroom, and get comfortable in my chair. To me, the single candle represents the light of God in my life, lighting the world. Sometimes I would listen to meditation music at a very low volume— mostly not, though. A major feature of my prayer practice in the evening was to send Reiki healing energy to Marilyn remotely from my bedroom to the adjacent room where she has already gone to sleep. Sending God's life energy across space is just as effective as if I had my hands on her during a traditional healing session.

Early in my prayers, I always invite the Holy Spirit to "come about me, surround me, and enter my being with Your love and guidance." Often at this point in my prayers, I am overcome by a strong and extremely pleasant tingling sensation that starts at the top of my head. It travels down my body, all the way to my feet. This tingling wave comprises such good feelings that I wish it would never stop. Its presence embodies a definite sacred character as the multiple waves of blissful tingling make their way through my physical body, usually in three strong waves. Once, the sensations were so intense and full of ecstasy that I told our Father that He could take me to heaven that very instant. At that time, I was not at all sure whether I was in my body or not, for I was not aware of anything in the room. But like all things on this earth, the sensations fade away all too soon, and my Reiki prayers continued for the benefit of sending life energy to Marilyn.

I tell you this story to illustrate the realness of the presence of the Holy Spirit and how accessible He is to us if we surrender ourselves to Him and listen to what He has to tell us. The Holy Spirit does not appear each and every time I perform Reiki healings. I cannot feel His presence all the time. As my spiritual advisor always says, "God gives to us what we need and not all the things we want." So even though I would like visits of the Holy Spirit to bless my body with these wonderful blissful sensations all the time, that does not happen. They occur when God thinks I need it for reasons He sees.

By the way, He will not use English, and your ears will not hear voices. Rather, He will infuse thoughts and feelings directly into your heart and mind. I have been blessed to have had many of these humbling experiences with the Holy Spirit. God is real. The Holy Spirit is real, too, and they both are immediately accessible to all of us. God and the Holy Spirit are among us right now, for that matter. Think about how wonderful that is. I am not special; I am just like everyone else. All this is available to everyone, not just me. Jesus said that if you seek, you will find. I actively sought to become a Reiki healer and am disciplined in its practice, resulting in these experiences. I am sure that other healers have their own unique experiences. Be active in your prayer life, and subtle spiritual experiences will show up in your life, too.

Other Kinds of General Prayer: One Size Does Not Fit All

ONE THING IS FOR CERTAIN: there is no best way to pray. They are all good. All of us have different personalities and are at different points in our spiritual journey. Over the years, different types of people have found various kinds of prayer helpful. Certain kinds of prayer feel more natural to certain personality types.

Fundamental to all types of prayer is complete honesty. We must bring our true selves to prayer, warts and all, acknowledging our faults. This does not mean we accept our faults; we just have to recognize their existence and ask God to help us with them. God meets with us wherever we are on our spiritual journey. Everyone is worthy to pray to God; there are no requirements. In pastoral ministry school, it was said, "Prayer is bringing as much as I know of myself to as much as I know of God." Prayer then becomes an honest conversation with God.

We also need to quietly listen for His responses to us. We must learn how to get past the clatter and banging of our own stream of thoughts and feelings by becoming silent in a quiet place where we can hear the subtle, loving movement of God within our hearts.

The principal kinds of prayer are intercession, penitence, petition, thanksgiving for His blessings, and adoration. Basically, we are either praying for someone else, praying for forgiveness from God, praying for ourselves to receive a blessing for something, giving thanks for blessings we have, or just saying "I love you" to God.

Prayer for Different Personalities: There Is One for You, Too

CHESTER P. MICHAEL AND MARIE C. Norrisey matched different personality types with the different kinds of prayer. We all have different personalities that make us unique; no news there. The news is that certain forms of prayer naturally lend themselves better to certain personalities. There is a prayer type that fits you the best; this is good news! This wonderful work allows people to pray to God in a way that feels more natural to them.[95]

Each of us perceives the world differently and processes the information we get from the world differently, too. God made us this way, along with the life experiences we have gathered along the way. As individuals, we do

---

[95]   Chester P. Michael and Marie C. Norrisey, *Prayer and Temperament* (Open Door Publishing, 1991).

not even notice the manner in which we take in data from the world and process it for future reference according to our individual temperament.

We choose from four pairs of preferences when we interact with our world. You can lump all the people in the world into one or the other of each pair listed below. Briefly, the preferences that constitute our different temperaments are as follows, though these preference represent a spectrum, not a black-or-white option. Each of us tends to lean one way or the other.

Extrovert vs. Introvert: The extrovert uses the outer world as a source of the psychic energy he or she needs to live. The introvert, however looks to the inner world of concepts, the spirit, and other inner resources to capture the energy to live.

Sensing vs. Intuition: Sensing people rely on the five senses to inform them about the external physical world. Intuitive people, however, envision new possibilities in both the external and internal worlds of spirit and ideas.

Thinking vs. Feeling: The thinking person uses data, logic, and methodological processes to arrive at a decision. The feeling person, on the other hand, centers on more subjective personal values, along with the effects any decision may have upon themselves and other people.

Judging vs. Perceiving: Judging people center on making assessments about how things should be according to a structure that they feel will make things work. On the other hand, perceiving people are mostly concerned with getting more data and information without necessarily getting to a rock-solid conclusion. They are more flexible and open in their thinking than the judging people.

Briefly, using the above terminology, there are four basic temperaments:

Sensing-Judging, or SJ

Intuitive-Feeling, or NF

Sensing-Perceiving, or SP

Intuitive-Thinking, or NT

Now let's explore in more depth these different temperaments and the prayer type best suited for each of them.

Christian Prayer Types

Sensing-Judging (SJ)

For sensing-judging people (SJ), the Ignatian form of prayer will feel the most comfortable. SJ people are structured, with a strong sense of duty and obligation. This lends itself well to Ignatian prayer, which advocates taking a biblical story and putting yourself into the story as one of the characters of your choosing. Use all your senses to feel what it must have been like to be that character at that time. Then follow St. Ignatius's ten-step meditation process, which is very structured to achieve our goal of coming closer to God.[96] Notice the use of structure and of all the senses; both aspects of this prayer method are important.

Intuitive-Feeling (NF)

The second form of prayer is for intuitive-feeling people (NF). This is me, folks. I am what the Myers-Briggs personality approach would call an INFP. In more detail, I am a healer by my basic nature. So it is no surprise that I am also a Reiki practitioner. This is hands-on healing where I am honored and humbled to channel the life force from God to someone who is sick in some way. My prayer life is as an intuitive-feeling person.

Basically, this type of prayer brings forward the meaning of scripture into today's situation. For example, I constantly ask myself, "What would Jesus say?" This kind of prayer applies the ancient words of the Bible to today's issues. A person with intuitive powers can better discern which messages are applicable to today's world and preserve the meaning in a way that makes sense to the people of today. NF people need to find meaning in everything. We feel that there always is an underlying meaning behind everything we experience. NF people need more quiet time alone to meditate and pray. When I tell people that I pray for more than an hour a day, most people are surprised; many ask how the heck I can concentrate that long. It's just part of who I am.

---

[96]   George Ganss, *The Spiritual Exercises of Saint Ignatius* (Loyola Press, 1992).

Sensing-Perceiving (SP)

THE THIRD GROUP OF PEOPLE is the sensing-perceiving group (SP). Unlike the Ignatian types, who value structure, this group must feel free to do what the spirit tells them. They can be impulsive, but they live very much in the present. *Carpe diem*, or "seize the day," would be their motto. They have a high level of energy and can be the life of the party.

St. Francis was a sensing-perceiving person. Franciscan prayer certainly fits this group of people who make full use of the five senses and can see God in the whole of creation. A key descriptor of Franciscan prayer is "celebratory"; they love to celebrate things. Notice how lately, Mass is increasingly being called a celebration, not a sacrifice. Funerals are now designed to celebrate the life of the deceased, not to mourn a loss. Free-flowing prayers help the sensing-perceiving people best commune with God.

Intuitive-Thinking (NT)

THE FINAL GROUP OF BELIEVERS falls into the NT category, or intuitive thinking. St. Thomas Aquinas was greatly involved with this kind of prayer. NT prayer has an orderly feel to it; these people have a tendency to be perfectionists. If an NT has a bad habit— smoking, perhaps—much effort and analysis will go into finding out what that is. The NT will then set goals and systematically proceed to accomplish them.

The best prayers for this group include an orderly progression of thought or rational thinking from the initial cause all the way to the subsequent effect. Intuitive-thinking people want to understand things (and thus control things) to be a success, whether in liturgy or business. Their spirituality should be neat and clean. Lectio Divina is an excellent form of prayer for NTs.

Other Types of Prayer

Lectio Divina

LECTIO DIVINA MIGHT BE PERFECT for NTs, but the other three temperaments can make use of it as well. This type of prayer goes back to the fourth and fifth centuries, and the basics are simple: read a sacred text while inviting the Holy Spirit to be with you. (*Lectio* means "reading" in

Latin.) I suggest taking a small section of verses that addresses a particular topic you are interested in. Read the text slowly, and listen to what God is saying to you through the text you selected. Meditate on this text; keep your mind open and fixed on what you read. A single word or phrase may stick out in your mind; take that word or phrase with you. Rest with God with that word or phrase in mind. Listen if God has anything to say to you. Pay attention to your thoughts or feelings as you relate to the text. Thank the Lord, and continue with your day. All this should take about twenty minutes.

If you are interested in more details about prayer methods for different personality types or temperaments, I highly suggest you get the book *Prayer and Temperament* by Chester P. Michael and Marie C. Norrisey.

Centering Prayer

CENTERING PRAYER IS BASED UPON Lectio Divina; it has been around for a very long time. In this kind of prayer, you choose a sacred word or a phrase that is meaningful to you. The intention here is to submit to God's action within your spirit. Then sit in a quiet place and close your eyes, as in any other meditation. Introduce the word or phrase as a symbol to God's presence. Focus on this symbol. The words could be anything, like "love," "Jesus," "God our Father," "Mother God," "peace," or anything that is relevant to your life. As with any other kind of meditation, when unrelated thoughts enter your mind, gently push them aside and resume your focus on the sacred word. At the end of your prayer, just sit still for a few minutes, slowly returning to the reality that surrounds you. One of the benefits of this kind of prayer is that it leads to contemplative prayer.

Contemplative Prayer

ROMAN CATHOLIC MONKS THOMAS MERTON, Thomas Keating, and Basil Pennington have taught the method of contemplative prayer, which is almost identical to centering prayer. Contemplative prayer dates back to the ancient prayer practices of the Christian contemplative heritage, with the Fathers and Mothers of the Desert and Lectio Divina. This prayer method takes the believer into silence, both mental and physical. Praying in silence or thinking on scripture in silence is normal, but mental silence is generally not considered superior to mental dialogue while praying. Some consider contemplative prayer not to be prayer at all, since there is no biblical reference to silence in prayer. But many famous Christian leaders throughout the years have used this advanced method to their success.

Use of Feelings in Prayer

OTHER KINDS OF PRAYER UTILIZE our feelings. Imagine, for instance, walking through a beautiful countryside. As you feel all the beauty that surrounds you, you will appreciate that God created everything you are feeling at this moment. No matter where you are—the beach, the mountains, the forest, or even your own flowerbed—the appreciation of the beauty that God has given you can be felt within your spiritual being. This gratitude is legitimate prayer. I personally love to sit in my lounge chair next to the window in the winter. The sun brings in its warmth as I lie on my side and absorb its glow with my eyes closed. I feel closer to God, many times drifting off to sleep while I pray in the sunlight.

Similarly, singing hymns in a choir or singing hymns to yourself throughout your day might create a feeling of love or awe. These very pleasurable prayers can uplift your soul and heal many wounds. An example of a similar prayer is connecting with other people in support of their life situation, encouraging them, showing them compassion, and radiating warmth toward them while displaying interest in their well-being. One big form of prayer for me as a Reiki practitioner is healing prayers for other people. This is based on God's infinite supply of life energy that can be channeled through Reiki to someone who is ill and needs this kind healing for mind, body, and soul.

Notice that you are not directly talking to God in some of these instances, but I believe that you are praying nonetheless. Your prayer is your action within God's creation for the benefit of His other children.

Inward (or Thinking) Prayers

THE LAST GENERAL TYPE OF prayer is more intellectual or thinking in nature. The three prayer methods described by St. Ignatius of Loyola are of this nature—the same man who practiced putting himself in each Bible story, as described earlier. The first is to think about each of the Ten Commandments, one at a time. Examine your relation with each commandment and how you have or have not kept it. From this, make personal resolutions to amend yourself. The second method is to examine each word of a prayer, like the Lord's Prayer. Explore its meaning. The third method is to turn a prayer into a breathing exercise. On inhaling, recite a word from the prayer; on the exhale, think about that word and its meaning. On the next breath, select the subsequent word in the prayer.

Richard Ferguson

It's Your Choice

ULTIMATELY, PRAYER IS TALKING TO God in any way you want. You do not have to follow any of the above methods for God to hear you. God wants to hear from you just as you are. Just pray the way you already know how—or you may feel more comfortable following one of the prayer types because of who you are. Go ahead and try a few of the ones above and see how well they fit. If you don't feel comfortable with them, keep trying until you find a way that suits you better. The main point is simply to pray. Pray every day of your life, and you will start to see this world differently—more positive, more loving. This will be the case no matter which prayer method you use. God will be as pleased with your individualized method of prayers as He would with something invented by some saint long ago.

A Reflection for Your Prayer Type

This reflection is a bit different than the previous ones. The goal is to identify which prayer type probably fits us the best. The standard reflection steps are not needed here, nor is a mantra.

There are no right or wrong answers here. All are acceptable in God's eyes.

Ask yourself the following questions:
How much of a sense of duty and obligation do you have?
Do you feel that everything needs structure to be successful?

If you have a compelling sense of duty and a strong longing for structure, you may want to look at prayers for the SJ, or sensing-judging.

Are you optimistic?
Do you communicate well?
Do you search for meaning in things?

If your answer to the above questions was yes, look at prayers for the NF, or intuitive-feeling.

Would you consider yourself a free spirit?
Are rules just guidelines for you, rather than law?
Do you live in the moment and feel that the future will take care of itself?

If this describes you, look at prayers for the SP, or sensing-perceiving.

Do you feel that rational thinking from cause to effect is very important?
Are you very logical?
Do you want to know how everything works?

If this describes you, look at prayers for the NT, or intuitive-thinking.

If you are interested in pursuing this topic further, you may want to read *Prayer and Temperament*.

Richard Ferguson

There Was Thunder in My Heart, and I Ran to Prayer

I DIDN'T HAVE OCCASION TO pray for real until I was about twenty-one years old. Sometimes, we forget to turn our attention upward to God until tragedy strikes. When all else fails, and we feel powerless, something inside us brings us to pray to God. There is an Old Russian Orthodox saying that people do not fall to their knees until they hear the thunder. So it was with me, too.

My engagement to a girl from Hawaii had just broken up. I loved her deeply. She had left town after graduation from the college we both attended, moving in with her mother about fifty miles away. Then something happened that ended things—I wasn't sure what. She went back east to live with her brother in Kansas. Even a doof like me could see the writing on the wall. I could not believe this had happened.

After a summer class one evening, I found myself distraught, terribly lonely, and feeling totally abandoned, with nowhere to turn. My heart was filled with grief; I could not bear the thought of living the rest of my life without her, yet I would have to.

I took the little red hammer, broke the glass, and pulled the handle marked "Call God." My little handle was bright and shiny, since I never used it before. But that evening, I went to the church on campus and prayed until late that night. God was the only thing left in my life, and I did not know Him very well at all. Alone in the mission church, I cried in the pew for a while. I felt secure, all alone in a big church, surrounded with statues. At first, I prayed that she and I would get back together, but somehow I knew that was never going to happen. So eventually I prayed for "things to work out for me."

After an hour or so of praying and crying, a distinct feeling came over me that did not come from inside me. Something mystical was about to happen. Everyone has feelings; we all know what they are like. But in this case, the feeling came from outside myself, attracting my attention with its appearance in my mind. Without words, this feeling told me that everything would be okay. That was all—just that things would be okay. I did not hear voices; I saw no angels. I just received the knowledge that things would be all right. I had never experienced anything like that before in my life. After a little while longer, I left the mission. I still felt rotten, but I also carried some new little measure of peace in my heart. I was bewildered by this certainty; I did not understand how to respond. I went home, and that was that ... or so I thought.

266

A few days later, it was my birthday: another normal day of working at NASA and then going to class in the evening. No one knew that it was my birthday, and I felt very alone again. I felt as I usually did, insignificant and invisible. Walking from class to the student union building, I spotted a female classmate of mine going the other way. She was an Asian girl with long, black, flowing hair. I had seen her before, and we had chatted after class now and again. On this particular day, we said hi and talked for a few minutes. I told her it was my birthday and casually asked her if she would like to go have coffee with me. She said yes; we went to a place called Sambo's and talked for a very long time. Talking to this friend of mine was wonderful; it felt good to be with her. She laughed at my silly jokes, and we enjoyed each other's company. To make a long story short, this student friend of mine became my wife the next year. We had been married for thirty-eight years when my beloved Marilyn passed away early in 2009.

Had my feeling of certainty in the mission church been a coincidence? Had God really answered my prayer? That is something you must decide for yourself. As for me, I have come to believe that there are no real coincidences in God's creation. God did talk to me that night in the mission. God communicates in feelings, not in audible language.

Loving spirits are constantly working behind the scenes to bring about what we need in our lives for our benefit and learning. This often happens without us receiving any hint that this is going on in our behalf. The universe is more loving than we think, even in spite of all the suffering that we see every day in this world.

Benefits of Prayer: Too Many to Count

PRAYER IS SUCH A CLOSE commune with God that each prayer seems to be different for me; no two are the same. My grandmother would pray the rosary every day; I remember hearing her rosary beads clicking together as she prayed. Repetitive prayers are not my personal style, but it worked for her. Ultimately, each of us will find a style of prayer that fits us best.

During prayer, the increasing awareness that He is actually listening to you and the feeling of closeness to Him are great blessings. When I first started to pray, I encountered some of the roadblocks to prayer that we all experience. My brain just was not used to prayer, and I did not really have any understanding of how to go about it. I felt very awkward and unsure of what to do. But I knew God was with me, listening and loving me through my bumbling words to Him.

The evening that I went to the mission church to plead with God to bring back my fiancé, I had felt very out of place, with no idea what to say. Words just stumbled out of my brain without eloquence. Yet over the subsequent years, I came to realize that my decision to go to the mission church and pray that night was in reality a response to God's call for me. God was calling me to pray, and for the first time in my life, I was open to hear that call. He already knew what was in my heart, and He had a mystical message for me—a message that everything would be different, but everything would be okay.

Prayer is one of the easiest things you will ever do; God never makes things complex for us. That night in the church, I ended up just talking to God and telling Him what I was feeling and how miserable I was. Just talk to God as if He were your best friend. Do this because He is just that: your best friend. When all is lost, you will turn to God, and He will be there. Besides, when you really think about it, nothing in your life today is yours forever. Everything will change. Things will pass away and out of your life; new things will enter. Nothing will remain the same in this life, except one thing: God. In the end, the only constant in your existence is your relationship with God. Everything else in this physical life is temporary, no matter how hard we try to resist change. No matter—God is sufficient for total bliss.

God is always with us, even if we do not feel it. After praying daily for some time, you will notice changes within your inner being. Subtle changes in your attitudes and feelings will evolve within your spirit. You will become more aware of just what is bothering you, what you pray for, your expectations, your hidden desires, and your fears. All of this will float to the surface of your consciousness. Prayer reflects real life and is not meant to be ritualistic with set wordings that should be recited by rote. No—real, honest prayer is an outpouring of what is in your heart: your worries, your aspirations, your needs, your fears, and everything else that makes up your life. Prayer can get noisy at times, with many thoughts vying for attention. In part, these thoughts define your life. Gently push the unwanted thoughts to the side and focus on God and what your intentions are. Prayer is not an escape from life; rather, it is central to life and exposes the inner parts of our being. Prayer is honest and reveals you to yourself. God already knows you better than you do; as you get to know yourself as well, you will recognize a unity between you and God. What a wonderful realization!

There is a heightened sense of honesty of self in all this. In their book *Primary Speech*, Ann and Barry Ulanov say the following: "In prayer we say who in fact we are, not who we should be, nor who we wish we were, but who we are. All prayer begins with this confession."[97] If we are more aware of our real selves, it follows that we will also become more aware of our relationships with others and cherish them more than before. I have always said that the fabric of the kingdom of God is woven of the relationships we have with God and others.

You will grow over time to discern the proper priorities in life. You will give less attention to material wealth, instead fostering relationships that are based on mutual love and respect. Your respect for others will grow, and you will realize that everyone is truly equal, regardless of position in society. God loves Joe the beggar just as much as the president of the United States.

With your increasingly compassionate and loving attitude, you will be more able to forgive others—and forgive yourself, for that matter. A certain amount of spiritual peace comes when you are able to forgive and understand more. You will become the human that God intended you to be from the beginning as love takes its rightful place in the center of your life. Praying for the well-being of someone else shows you the love within you; self-knowledge increases through prayer.

In my prayer practice, I have started to understand in a deeper way that what we see in this life is just the tip of the proverbial iceberg. There is far more to ultimate reality than we can perceive with our five senses, and that reality influences everything we experience. Call this the kingdom of God if you want, but what I am speaking of does not define God's kingdom; this bigger reality is just part of the infinite kingdom. As you pray, your perceptions of reality will expand, and your mind will open to the wonderments that God has in store for us. Prayer does not let us escape from this reality; rather, it reflects our increased participation in it as we pray for ourselves and for others. A prayer for guidance is one of the most powerful requests you could utter, in my opinion. I say such a prayer daily as part of my personal ritual. Such prayers will help you discern your proper direction according to God's will for you.

Prayer leads you to understand that we are all limited in what we can do. Some things that will happen in your life you can do nothing about, and you will feel powerless. This feeling was a very hard thing for me to accept when it came to my wife's illness. Through prayer and the help of

---

[97] Ann and Barry Ulanov, *Primary Speech* (John Knox Press, 1892), 1.

other people far more advanced spiritually than I am, I have come to know myself as a healer. I hurt when others hurt, and I want to heal them and put smiles on their faces if I can. My inability to heal my wife prompted the most horrible feeling of powerlessness you can imagine, but I had to accept it. My internal healer groaned with agony, but I knew that curing my beloved was beyond me.

Fortunately, prayer also leads to humility and acceptance. This letting go was agonizing for me. Ann and Barry Ulanov offer the following powerful message:

> How can we entrust to God's providence those we love most dearly? How can there be such pain and misery in a universe of goodness? Whatever the question, it is there we will meet our crucifixion and resurrection. There we are identified. There we will be forced to let go. There we will be tried and brought through the many deaths of disidentifying to a life in many ways altogether new to us. That new life comes from the discovery that when we have entrusted to God what we hold most dear or most frightening, we gain one entirely new life made over and made for our own true self. [98]

In other words, when we let go and trust God, our lives will change for the better. Our false identities will fall away to reveal our true identity as children of God and beings of love made in the image of God, forever growing toward our full identity within God's embrace.

When life spins out of control, our close relationship with others and God will make it easier for us to accept the things that we cannot change. Throughout my prayer life, I have learned that I have a much stronger will than I thought, even if I could not heal my wife or change many other things in my life and the lives of those I love. The lesson of acceptance is a very hard one—and an ongoing struggle. Frankly, I do not accept things very well at all. I still try to heal everything in sight, fix what is wrong, and be Mr. Gooddeed. I have not yet managed to accept all that is imperfect and painful. I still am a work in progress in learning to accept that which I cannot change and trust God in all things.

I have come to understand that the biggest prayer of all is life itself. The way you lead your life is a prayer to God in that it reveals you in your

[98]   Ibid., 48.

entirety and fullness. It reveals the true you, both to yourself and to God. Our actions are powerful prayers; each of us pray through the kind of life we lead and the intentions behind what we do and say.

Does God Answer Prayer?

YES. BUT HIS ANSWER MAY not arrive within the desired time frame, and the answer may not be what you want, either. But yes, God answers all prayers. His answers are designed for your spiritual growth; if the answer is no, you will eventually see that it was the best thing for you. I have come to believe that God prioritizes our eternal best interest, and that means saying no sometimes if granting our request would harm our spiritual journey. God says yes many times too. You may receive what you asked for—or something better. It is up to us to discern the manner in which His answer comes to us. We do this by paying attention to the events in our lives and by praying. This is where many people have difficulty: God answers their prayers, but many times, they are looking in the wrong direction and miss the subtle answer.

Now, a cynic might say, "Well, if I prayed for world peace, what are the chances of that getting answered?" I would say 100 percent. If one person prays earnestly for this (and many people do just that), I believe that this nudges the world in the direction of peace. We may not be able to discern the exact effect of a single person's prayers, but I believe that such an effect exists. If everyone in the world prayed for world peace, what would the result be, if not world peace? Further, a prayer like this will benefit the person who prays as well. Love, compassion, and empathy will grow in the heart of a person who prays for peace in this world.

If we pray for something specific, we need to be attentive to the events, feelings, and thoughts surrounding the issue at hand, in order to witness the subtle changes taking place. God may act through other people. A seemingly coincidental event might happen that sends the situation into a new, more positive direction.

Before my darling Marilyn died, I prayed countless times for God to take away her illness. Each time, I felt the same answer in my heart and mind: no. The answer to the most fervent prayer in my life was no. That was excruciatingly hard to accept. How could God say no to something that was so obviously good? How could He say no to curing my dear wife? It hurt terribly.

Yet there must be a higher purpose in this. God never acts maliciously, but always with love. Now, you may ask, "How can refusing to take away a grave illness be an act of love?" It comes down to perspective. All of us have a very limited view of ultimate reality. We see only a tiny portion of creation. We cannot understand the totality of any particular situation. The part we can see looks terrible and extremely painful through our limited perspectives; suffering is painful. There is no getting around the fact that painful and awful things occur on this planet.

On Earth we experience night as complete darkness, with no sunlight anywhere. However when the Apollo astronauts went to the moon, they saw that part of Earth was in light and the other part in darkness. We may not be able to see it, but even during our darkest nights, light is coming. Light is already here.

Either God is a loving God, and all this pain we experience in our lives will make perfect sense to us one day after we pass … or the universe is the worst cosmic joke in all existence, and we all are doomed but don't know it. When you really think about it, those are the only two choices; I certainly prefer the former. If you ever read about the saints, true mystics, and others who have been given extraordinary spiritual gifts, you will come to understand that there is more to reality than we can sense. But all of the events in our lives, both pleasant and painful, will be revealed to us, along with the reasoning behind them. Luke 12:2: "Nothing is covered up that will not be revealed, or hidden that will not be known."

Liberty of the Seas: A Real Mystical Story of Answered Prayer

Two years before Marilyn passed away, I took our whole family on a Caribbean cruise on what was at the time the largest cruise ship in the world. It was a very special trip, as we had our granddaughter Isabella with us too. Watching her enjoy the activities on the ship was a delight. During our cruises, I find that spiritual reflection comes easily for me. I sit on the balcony, watch the sea pass by, and hear the water rush past the hull of the ship. Something about the ocean enhances life's reflections for me.

I felt horribly torn during that trip, because we had interrupted Marilyn's chemotherapy so she could feel well on the vacation that she had been looking forward to for at least a year by then. I could see that her excitement to go on a cruise with the whole family was holding her together while she endured the intense side effects of the chemotherapy. Marilyn said a number of times that this trip was the only bright spot in her life.

Going on this trip was the one thing that she had to look forward to, and it gave her great joy to anticipate the fun Isabella would have.

Marilyn and I would walk around on the deck, feeling the sunshine and hearing all the kids splash in the kiddie pool, including Isabella. Marilyn was wearing the sun-blocking bandanna that was required for all cancer patients. I was so proud to be by her side and hold her hand. The sky was blue, and the ocean was beautiful. The sight of Marilyn smiling among all this almost made me forget my shattered heart … but I knew the reality of Marilyn's prognosis. Only I knew the terrible truth of things and had to put on a happy face for everyone else's benefit.

Marilyn's hopes were fulfilled the second day on the ship in one blissful moment that will live in our memories forever. Isabella was swimming with Ria, our oldest daughter. She had on those little swimming goggles and her new swimsuit. When she saw us by the pool, Isabella swam over to us and poked her head out of the water. Dripping wet and grinning, Isabella told Marilyn, "I love you, Lola." (She called Marilyn "Lola" because that is the Tagalog word for "Grandma.") She tried to splash us, but missed. My beloved wife lived for moments like this; it was priceless. Just that one moment of love from our granddaughter made everything worthwhile, including the chemotherapy treatment interruption.

During the trip, I was beside myself emotionally; I cried every day for my wife. I was very good at hiding my red eyes from everyone, however. The contrast between the beauty of our surroundings and the reality of what was growing inside Marilyn's body was just too much for me to bear. How could such a contrast exist so vividly in this world? How could the ugliness of cancer live right alongside such beauty? I would sit out on our balcony, reading a book and gazing out over the ocean, and feel such a sense of helplessness—and, frankly, dread—of what was waiting for us at the end of the trip. Yet for a brief moment, all was well, and Marilyn was the happiest I had seen her in years.

I had a hard time connecting with God or feeling His presence while I was on the ship. I could reflect on things, but deep prayer was escaping me. Something told me that I should go to the ship's chapel. Five days into the cruise, I located the chapel and went there. The chapel was located toward the rear of the ship and was on the highest deck. This seemed like the highest point on the ship; I thought it was very nice of the builders to pay respect to God in this subtle, yet profound, way.

The chapel was small, holding perhaps forty people. Little alcoves big enough for about three people surrounded the perimeter of the main seating area. Behind the altar, sunlight poured through stained glass. The glass depicted clouds and blue sky, giving the feeling of eternity and peacefulness. The silent chapel held such a sense of peace. It was a joy to be there, yet my heart was so burdened with the stark reality of cancer.

I sat inside one of those little alcoves, hidden from sight, and my tears flowed like a river as I started to pray. I kept asking God to heal Marilyn. Distraught, I strained to sense any response from God at all. My tears kept coming and coming, it seemed. At that moment, I remember thinking that I must have been the most miserable passenger on the boat.

Then something very mystical happened to me. While my prayers continued, and without any warning, I felt as if I were being lifted up. I felt as if I were going out of my body and being lifted higher and higher at a faster and faster rate. I no longer had the sense that I was in the chapel at all. As I felt this upward movement, I remember thinking, *Thank you, God*. A moment later, I was in the presence of two beings dressed in white robes. I perceived that they had great authority. Through my dim vision, I could not readily make out their features or perceive where I was. I remember pleading with them to spare Marilyn's life, asking them what good would it do for her to die of the disease. I repeatedly asked why this was happening and begged them to please let her live. I was extremely emotional, frankly; tears flowed down my cheeks while these two beings listened and looked at me.

Then the two beings looked at each other as if to acknowledge that they had both heard what I had to say. They disappeared from my view, and I regained a sense of where I was. I felt no descent, just a renewed sense of the chapel. The two beings had not actually responded to my pleas or given me any assurance of what would come next in our lives. But, unmistakably, they had heard me. I could not ask for more than that.

I had hoped that I would come away from my prayer with certainty that everything would be just fine. In truth, I still felt empty and still had a feeling of dread of what was to come next regarding Marilyn's illness. But I thank God that He sent two beings to let me know that my prayers were being heard. I now believe that God was asking me to have more faith in the eternal scheme of things and to remember that this life is not the entire picture.

This concept is monumentally important. Life events may not make any sense at all. They may seem cruel, miserable, and pointless. But if we could see the whole picture of existence, events that make no sense to us today will make total sense when the entire picture is revealed to us, as the Bible promises.

When I told my spiritual advisor of the two beings of light I had seen, she said that God was being very kind to me by sending the two beings to me. I think she must be right, even if not all requests are granted.

Roadblocks to Prayer

IF THERE ARE SIX BILLION people on earth, there are six billion ways to God and six billion ways to avoid prayer. The reasons not to pray are many; resistance can be rooted in many different causes.

Some of the causes of prayer avoidance include the fear of God. Lots of people my age were taught as children to do just that: fear God. Guilt is a big reason too; many people feel guilty about something and want to hide it from God. Since prayer is truth, guilt forms a barrier between God and that person. Other people may be opposed to the sense of surrender inherent in prayer; praying involves giving yourself over to something you cannot see and do not yet know the nature of. Others may worry that they will ask for the wrong thing and anger God in some way. Some people feel they are not good enough to approach God. "Why would almighty God be interested in little meaningless me?" they might ask. Others may feel that God is just not listening. Other barriers to prayer can include a lack of free time or the perception that past prayers didn't result in anything. Past prayers may have resulted in anticlimactic silence or a lack of the increased peace that so many had talked about.

Some people are just not the religious type, or so they say. Others avoid prayer to avoid looking silly in front of people or even themselves. I have heard people say that prayer is for sissies. Sometimes, prayer seems too profound for people. Addressing the infinite is overwhelming to them, so they do not pray. Prayer intensifies life by addressing it directly; some people want to skate through life without a lot of drama, so prayer gets avoided. I have met people who have a detached intellectual perspective on life, and prayer just does not fit that mold at all.

Ultimately, two things define us all: our relationship with God and our relationships with others. Prayer enriches our relationship with God and deepens our relationships with others as well. Prayer enriches our lives, leaving us more vibrant and more in harmony with our true selves and the will of God.

If you find yourself, for any reason, being blocked from prayer, do not despair or feel guilty about that. Be gentle with yourself, and simply say something along these lines:

> My dear Father in heaven,
> I have not prayed much to You in the past.
> I feel a desire to change that, but I don't know how.
> Please guide me and teach me to pray, for
> I want You in my life, Lord.
>
> Amen.

Use your own words, and say what is in your heart; that is all there is to it.

Even after praying becomes a habit for you, roadblocks will arise along the way. I have found that emotions can get in the way of prayer as my mind focuses on what is bothering me rather than on my intended communion with God. But as always, we all need to be gentle with ourselves and just refocus our minds on our prayers as best we can. By the way, when you pray, you don't have to use words. At times, when I have felt really emotionally rotten about something, I have simply looked to God and offered the emotion to Him without saying a word in my own mind. If I say anything at all during those times, it usually is simply, "Dear Father, guide me through this, and give me strength."

Set aside a quiet time each day for prayer, even if just a few minutes. After a while, you will realize the typical response to your prayers is silence. Well, then you wonder whether God heard you. Are you going to get an answer? Does this silence mean that nothing is happening? Prayers do get answered in different ways. It is up to us to be attentive for how answers appear in our lives.

Prayer will change your life for the better in ways that right now you cannot think of. This has happened to me. I am ever so thankful to God that He led me to this point in my life and the relationship I have with Him now. I very much enjoy my time when I pray at the end of my day before I go to bed.

Pray in a way that is natural for you, and you will start to see both the world and yourself change in ways that increase the joy and peace in your heart.

CHAPTER 16

Death and Dying:
The Great Journey Back Home

The Spiritual Lesson of Grief

THIS CHAPTER IS FOR ALL those losing a loved one as they pass away into heaven. Take heart—heaven is more beautiful, peaceful, and loving than you can possibly imagine. We all were there before we came here but have agreed to forget in order to perform our life's work before returning.

As Mother Teresa (1910–1997) said, "Death is nothing else but going home to God; the bond of love will be unbroken for all eternity."

Nonetheless, the death of a loved one is a crisis so intense that sometimes you lose control of your emotions completely; I did many times and mostly still do. I have never experienced such intense pain as the loss of my dear Marilyn. As our loved ones return to heaven, we must remember that every person's path through life is different. Simply put, your loved ones are on a different path to God than you are. As we go through our lives, we tend to operate under some unsaid and unconscious assumptions; certain human relationships sometimes cause us to forget that we are individuals.

When we get married, for example, both spouses' lives become inexorably entwined. What happens to one spouse happens to the other, too; everything is essentially experienced together. If one suffers, so does the other. Love creates a unity between people, a kind of oneness. There is a beauty in this unity that, in my opinion, transcends human understanding. When something makes your spouse happy, you also genuinely feel that happiness too. This can be true between brothers and sisters or parents and children as well.

The basic Catholic theology of marriage was written during the days of Pope John Paul II. It says that

This is from Vatican II and canon law.[99]

> Marriage is the closest and most intimate of human friendships. It involves the sharing of the whole of a person's life with his/her spouse. Marriage calls for a mutual self-surrender so intimate and complete that spouses—without losing their individuality—become "one," not only in body, but in soul.

Yet, as close as a husband and wife are in this life, it is my opinion that both the husband and the wife still retain their individual paths toward God. His sacred plan for each spouse remains different according to each spouse's individual need.

When certain events come into the lives of a husband and wife, the separateness of their paths in this life becomes more apparent. When my wife, Marilyn, was diagnosed with cancer, her journey in this life became much different than mine. Our lives remained completely intertwined, but the experience, including the emotional and physical impact, was profoundly different for her than it was for me, her caregiver.

So I believe the spiritual lesson here is that no matter how close you are to another person, no matter how much you love another person, and no matter how much time you spend with your loved one, they are still on a different path toward God than you are. I believe that God has lovingly designed each path. The purpose of this is to bring us closer and closer to our full divine potential, as God has ordained for each of us from the very beginning of creation. This is a manifestation of God's will, which will be done for each of us. In the end, each of our paths leads to a place that we will most certainly want to be. We will look back at the rough road behind us and say that it was worth the struggle and suffering to get where we are. This is God's promise to each of us: that there will be joy on the other end of our pain, and we will definitely be reunited with loved ones who went to heaven first. Love remains eternal, even when one partner is here and the other is in heaven.

---

[99] http://www.catholiceducation.org/articles/sexuality/se0096.html

In the meantime, while your loved one is still here, you must still treat them as you always have. Connect with them by talking when they are awake. Touch them, kiss them, and hug them, but keep your tears to yourself. Don't be a fake; be yourself, and talk about death if they want to. (Don't bring it up yourself.) Listen to whatever they have to say, and respond as if you were both in a restaurant, having lunch. In other words, treat them as a priceless human being, just as you always did.

The following prayer acknowledges that God loves us no matter what happens to us on our journey back to heaven. No matter what our circumstances, we need to give a prayer of gratitude and be thankful for the time we had with our loved one. As of now, I do find it very hard to say this prayer. The grief is still just too strong. We need to always remember that we will see them again in a far better place.

Dear Father in heaven,

I thank You and praise You for the time You have given me with my loved ones.
The love we share is a reflection of the love You have for each of us, for You loved us and knew us before we were born into this life.
I know too that each of us is on a path that leads back to You.
I know that our paths must be different, since You made each of us different.
Each of us is on a different part of our path that is our journey back to You.
I know that we, in this life, must endure certain things along our path.
These things we must endure are there for our learning and spiritual progress;
this is true no matter how painful the suffering may be.
I also know that the suffering will pass, though it will seem like an eternity.
When things do not make sense, I know that You are not finished yet, since only good things come in the end for those who believe in You.

Amen.

A Loving Caregiver and Dark Moments

IF YOU FEEL ROTTEN MOST of the time as a caregiver of a very sick loved one, you are a normal human being. How do you survive when a crisis is so intense and painful that you can barely breathe, and everything around you is dark—when you do not sense the presence of God at all, and you are scared to death? This is such an important question for caregivers. A number of caregiving advice books are available. Two are listed in the reference section in the back of this book; they are more practical and do not center on spiritual aspects.

When my wife, Marilyn, was diagnosed with cancer, I knew I had to carry on and do what must be done, for my beloved wife and I are eternally joined together as loving, married partners. God must have had a lot of confidence in me to give me this to deal with. It was almost too much to bear, and I felt as if I was very close to the edge all too often. As Mother Teresa said, "I know God will not give me anything I can't handle. I just wish that He didn't trust me so much."

The only thing I can say is that only by the grace of God I go, even though I cannot feel God's presence in these times. Somehow, He holds me up. I really do not know how; this is beyond me. I do cope somehow, even if it is a struggle at times. Before Marilyn passed away, I often felt like a robot going through the motions, barely conscious of even who I was. I was her caregiver and loved her deeply while in this emotional fog of pain and depression. I could not see what was around me—only this movie playing on the screen of my mind, depicting the life that had me by the throat.

No caregiver ever is alone. God walks with him or her. You are not alone in crisis. I know I have spiritual help. I have been told by people who have true psychic gifts that I have two (sometimes three) spirit guides and five angels here to protect me. I am enormously grateful to God for caring for me this way. But perhaps God thinks, "Rich is a basket case. Let's give him more help than normal people." As you care for your loved one, do not forget to care for yourself. A sick caregiver is not worth much to the terminally ill.

Pray to God and ask Him to give you the strength to make it through the day. Center your heart upon God as you try to make it though the day. If an entire day seems too much to ask for, then pray that He gives you the strength to make it just one more hour, just one more minute, just one more breath. God already knows your pain; He is there with you and in your pain with you. After your crisis has passed, you will look back and wonder how you survived it. The answer is that God was there for you and silently gave you what you needed.

God will not allow you to suffer forever; there is light on the other side. My spiritual advisor said that in the darkness there is still enough light. This simply means that things will never be so dark that you lose your way. God will not allow that. Abundant light awaits you on the other side; God will not disappoint.

At times through my experience as a caregiver, I was so extremely upset that I could not even pray; all I could do was cry with complete despair. I could not see any light; I could not feel God's presence. My mind was in the darkness, and I was paralyzed; I could not even think. My physical surroundings seemed almost like they were not really there. All that existed was Marilyn's suffering, my anguish, and me—nothing else. I felt isolated in a desert of agony, with no relief from the hot sun of Marilyn's cancer beating down on me relentlessly. Yet I was not alone; you are not either. I had and still have many loving people praying for me every day; I know that you will too. You will be on loving people's minds throughout their day, and they will pray for you.

Spirit Guides

ANOTHER WAY YOU ARE NOT alone is that your spirit guide is with you every second of your life. I know that each of us has a spirit guide given to us by God. I know this for two reasons. First, it is in the Bible. There are numerous stories in the Old Testament where angels intervened with a believer to help him avoid something not of God. Second, I can feel my guide's presence most of the time. I talk to him, and he answers me with telepathic thoughts infused directly into my mind. With practice, you too will be able to hear your spirit guide and discern whether the response you hear are the words of your guide or an echo of your own imagination.

The idea of a spirit guide may seem strange, if you have not heard of it before. But spirit guides are real, and they are on your side. They were assigned to us before we came to earth. Christians call them guardian angels. They are here to help us surmount the challenges and troubles in our lives. You can ask them questions, and they will answer.

He or she is with you in your darkest moments, on one side of you or the other. My spirit guides accompany me, both on my right side and behind me. Their names are Martin and Randal. Martin is an English gentleman who lived in a small town some distance from London. I can't understand the full name of where he lived when he tries to tell me—it's Huffingstone or some English name like that.

Do not pray to your guide; simply talk to them. Spirit guides are wonderful, but not divine. To talk with your spirit guide, prepare as you would a prayer session. Find a quiet place free of interruptions; use earplugs if necessary. Darken the room if you desire, ask God to surround you with the light of the Holy Spirit, clear your mind as best you can, and just relax. After a suitable length of time, talk to your spirit guide as if you could see him standing there, holding your hand. Tell him or her of the problems you want help with. You don't need to speak out loud; speak with your mind, and your spirit guide will hear you clearly. Ask your guide for advice to lead you out of your problems, and your guide will respond. Guides have a way of suggesting ideas to our minds. Listen for the stirrings of new thoughts about your struggle. You may be surprised at how quickly this will happen.

Since I have been talking to my spirit guide for quite a while now, Martin responds very quickly with thoughts that clearly originate outside myself. Thinking for yourself takes effort; external thoughts are effortless and can accompany your own thought process. If a thought appears in your cleared, blank mind, your spirit guide is likely the source. When a new thought appears and you wonder where it came from, it's probably from your guide.

I have talked to my spirit guide during many difficult moments. Many times, a tingling sensation over most of my body will confirm his presence. If you are interested in pursuing this in detail, read a wonderful book called *Contacting Your Spirit Guide* by Sylvia Browne. For more details on the book, please see the reference section.

Take Care of Yourself

WHEN YOU ARE SUFFERING THE emotional agonies of caring for a terminally ill loved one, remember to pray if you can. Sometimes praying can be hard; emotions get in the way. Praying was a struggle for me during Marilyn's illness and is still difficult now that she has passed. When I tried to pray, my emotions would often take over, and I could hardly say the word "God." What I did was just say, "Here, God. Feel my horrible emotions with me." Your emotions will probably be so intense that they prevent you from feeling the presence of God. My spiritual advisor says all this is normal.

As a caregiver, it is vitally important to take care of your physical needs. I failed in this regard; my appetite disappeared, and I lost weight. All this did was make things harder. If you start losing weight, go ahead and eat the high-calorie stuff that tastes good. I still do while I continue to mourn my beloved Marilyn. As I write this, my appetite has still not returned.

You also need to be gentle with yourself. Give yourself a rest during the day whenever the opportunity occurs. Do not shoulder the responsibility 24/7 or you will burn out for sure. Allow others to fill in for you for certain lengths of time.

Make life as easy on yourself as you can. For example, I got a doorbell and put the button on Marilyn's bedpost. All she had to do was press it, and I could hear it anywhere in the house. This way, I felt free to roam the house without worrying that she might need something.

Get out of the house and do something that you enjoy. You will not feel like it, but you must. Get some exercise, even only if it is only walking around the block a few times. I played golf once a week on the weekends when my daughters were home from work.

Get the proper amount of sleep, even if it means going to your doctor for a sleeping-pill prescription. I did, and I am glad I did. My doctor also gave me some medicine to lessen my intense anxiety. You will be helping yourself and everyone else if you take medication as necessary. Your mind must be clear, or you could make a mistake in drug dosage; that is serious. To reduce the risk of this, go to the drugstore and get one of those multi-day pill containers; some even have four separate slots per day. Get a big calendar for all the doctor's appointments and changes in medicines.

Try to keep your mind from racing ahead to what may come; it will drive you nuts. I had a very hard time with this, but try your best to live just one day at a time. Do whatever you have to in order to revive yourself and get your mind off the situation. I pray that you do better at this than I did. I would fly my airplane, but my emotions would overcome me before I could get the plane safely on the ground. So my new airplane sits on the ground and looks like a very aerodynamic paperweight. It may seem impossible, as it did to me, but you will get through this. Yes, you will! Remind yourself of this constantly, even if you have to make a sign and hang it in the kitchen.

The idea of your loved one suffering is an incredibly upsetting one. Remember that the person who is passing away is unconscious most of the time; during their waking moments, they usually are filled with morphine and other painkillers that make them very comfortable. Their confusion also protects them from what is happening. This is God's way of easing the transition to the other side. Remember this quote from Irish essayist Jonathan Swift (1667–1745): "It is impossible that anything so natural, so necessary, and so universal as death, should ever have been designed by Providence as an evil to mankind."

A Jesuit Priest

A JESUIT BROTHER WHO HAS been my close friend for about forty years told me of the death of a Jesuit priest.

It was about three in the morning, and my friend was tending to the priest's needs. The old priest could barely breathe and had been too weak to sit up or feed himself; he was very close to passing away. Suddenly the elderly priest somehow managed to sit up in bed. His eyes opened wide as he looked upward with an expression of peace and wonder on his face. Then the old priest looked at my friend with an astonished look on his face and said these exact words: "It's beautiful!" His face had a glow about it as he spoke. Then the priest lay back on the bed, took one more breath, and passed away.

Marilyn Passes Away into Heaven

THE CLOSER ONE COMES TO passing away, the more often they will see heaven and heavenly figures: family members who have already passed away, angels, and other sacred beings. If you are tending to a dying person, and they appear to see something that you cannot, I can tell you with certainty that what they are seeing is from the other side and very much real. A feeling of peace and joy accompanies these visions. They are not hallucinating; never believe the people who attribute such visions to a lack of oxygen to the brain or other medical causes. It's not that at all. Doctors especially say things like this, because the desire for a scientific explanation stems from their medical training.

About two weeks before Marilyn passed away, she asked me if I saw the two angels sitting at the foot of her hospital bed. Well, I saw absolutely nothing. I asked her to describe what they looked like. She said that they both were dressed in white. One of them had curly hair, and they had peaceful looks on their faces. She also commented that they looked "effeminate"; they had both male and female characteristics. Marilyn told me that they had visited her a few days before, but she had told them to get out of there. They obeyed, but returned when I was there.

You can expect these kinds of experiences as your loved one's passage into heaven draws near. These visions are often a very positive experience for the ill person; the visions can be positive for the survivors as well.

The evening Marilyn died, we were back home, and I was in the room with her. I told everyone else to stay out, as I suspected that her passage was near, and I did not want it to be chaotic. I sat in a recliner chair at the foot of her bed, listening to any sounds she would make. The TV was on very low, and her IV medications dripped steadily.

At about 8:00 PM, she started to wheeze, so I got up and ministered to her a modified form of Reiki. After about ten minutes, her breathing cleared up and returned to normal. After the Reiki, I placed my left hand on Marilyn's forehead and said, "I love you eternally, honey." I did this three times. In a sense, my words represented an acknowledgement prayer that she and I were eternally bonded in our deep love for each other.

I sat down in my chair again. After a few minutes, something caught my eye right above Marilyn. It moved slowly upward toward the ceiling and from right to left. I kept looking at it, but I could not really see what it was. Once it had proceeded to the ceiling, I could not see it anymore. I got up off the chair to check on Marilyn, and it was then that I knew she had just passed away. The last thing she heard on this planet was me telling her I loved her eternally. The last thing I saw of Marilyn was her spirit departing this world and silently going up to heaven. Yes, this is how it really happened.

The Mourning Process

AFTER A DEATH, THE REMAINING survivors experience such a mixture of deep-seated feelings. Not all of them are negative and painful; many times, survivors will have a feeling of completion and relief that the loved one suffers no more. But grieving, loneliness, and a sense of loss are also inherent in the process. You will feel off balance and succumb to fits of crying that may come upon you at odd times. You will wonder what is next in your life and how to pick up the pieces. I felt all of this, along with a strong sense of abandonment. I hope that my words will help prepare you for this difficult experience.

Grieving

GRIEVING A LOVED ONE IS just plain painful, and it will seem to take forever as you attempt to regain some balance in your life. But if you love, avoiding grief is impossible.

As social psychologist Erich Fromm (1900–1980) said, "To spare oneself from grief at all cost can be achieved only at the price of total detachment, which excludes the ability to experience happiness."

When grief strikes you, remember that your loved one suffers no more and is now in a place that is far better than this earth.

> There is no death! What seems so is transition;
> This life of mortal breath
> Is but a suburb of the life Elysian,
> Whose portal we call Death.
> —Henry W. Longfellow (1807–1882)

Right after Marilyn died, these two thoughts consoled me: she was in heaven, and she suffered no more. Amazingly, Marilyn appeared in two people's dreams the night she passed away. In their dreams, both my daughter-in-law and my future son-in-law heard her say the exact same words: "I feel so much better now." This was about ten hours after her death. This shared mystical experience brought the family great joy, showing God's care for all of us during this awful time in our lives.

During the preparations for the funeral services and immediately afterward, you will not yet feel the emotional impact of what just happened. You will feel numb and overwhelmed; what happened has not sunk in yet. After a week or two, when all the commotion calms down, the reality and finality of your loved one's death will strike your emotions very hard. Loneliness, feelings of abandonment, confusion, and the significant loss of energy usually occur. Crying spells may occur multiple times a day as well. All this has happened to me to the point that my doctor prescribed sedatives and some narcotic painkillers in order to prevent a total meltdown. As it is, I have had many panic attacks that literally take me out of my body; I end up doing things that I am not aware of until later, when I realize I am bleeding from my arms after digging my fingernails into my own flesh in anguish. Then I am totally exhausted and need to lie down for hours.

Tears can come upon you almost without warning. When it happens to me, I usually detect the initial signs five minutes beforehand, and I must retreat to a quiet room away from everyone before the inconsolable sobs set in.

Expect a lowered energy level in general in the months following the funeral. Some days will be better than others; enjoy the good days, and make the most out of them. As time slowly passes, you will find that the good days become more frequent. Time will bring many ups and downs, but slowly, signs of hope will emerge.

Proof that Your Loved One Is Still with Us—Really!

AFTER A PERSON PASSES AWAY, expect to experience some weird happenings, depending on your prior relationship with the one now in heaven. Much of this depends on just how open you are to the idea of mystical occurrences. It also depends on your level of spirituality, but spirituality is not totally necessary for a loved one from the other side to do something that says, "I am here—and very much alive!"

I hesitated to include this next passage, because it is very personal, and many people will think that I have gone off the deep end. But in the end, I believe that sharing my experiences will help many of God's loved children. During my prayers recently, I got the direct feeling that God wants me to tell the truth about what has happened to my family members and me since Marilyn has passed away. Everything I am about to tell you is the whole truth and has not been changed in any way for literary effect. I have had dozens more very personal and mystical experiences with Marilyn than what I will describe now.

Some people will be like my son, who said regarding spiritual matters, "I will believe it when I see it." One night, my son got what he asked for; in the process, he got the surprise of his life. Now, in our family room is a wonderful display case with about twenty cubbies for artwork. Marilyn designed this display case; each cubby had an individual light that shone down on what was inside. Marilyn kept beautiful glass sculptures there that she collected in our travels. She kept bugging me to fix five lights that were not working; she wanted all the lights on all the time. Since I was always exhausted tending to her needs, I never did fix the lights. I also could never find the hidden switch to turn them on or off, and Marilyn was in no condition at the time to tell me.

One evening after Marilyn's death, my son was watching TV and talking to his girlfriend on his cell phone in that room. Suddenly, all five of the burned-out lights turned on all by themselves—yes, all five simultaneously. This shocked my son, and he yelled out, "The lights! The lights!" He got really scared and ran upstairs to get my daughter to show her. Later, he said he had goose bumps all over his body; it really did shake him up. Marilyn undoubtedly had turned them on that evening. Those five lights stayed on for months—we wouldn't dare touch them!

After a loved one passes away, you can expect similar experiences in one form or another.

Marilyn and I have a very deep and entangled relationship; we both felt strongly that we were partners for eternity. When two people are that deeply in love with each other and one dies, the remaining one has a very hard road to travel. The one left behind needs spiritual help along the way. In my case, God increased the number of spirit guides I have from one to three, and I have five angels to protect me from spiritual damage. I really do know these things; I would never make this up.

One day, I got the bright idea that I should walk to the cemetery where Marilyn is buried. I was feeling as rotten emotionally as a person could, and I thought being physically close to her might make me feel better—big mistake. I cried during my entire two-and-a-half-mile walk. Several times, I had to stop, as I could not see where I was going through my tears. When I got to her grave, I could hardly stand. I lasted no more than sixty seconds before I just had to leave for home. As I walked home, sobbing, something mystical happened. I was walking on the sidewalk with my head down, looking at my feet passing across the sidewalk. Tears were falling onto the inside of my glasses.

Suddenly, a vision started to form above me and on my right. I saw a cloudlike structure forming. Then I saw the most beautiful female hand descend from the cloud, as if she were offering me a helping hand. I could not help noticing that the hand looked exactly as Marilyn's had when we were first married; also, she was wearing the most beautiful diamond ring on her ring finger. I took hold of her hand, and it indeed felt exactly like Marilyn's hand. I slid my hand up her arm past her elbow—yes, indeed, it was Marilyn for sure.

I asked her, "Where did the large diamond ring come from?"

She said in Marilyn's voice, "It's for all the wonderful things you did for me." I told her I loved her eternally; with that, the vision melted away.

I kept on walking, but I had stopped crying. I did not cry for the rest of the day. The ring she was wearing showed me that Marilyn wanted to remain my wife for all eternity. I know she will be the first person I see as I pass away, as she promised this before she passed away. I do look forward to that.

Another experience happened to me on the golf course. The night before, I had prayed to God to allow Marilyn to play golf with me the next morning. Marilyn had not liked golf and had never accompanied me to the golf course before. But as I walked down the second fairway, I suddenly felt Marilyn's presence very strongly. She was hugging me from behind, with her arms wrapped around my neck. At times, I could even feel her head resting on my right shoulder and her cheek pressed against my cheek.

I cannot begin to describe the peace and joy I felt that day. We spoke sometimes, but we usually simply said "I love you." I could feel her love for me and just how happy she was. Mentally (and spiritually), I ran my hand through her beautiful black hair, which shone in the sun. I could see that Marilyn had gone back to wearing her hair long, as she had when we met so many years ago. I was so peaceful that day that I shot my best score of the year. (For you golfers out there, it was a 76 from the championship tees.) Marilyn stayed with me for the rest of the day until I went to sleep that evening. I am truly blessed by God to have experienced this.

I am not alone in such experiences. The female client of a very good friend of mine had a son who was a rabble-rouser. He was always getting into trouble, and he always rejected anything to do with church. (Sounds like me when I was a kid.) This was a major concern for his mother. Eventually, the son joined the Army and found his way to Iraq as a helicopter pilot. One day, as he flew low and patrolled the area, his helicopter hit some wires and crashed to the ground within a second or two. No one survived the violent crash.

Afterward, his mother was extremely distraught about her son and whether he was "right with God." These thoughts consumed her mind and emotions for months.

One day, she was sitting out in the backyard, reminiscing about her son's childhood habit of spending a lot of time in the old oak tree. The tree was so large it dominated the entire yard, becoming his refuge from life.

Then it happened: there, standing on one of the large lower limbs, were both her son and Jesus Christ. She saw them with her eyes open. They were plainly visible, and they were just standing there, looking down on her with the most peaceful, loving expressions. This woman told my friend that she instantly felt peace in her heart, knowing that her son was with Jesus and that everything was indeed much better than she could have hoped for. She also got the strong feeling from Jesus that He knew her and she knew Him from times past; there was a deep pre-existing relationship there.

This vision lasted for a full twenty minutes, with the three of them just looking at each other. Nothing was said, but the essence of peaceful thoughts was exchanged. When she got up to go to the bathroom and got back to her lounge chair, they were gone. From that moment on, she felt a profound peace in her heart for her son, and she no longer feared death.

The world is full of these kinds of stories; I suggest that you seek them out. They will comfort you as a caregiver and as a mourner. Be open to these mystical events happening to you, too. Don't think it cannot happen, as my son did. The result was the biggest surprise of his life! After that happened, I asked him if he now believes in spirits. He said yes.

A Very Personal Vision of the Reality of Heaven

THE LAST MYSTICAL STORY I will tell you involves a vision of heaven, Marilyn, and my spirit guides (Martin and Randal). One day recently, I was just feeling rotten. I had already cried three times that day and had exhausted myself by evening; emotions can really take your energy away. After sundown, I went into Marilyn's room to sit on the recliner at the foot of her bed, where I had been when she passed away. I cleared my mind as best I could, then thanked God for all He had done for me and prayed for healing. Then I started to talk to Martin and Randal, my two guides at the time. My mind asked a simple question: "Martin, what is Marilyn doing now?" He instantly answered, "She is preparing a place for you." Well, I certainly not had expected this answer.

By the way, surprise is one of the markers of a true mystical answer. If you are told something unexpected or something you never heard before, the chances are high that you have received a mystical answer.

I was not sure what Martin meant, but mystical answers are almost always short and very much to the point. I then asked Martin, "What do you mean—how?" Martin did not answer with a thought this time.

Rather, he showed me a vision of Marilyn and what she was doing. This is what I saw: Marilyn was dressed in a white robe. I could see her as if I were about fifty feet away; I saw her long, black hair. She was planting flowers in a garden bed in front of what I took to be a house. I have to say, this was the most beautiful sight I have ever seen in my life. Light seemed to come from everywhere; there were no shadows. The garden seemed to be terraced, leading up to the house which was on top. A paved pathway led from where I was standing, around to the right, and up to the house.

I have never seen anything like this house. It glistened in the light; it seemed to be made of beautiful marble and crystal. The crystal sparkled in the light against what I thought to be a blue sky. Mountains rose up in the distant background. The house's crystal spires reached up into the sky. Surrounding the house was the most beautiful garden I have ever seen. Marilyn always loved flowers and was always tending to our garden around our house; she continues to love flowers and was doing something she loved. How appropriate.

After a very short time, the vision passed. I thanked Martin for showing me this. I lost my focus, and my mind started to cloud over with other thoughts. So I ended my meditation with a prayer and felt better for the experience.

Days later, during another meditation session, Marilyn showed me the inside of the house. When I entered, I saw that the interior was at least ten times as large as the house appeared from the outside; the laws of physics are apparently different in heaven. I will not go into detail of what I saw then; that is for another time.

And Our Life Cycle Completes: We Are Back Home with God

WE ALL STARTED IN A heavenly place. There were billions of us, and we all knew each other and loved each other. We had our eternal names, but no bodies yet. God gave us His unconditional love. He offered us the opportunity to expand our spiritual wings and go to other parts of His creation, where we would live a life that would change us. He would help us; we would not be able to see Him directly, but He would be with us all the time.

Those who love God enough to live good lives will go back to heaven— back where we started, but changed in a divine way that will allow us to experience in a much deeper way all the joy, bliss, and love of the kingdom He has created for us. Upon our return, we may enjoy more of God's infinite creation by means of what we have learned and experienced on this earth. This is what God promised us in the beginning; our existence has come full circle as we cross back to the other side, and so too has this book.

I pray that these true stories will bring peace and joy into your heart and increase your understanding of what happens in all phases of life on this earth. Dying is not to be feared; it is simply part of a cycle. Remember the following:

"Death is the gate of life."

—St. Bernard of Clairvaux

So it was with Marilyn; so it will be with me; and so it will be with you.

May God richly bless you and all your family.

References

Arntz, William, Betsy Chasse, and Mark Vicente. 2005. *What the Bleep Do We Know!?* Health Communications.

Bloom, Anthony. 1970. *Beginning to Pray.* Paulist Press.

Brennan, Barbara Ann. 1987. *Hands of Light.* Bantam Books.

Bridgewater Book Company. 2004. *Buddha: His Life and Teachings.*

Browne, Sylvia. 2005. *Contacting Your Spirit Guide.* Hay House.

Burklo, Jim. 2000. *Open Christianity.* Rising Star Press.

Dawood, N. J. 1956. *The Koran.* Penguin Books.

Ehrman, Bart D. 2005. *Misquoting Jesus.* San Francisco: Harper.

Erikson, Erik H. 1950. *Childhood and Society.* W. W. Norton and Co.

Erikson, Erik H. 1980. *Identity and The Life Cycle.* W. W. Norton and Co.

Fowler, James W. 1978. *Stages of Faith.* San Francisco: Harper Collins.

Frankl, Viktor E. 1959. *Man's Search for Meaning.* Washington Square Press.

G., Phil. 2007. *Soul Matters: The Voice Within.* Self-Published.

Ganss, George E. 1992. *The Spiritual Exercises of Saint Ignatius.* Loyola Press.

Garrison, John C. 2001. *The Psychology of The Spirit*. Xlibris Corp.

Green, Glenda. 1999. *Love Without End: Jesus Speaks*. Spiritus Publishing.

Hawking, Stephen W. 1988. *A Brief History of Time*. Bantam Books.

Hennessey, Maya. 2006. *If Only I Had This Caregiving Book*. AuthorHouse.

Hirsh, Sandra Krebs, and Jane A. G. Kise. 1998. *Soul Types*. Hyperion Publishing.

Hunt, Valerie V. 1997. *Mind Mastery Meditations*. Malibu Publishing.

Keating, Thomas, and Basil Pennington. 1998. *Centering Prayer*. Continuum Publishing.

Laitman, Michael. 2007. *The Zohar*. Laitman Kabbalah Publishers.

Laszlo, Ervin. 2004. *Science and the Akashic Field*. Inner Traditions.

Lopez, Donald S. 2004. *Buddhist Scriptures*. Penguin Books.

Mascaro, Juan. 1962. *The Bhagavad Gita*. Penguin Books.

Michael, Chester P. and Marie C. Norrisey. 1991. *Prayer and Temperament*. The Open Door Inc.

Nussbaum, Stan. 2005. *American Cultural Baggage*. Orbis Books.

Radice, Betty. 1979. *Confucius: The Analects*. Penguin Books.

Sanford, John. 1981. *Evil: The Shadow Side of Reality*. The Crossroad Publishing Company.

Smith, Huston. 1961. *The World's Religions*. San Francisco: Harper.

Smith, Linda L. 2006. *Called Into Healing*. HTSM Press.

Snow, Tiffany. 2003. *Psychic Gifts in the Christian Life*. Spirit Journey Books.

Soelle, Dorothee. 1975. *Suffering*. Fortress Press.

St. Teresa of Avila. 1997. *The Autobiography of St. Teresa of Avila*. Tan Books.

Ulanov, Ann and Barry. 1982. *Primary Speech*. John Knox Press.

U.S. News and World Report. *Mysteries of Science*, Special Collectors' Edition.

U.S. News and World Report. *Secrets of Christianity*, Collectors' Edition.

Walsh, James, ed. 1981. *The Cloud of Unknowing*. Paulist Press.